KU-753-008

Contents

Connect

Show Up

Survive and Rise

Radical Acts

Create

Inspire

Introduction
Feminist Book Society

This book is about action. It was inspired by a need to take action, even as global events in the spring of 2020 made so many feel powerless, or *more* powerless, and unable to move forward.

When the coronavirus pandemic hit in early 2020 it became horrifyingly clear, very quickly, that essential debate, action and forward movement in the fight for gender equality were going to be sidelined, silenced, even halted altogether. That hard-won progress was going to regress. A stark warning came not even a week into lockdown in the UK. We started seeing media reports of heightened threat: calls to domestic abuse helplines in those early weeks alone were up by 49 per cent. Killings – of women – doubled. And this is *just one* area where women and non-binary people, of all backgrounds and experiences, have been disproportionately affected by this crisis, and where gender inequality is, simply, a matter of life and death.

This book exists because of many, many small actions. In those early days of lockdown in the UK, we – the team behind Feminist Book Society (an author panel event that used to be held monthly in a London bookshop, and now happens online) – sat in our homes, at our new makeshift workspaces, feeling isolated and anxious. We decided to use what resources we had as people in the book industry, and reached out. We pitched an idea. We connected with two independent non-profit publishers, And Other Stories in Britain and the Feminist Press in the United States. At Feminist Book Society we challenge ourselves to bring together authors that you might not typically expect to see sharing a stage or an online panel. So we knew, for this book, that we wanted to hear from the broadest range of feminist voices possible. Together we approached feminist authors, creatives and game-changers we were inspired by, and along the way we were introduced to more. We made contact with the organisations the funds raised by the sales of this book will support – Women's Aid and Imkaan in the UK and the Third Wave Fund in the US. With each small action, each pitch, each email and each positive response, an engaged and committed community began to grow.

In summer 2020 our amazing contributors put pen to paper, or joined us online for 'in conversation' interviews. Our team of voluntary editors got busy shaping these pieces into a book. As a collective, working together, at pace, and in ways none of us had ever worked before, we pulled together the determinedly intersectional transatlantic feminist writing collection that you are now holding in your hands.

Each contributor was asked to capture a moment, to share what they, personally, were thinking and feeling, as feminists writing 'right now' and what 'coming back stronger' meant for them. When we first shared the brief with our contributors the defining global event of 2020 was the pandemic, and much of the world was in some version of a lockdown. By June 2020, the Black Lives Matter protests and action that gained huge, renewed international momentum following the deaths of George Floyd and Breonna Taylor in particular, were informing and shaping numerous responses to the brief in powerful ways. Every writer in this collection shines their own bright light on the numerous, varied and often woefully under-represented spaces where misogyny and other deep-rooted inequalities intersect. The defining events of 2020 were simply a starting point for our writers.

So what you'll find in these pages is a truly exhilarating and honest creative response to crisis. Each piece stands compellingly on its own, and was not commissioned as part of the 'theme' they're now arranged within. Authors did not know at the time of their writing what other authors would be contributing. And the way the pieces are curated here is only one of the many ways it was possible to bring them together.

One of the most exciting things about watching the project develop has been seeing how these various contributions interact with one another. Some themes are writ large across multiple pieces. Urgent questions are asked again and again, and answered with unique insight, from multiple perspectives. Some pieces can be read in dialogue with each other, some in conflict. This collection is a conversation starter, a catalyst for healthy, respectful but rigorous debate; it's also a listening exercise, a love letter, a warm invitation to connect and find closeness, perhaps a source of comfort; and it's a rallying cry, a polemic, an amplifier and a challenge. It's a book that rejects the search for, or acceptance of, a 'new normal' and demands a new *different*. It highlights the urgent need to drive feminist action forward, as the global pandemic crisis continues, and as the seismic local and global events of 2020 shape whatever our futures hold. It challenges what 'feminism' is in the twenty-first century, and what we want it to be.

A huge thank you to each contributor, and to everyone involved in this book, for your acts of creativity and courage, your kindness in giving your time, your words and support.

And thanks to *you* for buying this book.

As a result of your action, 20 per cent of the price you paid will go to Women's Aid and Imkaan in the UK, supporting their essential work on the frontline of the fight against one manifestation of ingrained misogyny and gender inequality.

This book is about coming through crisis and coming back stronger. It is about how we create what comes next. This book is about action – about every small act that leads to a connection, to something bigger, that creates something, that sparks something.

So now, it's over to you.

Cry Out

So Much Racket

Sara Collins

Sara Collins obtained a master's degree in creative writing (with distinction) from Cambridge University. She is the author of the critically acclaimed novel *The Confessions of Frannie Langton*, which won the 2019 Costa First Novel Award.

Sara supports Arts Emergency and FareShare. You can find Sara on Instagram @saracollinsauthor, on Twitter @mrsjaneymac and via her website saracollinsauthor.com.

t's an unbearably cold morning in February. For days now I've been feeling emergency in my bones, the way some people's ankles prophesy the weather. I'm scanning the news on my phone while waiting for a train. Eleven million people are still quarantined in Wuhan, China, but because the epidemic is affecting millions of non-white people who don't live in one of the 'hashtag-able' cities, it's barely shifting the needle on what I call the 'Western Tragedy Scale'. Why aren't we 'praying' for Wuhan the way we 'prayed' for Paris? Here in London, people seem (at best) mildly interested, and the virus is only an item on a news chyron. No one knows yet that these are our last weeks of eyeing each other as strangers rather than disease vectors. I step into the carriage, click on a link and slip in my earphones. A panorama of Wuhan appears on my phone screen, a night sky studded with faintly lit skyscrapers. Out of the darkness the residents call out, from one block of flats to the next, their shouts reverberating between the tall buildings. 'Wuhan, come on!' they're saying. 'Stay strong. Keep going. Wuhan, come on!'

Nothing moves at all on-screen. The only thing passing between the people is language, but as it moves back and forth it amplifies itself, and becomes an endless, echoing crescendo, an eddy of noise, disturbing the silence.

Stay strong. Keep going.

Little do we know how soon we, too, will need that message. In the weeks to come, the virus will sweep airily past the calcifying UK borders that the government is still ineptly and inexplicably busy trying to 'take back'. The Prime Minister will drag himself onto our screens and announce a lockdown. Overnight each of us will become either 'essential' or an epicentre of inertia, busying ourselves with Netflix and Joe Wicks and banana bread if we're lucky or, if we're not, with sickness and grief and unemployment. Every press briefing will remind me of a line in Arundhati Roy's powerful essay 'The End of Imagination': 'What do you do if you're trapped in an asylum and the doctors are all dangerously deranged?' Eventually we will call to each other out of our own windows; we will bang our own pots. Energies and emotions will narrow themselves down, and time will empty itself out, making us desperate to eke out small joys as a way to feel it passing – a meandering walk, a sliver of garden, a delivery of fresh-baked spanakopita from the neighbours. 'When will this end?' we will wonder, until the wondering seems to drive us mad.

Leaders whose compact with their people revolves around building walls to keep people out will find themselves stymied as the virus finds its way in. We will learn the hard way the value of intelligence and empathy and international collaboration. It will be no accident that countries led by women or non-white men, countries where the population is inclined towards sacrifice and collaboration, will fare better than most. In his 2019 book, *Epidemics and Society*, Frank M. Snowden writes: 'Epidemic diseases are not random events that afflict societies capriciously and without warning. On the contrary, every society produces its own specific vulnerabilities. To study them is to understand that society's structure, its standard of living, and its political priorities.' In other words, an experience like this can teach us something about what kinds of human beings we are. It's not just that our vulnerabilities cause pandemics, but also that pandemics reveal our vulnerabilities.

What kinds of human beings are we?

IN MAY, George Floyd will be murdered on camera, while millions watch.

It comes apparently out of the blue, this reminder of the old ways to die. That the world waiting outside closed doors is still one where a white man will kill a Black man for no reason other than his own wilful blindness, his ability to remain human in his own mind by convincing himself his victim never was. It's a story so old we've acquired the technology to record these murders before these men acquired the humanity to stop committing them.

But after George Floyd's murder something unusual does happen, in that the same people who scrolled past death when it was happening in Wuhan now cry out themselves, in a flood of anguish and black social-media squares. They march, they paint 'Black Lives Matter' onto cardboard in rainbow colours, they turn in dismay to their Black friends (if they have any) and say they can't believe this kind of thing could happen in the twenty-first century. And their Black friends (if they have any) may be privately or publicly annoyed that these people, who stayed silent after Stephen Lawrence was murdered, after Trayvon Martin was murdered, after Eric Garner was murdered, after *so many other murders*, fail to recognise what a privilege it is to greet these conjoined feelings of grief and rage like something new. But they also tell themselves that maybe it's better late than never, because among other things to be Black is to know how to wait, how to be patient. They hope this is more than just performative anger, a pandemic of outrage, a momentary strutting and fretting on an Instagram stage. They know that sustained energy will be needed for a revolution.

Maybe, at the very least, it is an end to the silence.

Part of the reason for the outrage is that before George Floyd died, he spoke; he did not go quietly, although no doubt those murdering cops wished he would have. And people around the world had very little to do when this murder happened. So, they listened.

For weeks I mull over his last words, thinking about how he reached out to his loved ones even though he could not move: 'Momma, I love you. Tell my kids I love them. I'm dead.' Months later, I read a full transcript released online, from the policemen's body cameras, which documents Floyd's mounting anxiety from the minute he was stopped, his fear that the officers were going to shoot him, and those words again: 'Momma, I love you. Tell my kids I love them. I'm dead.' It makes for agonising reading.

According to the *Guardian*: '[Floyd] told officers "I can't breathe" more than twenty times only to have his plea dismissed by Derek Chauvin, the white officer pressing his knee into Floyd's neck, who said: "It takes a heck of a lot of oxygen to talk."'

'Momma, I love you. Tell my kids I love them. I'm dead.'

It's not a transcription mistake. George Floyd did indeed say 'I'm dead' in the present tense. I wonder if his words landed like blows on those homicidal cops. I wonder how they could remain so indifferent, so *inhuman*, on hearing him. I read again the murderer's words to the dying man: 'It takes a heck of a lot of oxygen to talk.' It's clear what he was really saying, or at least what his words must be taken to mean: *Shut up. I don't want to hear you. Stay silent.*

Your silence will make this easier for me. *The more you speak, the more this looks like murder.*

But George Floyd did not remain silent, even if silence was the only state-given right he had. With the last of his precious oxygen, he cried out so that we would hear his words reverberating through the darkness, echoing from what was left of his life to what is left of ours. He spoke not in the present tense but the eternal one. And we heard him. We will keep hearing him.

'WE DIE,' said Toni Morrison in her Nobel lecture. 'That may be the meaning of life. But we do language. That may be the measure of our lives.' It's why one of the foundations of authoritarianism is the destruction of language, the insistence on silence, side by side with the creation of spectacles and emergencies that strip away our alphabets. Authoritarians love doing things we have no language to describe. It is one way of taking away our ability to speak. (How many times have you felt speechless over the past four years?) Sometimes I think of death as the loss of language. But until we die, we can cry out.

Sojourner Truth allegedly began her famous speech to the Women's Rights Convention in Ohio as follows: 'Well, children, when there is so much racket there must be something out of kilter.' I first came upon this speech as a young woman dipping my toe into feminism, when it seemed that feminism was yet another space that had been designed without Black women like me in mind. Later I learned that the version I'd read was said to be inaccurate, that Sojourner's words had been twisted into that Huck Finn dialect by Frances Gage more than a decade afterwards, and a different version had been published contemporaneously in which neither this line nor the famous exhortation,

'Ain't I a woman?' was present, but I clung to them anyway. Sometimes now, recalling them, I reverse the order of the words: when something is out of kilter, there must be a racket.

WHEN I WAS a girl, church was mandatory. I remember the fidgety silence of hard benches, of scratchy ankle socks, but there came a moment when I realised that the real source of my discomfort was that it was just one more way in which, to borrow Rebecca Solnit's phrase, I'd been tricked into having men explain things to me. I revolted against trying to understand myself as a young woman within an infrastructure that had, after all, been built around this Bible verse: 'But I suffer not a woman to teach, nor to usurp authority over the man, but to be in silence.'

That was never going to work on me. I was a mouthy little girl, filled to bursting with despair whenever I encountered an example of injustice. I simply could not stay quiet. And in any event, I preferred the fidgety silence of the library, broken only by the crinkling of plastic-covered books, where *novels* explained things to me. When I became a teenager and decided I would become a lawyer, a relative warned: 'Don't do it! You never going find a man! Women lawyers too damn cantankerous. It puts men off.' I suppose that was meant to scare me out of it, picturing myself in the future as some shrewish lonely spinster or a harpy of a wife, like Elizabeth Taylor had played in *The Taming of the Shrew*, which I had just watched on television – the play in which Petruchio utters these words: 'Say she be mute and will not speak a word; Then I'll commend her volubility and say she uttereth piercing eloquence.'

But of course that injunction didn't work on me either. I became a lawyer, although the only thing I liked about being one was the power of being able and equipped and unafraid to speak. I daresay it put some men off, which made it doubly useful.

Decades later, I became a writer and felt again the joy of making a racket.

WHEN AUDRE LORDE spoke of the transformation of silence, she famously asked: 'What are the words you do not yet have? What do you need to say? What are the tyrannies you swallow day by day and attempt to make your own, until you will sicken and die of them, still in silence?'

This world was designed as a place for women to be seen and not heard, and for all Black people to be unseen *and* unheard, which can make the experience of Black womanhood a kind of double silencing. But I have also learned that this makes it doubly joyous to find your voice, to refuse to be silenced. I think of writing, of all art, as a way of doing this: of trying to preserve the echoes of our crying out. We may be sitting in the dark, but it's always possible to reach out towards one another and say, 'Stay strong. Keep going.' I think of it as the opposite of death, for it is as close as we can come to saying something people can keep hearing forever.

I believe in my young-adult daughters and their feminist contemporaries of all genders, because they are a generation of noise-makers. Before the pandemic shut them away, they were busy sounding the alarm in art and in activism about the climate emergency, about intersectionality, about body positivity, about harassment, about sexual violence, about the resurrection of fascism, about white supremacy. Even during a pandemic, they were angry enough to come out in support of BLM protests all over the world. And though I worry about what life will be like for them after

we emerge from this, about how they will get the oxygen –
fairly paid work, shelter, safety, platforms – that they will
need to continue to speak, though I mourn the fact that
Covid-19 forced them into a temporary silence, I believe
that together we will find new ways to keep doing the old
work. Because it is our obligation to make a racket when
there is something out of kilter.

11 June 2020, 4 a.m.
Notes App.
Sophie Williams

Sophie Williams is a leading anti-racism advocate and activist, and the founder of the @officialmillennialblack Instagram account. Sophie is a regular panellist, speaker, consultant and workshop facilitator, with a focus on anti-racism, and diversity and inclusion. Her writing has appeared in publications such as the *Guardian*, *Bustle*, *Refinery29* and *Cosmopolitan*. Before beginning to write, Sophie had a career in advertising, particularly in social agencies, where she held the position of chief operating officer. In 2019, Sophie left traditional agencies in order to create her own business, working with clients such as Netflix on projects combining her professional advertising experience with active anti-racism work. Sophie is the author of *Anti-Racist Ally: An Introduction to Activism and Action* and *Millennial Black*.

I wrote this piece on my phone, in one sitting (lying?) as a single stream of consciousness, one morning in June 2020 – a month when finding restful moments was proving difficult for me. I decided not to make edits later, instead preserving that morning and those feelings in amber, fossilised tree sap, as a personal record of the moment.

At first it seemed unreal.

'We'll just get a few bits. Just in case,' we told ourselves.

He can pop out on his lunch break. It will be good to get out of the office for a while.

What do we need?

A little bit of oil.

Maybe some avocados.

Lots of cat food.

No toilet paper. We're not monsters.

Walking down the aisles, shelves were empty. People were wearing masks, the first time we'd seen it. 'Look at them,' we said, shaking our heads. Overreacting. A trolley piled high with bottled water and loo roll. Selfish. They're going to feel silly in a few weeks.

'Will this be a time we always remember?' I ask. 'No,' he says, 'I don't think it will be that serious. It's not like it's Ebola.'

We didn't know.

'Ah, fuck it,' we said. Let's get a Zipcar. Let's go to Costco. We're not panicking. No. Of course not. It will just be a laugh.

'These things won't help with the virus.' The cashier laughed, ringing up our stuff. A giant cake with 'Happy Birthday' written on top, in the kind of icing that you only see in American films. The biggest bottle of tequila.

We're not worried. This will be over soon, and if we're going to stay inside for a week, we may as well have fun doing it.

That doesn't last.

People die. Thousands of them.

How can we stay connected?

I start an online dinner party. Once a week? We can do it on Instagram Live. We'll share a recipe in advance and we can all cook the same thing and eat together. We'll be together, but apart.

We think we've caught it.

I cough and cough and cough until the pain shooting through my head goes down through my right eye, into my jaw, making me see stars.

I have a temperature. I feel like I'm burning. How hot am I? We can't know; our only thermometer is for cooking.

I sleep sitting up. Maybe that will help me cough less. I sleep all the time, waking every few hours with a coughing fit. Gasping for breath at the side of the bed.

What are we supposed to do now?

There's no advice for what to do if you're sick. Stay at home. Don't spread it to others. Reduce the R number. You'll never know if you really had it, not for sure.

I saw it in the news. A Black woman in London was sick. Her husband phoned 999. She's not a priority, they say.

No ambulance is coming. No hospital will take her.

Stay at home. Protect the NHS. Save lives.

He washed her, dressed her, sat her in the living room whilst he got dressed himself. When he came back, minutes later, she had died. Alone in her living room. I think about her every day. And him.

The people came in hazmat suits, took her away. In and out as quickly as possible. They stood outside, posted a report through the letterbox. No one told him what was happening.

Oh fuck. I think I could be in real trouble.

The Queen looks wrong. Like she's done her own make-up. Like she's had to mix a few foundations together on the back of her hand to get her shade. Like every Black teenager in Boots in the days before Fenty. But, unlike Black teens, she's not used to it; she doesn't have the knack. She looks weird.

'We'll meet again,' she says. Everyone is talking like we're at war.

How are people getting things? Supermarket shelves are empty and deliveries are gold dust. Maybe we'll just figure out how to do this ourselves.

Have I become a wartime housewife? I scrape the seeds out of a tomato, carefully, with my fingers, onto a piece of kitchen paper and place it on the windowsill, in the sun.

Is this how it works? How long does it take for a tomato plant to grow, anyway? Ages, it turns out.

I'm not a wartime housewife, I reassure myself as I cut the bases off spring onions, celery and leeks, fill a glass with water and stand the root ends in them. I'm finding a way to be self-sufficient. I'm getting stuff done.

Slowly the roots will fill the glass, then you can plant them and they'll regrow. Don't forget to change the water.

I order more soil.

People clap for the NHS. Every Thursday at 7 p.m. At first it's gentle, but as time goes on it becomes cheering, whooping, banging pots and pans, whistling, and shaking tambourines.

The NHS are heroes. Thanks for them are splashed across newspaper front pages. There are photos of smiling doctors and nurses in their uniforms. They're saving lives.

Something is wrong. What is it? 'Everyone's white,' someone points out. Forty-four per cent of NHS medical workers are 'BAME'. Seventy per cent of front-line workers who die of it are BAME. But almost every hero's face we see is white. What happened to the Windrush nurses?

Heroes so white.

'I have it,' a man claims. Then he spits in Belly Mujinga's face whilst she's at work for Transport for London. She dies. The case is closed. No one is prosecuted.

Ahmaud Arbery is out jogging. Two white men lynch him in broad daylight. Lynching was only made illegal in 2018. It doesn't seem to have sunk in yet.

Breonna Taylor is sleeping. Police break down her door and shoot her eight times. They're looking for drugs, but there are none. They've made a mistake. It's the wrong address.

We say her name. We celebrate her birthday. Twenty-seven today, except not.

A police officer kneels on George Floyd's neck. Three other officers watch. George is forty-six years old. He calls for his mom. He begs them to stop. He realises they're going to kill him. Eight minutes and forty-six seconds is such a long time. Count it.

We feel these things as though it's our own skin. I cry for days. I bury my face in a cushion and weep in the toilet. The house is open plan, and he has conference calls to make.

He knocks softly on the bathroom door. 'Are you OK?' he asks. 'What's wrong?'

I can't breathe.

The world is watching.

No justice. No peace.

We take to the streets.

Black Lives Matter.

We're meant to be in lockdown, no gatherings of more than six people. Black people are the group most likely to die of it. We know. But how can we not gather? We can't go on this way.

We ask our allies to support us. We ask our friends to pull up. We didn't make this mess, we tell them; we can't fix it on our own. The young turn out. But the baby boomers who have turned out to march against Brexit and every other injustice are conspicuously absent. They do not send their apologies.

We make posters and banners. We shout into megaphones. We deserve to be here, we say. We're people too. We didn't ask for this, for any of it. Enough is enough.

We take a knee. The meaning has shifted. Eight minutes and forty-six seconds is a lifetime.

People want to hear from us. People follow us. They're looking for teachers, they want us to guide the way. They forget we are tired. Maybe they never knew. We have had skin in this game for as long as we have had skin. Our very bones are tired. We need them to join the fight this time.

My followers explode. Nearly 200,000 people want me to tell them what to do. How am I supposed to know?

I am in a daze.

I don't sleep for a week. I feel like if I stop, if I let the feelings back in, I'll be sick, right onto this pink velvet sofa that has become part nest, part mission control of an empire I didn't mean to build.

The eyes of the world are suddenly on Black women. Is it the first time ever? They buy our books. They are thirsty for our words. We wanted them to listen, but not like this. Are we helping, or are we profiting from other people's pain? Everything feels wrong.

Will we keep the momentum or will it fizzle out?

People want to get back to normal, to the good old days. We want to scream that normal wasn't working. That normal was killing us.

We keep moving.

A Matter of Life and Death

Laura Bates

in conversation with Feminist Book Society

Laura Bates is the founder of the Everyday Sexism Project and bestselling author of *Men Who Hate Women*, *Girl Up* and *Everyday Sexism*. A fellow of the Royal Society of Literature, she writes regularly for the *Guardian*, *Telegraph*, *New York Times* and others. She works with schools, police forces, MPs and bodies from the Council of Europe to the United Nations to tackle gender inequality. She is a contributor at Women Under Siege, a New York–based project working to prevent the use of rape as a weapon of war in conflict zones worldwide. bio

As we speak, it's early September 2020. The UK has seen nationwide and regional lockdown restrictions imposed, and eased, and as we enter autumn, imposed again. What feminist issue is most in your mind right now?

Foremost in my mind at the moment is the issue of domestic violence. The form of everyday terrorism that was briefly and belatedly highlighted during the early days of lockdown, only seemingly to be forgotten again in the weeks that followed. Women were already subjected to shocking levels of intimate abuse before the pandemic hit, with a phone call to the police every minute on average about domestic abuse. But mandating a national lockdown was a literal death sentence for some women, as well as exacerbating horrendous abuse for many more.

We know that calls to UK domestic abuse help-lines jumped by 80 per cent during lockdown, and that charities around the world reported similar statistics. We know that in one county in the Hubei province in China, where the virus originated, domestic violence reports to police more than tripled during the February lockdown. But we don't know, can't know, about the grinding, daily terror that lengthened every minute of those agonising weeks for thousands of silent victims. We don't talk about it much anymore, even though restrictions on travelling and visiting, and the continuation of home working for millions of people, has meant that, for many, the nightmare never ended, even when national lockdown lifted.

In 2012, you founded the Everyday Sexism Project, a place to record stories of sexism faced on a daily basis by ordinary women in ordinary places. To date, more than 100,000 women around the world have documented their experiences. How has everyday sexism manifested in the UK during the coronavirus pandemic and 2020?

Coronavirus has provided a perfect microcosm for the existing inequalities in our society, horribly highlighting and deepening the fault lines that were already there, but which many people chose not to see. This has been true in the case of racism: the virus disproportionately affected Black, Asian and minority ethnic communities. The Institute for Fiscal Studies (IFS) think-tank estimated that when factors like geography and age are taken into account, deaths of Black Africans were 3.7 times higher than might have been expected, with deaths of Pakistanis 2.9 times higher than expected and of Black Caribbean people 1.8 times higher. And the Office for National Statistics concluded that Black people, Bangladeshis and Pakistanis were almost twice as likely to die with the virus as white people, and Indians around 1.5 times as likely. Asian women reported an enormous spike in racial harassment early in the pandemic (one woman was walking down the street when a man shouted at her, 'Keep your Asian disease away'). It has been true in the case of class inequality, with the death rate in the poorest communities in England and Wales twice as high as in the wealthiest, and those in low-paid jobs often the ones expected to risk their lives on the front line to keep the country running.

And it has been the case, too, with sexism. Emerging research suggests that the burden of unpaid care already disproportionately shouldered by women was dramatically increased by the crisis and subsequent lockdowns. A Boston Consulting Group study found that mothers in Europe and the US took on an additional thirty-one hours of housework per week on average during lockdown. And a report by Citigroup found that of the forty-four million expected redundancies worldwide, thirty-one million – 70 per cent – would be women. Submissions to academic journals from men soared during lockdown, while those from women plummeted. Mothers were already discriminated against in the workplace, but as the pandemic took hold, they were twice as likely as fathers to lose their jobs or quit, and charities reported an enormous spike in maternity discrimination cases. The IFS found that mothers were only able to do one hour of uninterrupted work for every three hours done by fathers. As social media wags joked that people would be learning new languages or writing novels in the extended leisure time afforded by quarantining at home, mums everywhere knew they'd be lucky to manage a single solo wee.

And some of the deepest impact was felt in the lives of those for whom these many different inequalities intersect. In America, for example, a study by the organisation Lean In found that 54 per cent of Black women faced job or income loss during the pandemic, compared with 27 per cent of white men. When it came to Covid-19, inequality, it turned out, was a pre-existing condition.

Of course, none of this was intentional. The British government didn't set out to exacerbate domestic violence, to arrive at unequal career outcomes or disadvantage mothers. But that was the impact nonetheless. So it is significant that there seemed to be so little diversity in the groups of decision makers steering our national ship through the crisis; that vanishingly few of the government spokespeople leading the daily news briefings, for example, were ever women. Because people bring their own experiences to that decision-making table.

It isn't an exaggeration to say that representation was, in this case, a matter of life and death. It took the government nineteen days after imposing lockdown restrictions to implement a social-media and funding campaign to tackle the potential domestic abuse crisis that would follow. But by that point, eleven women, two children and one man had already been killed in suspected domestic abuse cases.

When lockdown ended in late summer and the government attempted to cajole those who had worked from home for several months back into the workplace, there was little acknowledgement of the fact that a return simply wouldn't be possible for a huge number of caregivers and parents, the majority of them women, whose usual support systems, school clubs or holiday play schemes simply weren't available.

And there was no recognition at all, when the A-level results fiasco concluded with most students receiving predicted grades, that studies have repeatedly shown gender stereotyping leads teachers to mark girls down in subjects such as science and maths and to overestimate boys' abilities.

All this is to say that sexism and other forms of inequality have manifested themselves in a thousand ways during the pandemic, just as they did in daily life before Covid-19. But the problem has been exacerbated by a lack of diverse representation or gendered analysis in our national policy response. The results, in terms of our progress towards equality, are potentially catastrophic.

What do you know now that you didn't know at the beginning of 2020?

The lessons I've learned from 2020 have been very simple ones – things I am surprised I hadn't learned before – prompted, I think, by a crisis that felt very timeless, in which we were powerless as individuals and forced to trust in (or at least to accept) the decisions of a tiny group of people in the face of a global tragedy.

I was powerfully struck by the extent to which each of us experiences identical events wildly differently. Nobody had it easy during the pandemic. But people's personal tragedies, fears, pain and burdens were so very diverse. There was a gulf between the experiences of a front-line shelf stacker, an isolated person facing redundancy, a single parent with young children in a small urban flat with no garden, a family shielding to protect a vulnerable relative, a carer with no respite, a cancer patient with treatment suspended, a mourner without a funeral, a teenager suddenly stripped of the rite of exams.

I've learned that there are no one-size-fits-all solutions. That it is so very easy to forget and erase entire groups of people from the plan if those making that plan don't personally happen to have direct experience of their world.

So I've learned that using our hard-won vote and – for those with this privilege – our political voice is a matter of life and death, but that this may only become clear to us months or years too late. I've learned that local community action and kindness to our neighbours is the backbone of social survival. I've learned that sunshine helps.

As a writer, what narrative of this crisis would you want to create for yourself and for others as you look back now, and if you were looking back five years from now?

Even the idea of a narrative of the crisis feels dangerous and slippery. Who gets to write the story? Already we've seen protestors against racist state violence blamed for infections and deaths while beaches and pubs heaved. I hope there will be accountability.

Has the notion of a feminist support network been redefined for you in lockdown? What are the best examples you've seen of womxn supporting and empowering other womxn during this time?

In April 2020, a woman in Washington was walking in her neighbourhood. With fewer people on the street, fewer places to turn for sanctuary and a direct imperative to stick to less populated routes where possible, it was a period in which women around the world were particularly vulnerable to harassment and assault in public spaces. My Everyday Sexism Project saw a significant spike in reports during this period.

The woman briefly caught the eye of a man sitting on a stoop. He stared at her intensely, got up and began to follow her. She crossed the street. So did he. He moved closer, until he was less than a foot behind her. He started to shout at her. She didn't respond. He punched a street sign as they passed it, making a loud bang. She looked for an escape route. All the shops and cafés were closed and shuttered, lockdown was in full swing. She started to think about running, mentally weighing up the risks. Would it cause him to pursue her more aggressively? Could she outrun him?

Finally, with a rush of relief, she spotted a small corner shop that seemed to be open and raced towards it. The man followed her in. Her heart sank as she realised the shop was empty. Then, at the back of the shop, she spotted the owner, a woman. The two women exchanged a single look. She told the man to leave her alone. Furious, he left, slamming the shop door. She burst into tears. And the shop-keeper locked up, there and then, in the middle of the day, and walked her all the way home.

In the face of continuing and worsening violence and inequality, women continue to raise our voices collectively. And we continue to walk each other home.

What makes you hopeful about a feminist future?

We are furious. In the short term, I hope that anger is so powerful that it cannot be dismissed or denied. In the long term, the young people I work with in schools across the country give me enormous hope for the future. They have been painted as a generation of cowering snowflakes. It couldn't be further from the truth. They are a generation of young women who are strong, brave and determined. At one school I visited, where the girls had been forbidden from forming a feminist society because it would be too 'contro-versial', they carried on with an underground group instead. At another school, when girls were told they couldn't wear leggings because they might 'distract the boys', they picketed the school the following day with placards bearing slogans like 'Are my leggings lowering your test scores?' In spite of all they have faced this summer, these young people do not flinch away from their role as our future leaders and decision makers. Teenage girls are fighting back with humour, courage and determination, and they fill me with hope for the future.

Domestic Abuse: An Epidemic in a Pandemic

Jess Phillips

Jess Phillips was first elected as the Labour MP for Birmingham Yardley in 2015, before being re-elected in 2017. She was elected chair of the Women's Parliamentary Labour Party in September 2016. Before becoming an MP, Jess worked with victims of domestic violence, sexual violence and human trafficking, and she continues to speak up on behalf of those who struggle to have their voices heard.

Jess has worked with the Home Office, the Ministry of Justice and the Department for Communities and Local Government on issues of violence against women and girls. She is one of the women who launched the #NotTheCost campaign to combat the violence faced by politically active women, and the Reclaim the Internet campaign, which challenges online abuse.

Jess lives with her husband and two sons in Birmingham, where she was born and raised.

'The nearest bed I can find is in Hertfordshire.' These were the words of one of my caseworkers trying to find a refuge space for two separate women in Birmingham in the first week of the Covid-19 lockdown in March 2020. It is not unusual that in the second biggest city in the UK, we find there are no safe secure bed-spaces within a 150-mile radius for victims of domestic abuse and their children. In fact, it is more common than not that there is no room at the inn.

Research by the national charity Women's Aid 'Save Our Services' campaign found that 60 per cent of those who seek refuge are turned away. Imagine for a second that this was any other life-saving service, such as insulin for diabetics – can you imagine if the health service in this country said, 'We have decided only to provide every third person with diabetes with the insulin that they need to survive'? Yet when it comes to providing services to victims of domestic abuse, this is exactly what happens; we as a country are satisfied with the undersupply of services, and the government expects a gold star for helping anyone at all.

This is a normal-times gripe. I have screamed my voice hoarse trying to improve this situation. Covid-19 has finally shone a light on this but only by creating the perfect storm for domestic abuse victims and survivors.

The calamity facing some of the most vulnerable in our

society during the lockdown was threefold. First there was the immediate increase of risk to a woman and her children if they were locked in with someone who was abusing them. Without school, work, visits from family or access to services, a normal grim-and-terrifying existence turned into a potentially life-threatening one. The second problem stemmed from the fact that the availability of refuge accommodation relies on people being able to move out of refuge into other secure homes. This obviously immediately stopped, and for months the ability to make space in refuges by people moving on ended. A new blockage to an already impeded and difficult system ensued. The third came as perpetrators used the virus as a new threat and excuse for their behaviours. I spoke to many women whose perpetrators used the lockdown to flout family court orders and hold on to their children during lockdown, or to argue in court that they could not vacate their property as part of an occupation or restraining order because they had nowhere to go as a result of the lockdown. In the worst case of this I came across, a man who was convicted of a violent attack on his partner – kicking her repeatedly as she was balled up on the floor – avoided jail in large part due to restrictions on prisons and the heightened risk of catching Covid-19 in one.

The virus was sadly becoming a tool in the armour of perpetrators of domestic abuse to avoid justice, enabled by a system that already failed to clearly hear the voices and concerns of victims. In some of the cases I encountered, the virus was used as part of a direct threat: 'I will infect you and the kids with the virus.' Or, in other cases, perpetrators lied about having the virus in order to ensure their families would have to be completely quarantined without interaction with others for at least two weeks.

For anyone with half a brain, and even a fraction of heart, it was clear that as country after country went into lockdown, something would need to be done. Resources would have to be put in place, hotels would have to be turned into women's refuges, phone lines and support services would need to ramp up at the exact moment that everything else was ramping down.

In the first few weeks of the lockdown it felt a little like those of us who cared were screaming into a void. Every day I would have conference calls with charities across the country telling us what was happening. We teamed up in groups seeking to tackle each problem that arose. I was charged, along with two specialist charities, with creating new emergency beds in hotels and empty properties; so, we set about doing it. It is not often that the sort of politics I practise means I get to try to woo big hotel chains and landowners, but now was the time. What I found is that they wanted to help, and within a week we had lined up big, famous hotel chains, started to draft guidance and thought about which local organisations could act as the charity partner in each area. The only blockage was that we needed the government to agree to pay for it. This was not the price of the hotel rooms that you and I would pay for on a weekend city break; this was at cost. Refuge beds were needed, and we had found a solution.

But, as so often happens, the government computer said no.

Three weeks into the crisis, the home secretary announced a paltry £2m to provide extra phone lines for victims to call. Obviously it was welcome, but there is little point in a phone call to a friendly voice if there is nowhere for you to go. Like so many things during the crisis, it felt as though people were there and ready to provide a solution.

People had rolled up their sleeves and, in the spirit of the blitz, bombed through unanswered emails and calls to Whitehall. Yet from the government it felt that there was never a sense of urgency or speed to act. During the first month after the lockdown, which began in late March, sixteen women and girls were killed in suspected domestic homicides. This figure is more than triple the number from the same period in 2019.

The government does care about domestic abuse, I have absolutely no doubt about that; however, it seems to me, it is never its priority. It is always a policy add-on or a 'nice to have' rather than a 'need it now'. Some more weeks into women living in abject terror and the government, pushed by myself and others, announced a further £76m fund, a big chunk of which went to help domestic abuse charities function. Again, this was welcome, but it all felt like an afterthought. We, the campaigners, were meant to be grateful and gracious for funding that would not even nearly fully fund the need for support in normal times, let alone in a period of home imprisonment. It was, by way of comparison, not even half of what was spent on the scheme that gave everyone half-price dinners in order to help out the restaurant industry. It is without doubt that the local McDonald's and Nando's received more coronavirus emergency funding than the local women's refuge or community support service.

Domestic abuse services are always the bridesmaid in policy terms. The bridesmaid who is expected to be grateful that she got to wear a pretty frock and go to the party. I learned long ago in politics that it doesn't really matter what I say or do – my main job is just to be in the room and speak with the voice of a woman. If there is no woman in the room, you can bet your bottom dollar that a woman's experience of a policy will not be considered. Sometimes I am just merely a totem; carved in my flesh it says, 'Remember that we exist.' For victims of domestic abuse, it's not so easy to always be in the room.

If there is one thing I would like to change about our country's policy-making process, it would be that, when considering pretty much any policy, not only should government have to assess whether they have considered women's jobs, women's lives, women's welfare and women's health, but whether they have also considered how the policy might affect the one in three women aged between sixteen and fifty-nine who are living or have lived with domestic abuse. In the beginning of the pandemic, it felt as if in government there was no woman in the room. No strategy document existed in the weeks leading up to lockdown to try to manage and mitigate the epidemic that is domestic abuse. No one thought of it. I guess they just thought people would cope.

Slap-bang in the middle of this crisis, on 28 April, Parliament returned and with it returned the Domestic Abuse Bill – a bill so beleaguered it had survived two general elections and one illegal prorogation of Parliament. Good job it is not about anything life or death, eh? With the coronavirus crisis raising the profile of the plights of people locked at home, we now had a parliamentary opportunity to speak up, to come together as parliamentarians and to change our laws so that those living in fear and those whom we didn't save could have justice and peace.

The Domestic Abuse Bill had been a largely uncontentious piece of legislation. All 650 members of Parliament broadly agree (or at least are too ashamed to admit otherwise) that we need to tackle domestic abuse. For three years it has been kicking around the House of Commons, during which time it has been praised by all. An atmosphere of working together to make it better has been the standard. When the bill finally came back for its last outing in the Commons, I found myself no longer in the position of keen back-bencher with a speciality, but instead as the Member of Parliament on the front bench who would guide it through on behalf of Her Majesty's Loyal Opposition.

It is difficult to criticise something that you have spent years trying to get off the ground. I spent years pleading with the government to get on with enacting the legislation as it was slowly pushed from pillar to post. I became the bill's leading advocate in the country, asking for it to be debated, and I fought against the government every single time it was dropped. I felt like the protector of the Domestic Abuse Bill, because an opportunity to discuss the wide-ranging nature and effect of this abuse was too delicious an opportunity. I don't often feel like this about conservative government legislation.

When it finally was in my gift to stand at the dispatch box in the House of Commons and welcome this bill, I was straight off the bounce of feeling how badly let down the nation's victims had been during the crisis. I decided that I was no longer the bill's cheerleader and that, while I wanted more than anything for it to be a success, it couldn't just be window dressing for the government to point at to prove they cared while the domestic murder toll rose. So, I became its biggest critic. In a tough-love kind of way.

The fact that there is a bill in Parliament that is called the Domestic Abuse Bill is a huge stride forward. It is the first time that has happened. But words written on fancy scrolls will do nothing to save lives. The bill needed to actually provide decent refuge accommodation to a standard we would all want to live by. When the statutory definition of 'domestic abuse' was written into law for the first time, it needed to include children in the definition, as those who grow up with domestic abuse are the forgotten victims. It needed to overhaul the family court system that I had seen systematically retraumatise victims at best and at worst put them and their children in harm's way. The bill in its form as presented did nothing to protect migrant victims of domestic abuse. While on the news people were praising nurses and carers from abroad, in Parliament we were trying to pass legislation that would have discriminated against those same people had they needed a refuge bed. I was not willing to be grateful that we had a bill. It had to be a good one.

So, I went toe-to-toe with the ministers, with mixed success. I put in around forty amendments to the bill to improve it – a marked departure from the 'let's all be pals' consensual atmosphere. We won on a number of areas around the family courts, on the inclusion of children in the definition, and the government created a fund for migrant victims (although it still doesn't want to recognise them in the legislation). The government launched a review into domestic abuse in the workplace and gave in on the need to give domestic abuse victims priority for social housing. Every single thing that is good in the Domestic Abuse Bill was won by teams of campaigners from across the political divide, and, as it was laid to rest and sent over for those in ermine in the Lords to look over, it was in better shape than when the crisis began. But still not good enough.

At points during the process, I was looked at as if I were ungrateful. Eyes visibly rolled when on committee I rose to tell another story of another victim whom the bill would miss. I was accused by ministers of always acting with my heart where they have to act with their heads, which is a patronising way to say that I am emotional, and frankly an attempt to undermine my expertise (which is far greater than theirs in this regard). But I was emotional. I came back to Parliament from the pandemic having made a mission-control centre in my house, trying to think of every area where the pandemic would hit up against the epidemic of domestic abuse and attempting to solve it. I was tired and worried. My inbox was flooded with harrowing stories of women locked in with a man who would rape her each and every night, or of women whose children had been forced to stay in a home with an abusive father.

Victims all over the country turn to me for help with their cases of domestic abuse. They think that I have some power to stop the terrible thing that is happening to them in the courts, or with their benefits, housing, kids' school places, their police forces and courts. I don't. All I have is an outside chance to change the law, which is slow and usually shifts the dial just a fraction. The only thing that would truly change domestic abuse policy in the future was if it were given the political priority, the resources and the consideration in policy-making that an epidemic of its scale demands. We have grown too used to the harrowing statistics, too used to accepting the domestic murders. It's just 'one of those things', like rain on a bank holiday, or the fact that travel agents hike their prices during school holidays. We just accept it as a bad thing.

It is incredibly tiring to feel you are having a decades-long fight. The brilliant meme-worthy slogan spotted on a placard at the women's marches in 2016 sums it up perfectly: 'I cannot believe I still have to protest this shit.' But we can do it. Things have changed. Culture has changed in the decades I have worked in this field, so the attitude that it is 'just a domestic' is pretty much dead.

Police forces have special units for violence against women. Refuges will soon in this country have a statutory footing, meaning local authorities have to provide refuge beds.

The law of our land will now name in clear definitions this thing that victims have suffered for decades. It will exist in the law rather than just being 'an assault'.

Soon children in every school will be taught about healthy and unhealthy relationships, and all that campaigning, lobbying, begging and stropping will be for something.

It would be nice not to have to fight. It would be nice if it was just considered in the first place. Hope springs eternal.

As for the Domestic Abuse Bill, it has to be the beginning of something, not the end. I truly hope it will lead to fewer dead women, fewer traumatised kids, more refuge beds and a better court system.

Then and only then will I be grateful, and until then, I will continue to be too emotional.

The Woman in the Portrait

Juliet Jacques

Juliet Jacques is a writer and filmmaker based in London. She has published two books, *Rayner Heppenstall: A Critical Study* and *Trans: A Memoir.* Her short fiction, essays and journalism have appeared in numerous publications, including the *Guardian*, *New York Times*, *Frieze*, *Granta*, *London Review of Books*, *Sight & Sound* and many others. Her short films have screened in festivals and galleries worldwide. She also hosts the radio programme/podcast *Suite (212)*, which looks at the arts in their social, cultural and political contexts. Her next book, *Variations*, is a volume of short stories that tell the history of British trans and non-binary people.

I wrote this short story in 2014, after Tate Modern asked me to respond to a work in their collection 'from a trans perspective'. They held no works by openly trans or non-binary artists, nor any portraying such people. At the time, representation in media and the arts was improving – we were near Time magazine's famous 'transgender tipping point' – so I was thinking about the history of trans exclusion and erasure. Christian Schad's Self-Portrait with Model, painted in Germany in 1927 and on display in the gallery in London, seemed the perfect foil to explore these issues through fiction, given Schad's interest in the Weimar Republic's queer/trans subculture, and the horrific fate that many people in that subculture met once the Nazis came to power.

Writing 'The Woman in the Portrait', I identified strongly with my fictional protagonist, drawing on my own experiences of exclusion and erasure, harassment and objectification. When I presented it at C. N. Lester's Transpose event at Tate Modern, some of the audience found the sex scenes too traumatic. They drew on my experiences, too, and I wanted to share that disappointment on finding that people attracted to trans women – even the ones we trust – have often internalised transphobia, and the danger that can put us in. Of course, identification with that was painful, as was the realisation that *the issues that Heike faces in the story are not purely historical.*

In 2014, I was cautious about Time's *'tipping point' optimism: in the UK, austerity was hitting women and LGBTQI+ people hardest; the Russian 'gay propaganda' law had been passed and the forces of reaction against trans visibility were mobilising.*

Now, as numerous governments revoke laws that protect us, or threaten to do so, as an opening salvo in a wider culture war on women and LGBTQI+ people, the threat of the far right feels even more present.

As the old saying goes, history doesn't repeat itself but it often rhymes. Returning to this story now, I'm reminded of the need to remain vigilant against the fascists redrafting their old verses.

You can view the creative inspiration for this short story by visiting tate.org.uk/art/artwork/ schad-self-portrait-L01710.

GOOD EVENING ladies, gentlemen and everyone else, and welcome to the Tate Modern. The image you see is *Self-Portrait with Model* by German artist Christian Schad, known as 'the painter with the scalpel' for the cutting, forensic nature of his work, and it is on loan from a private collector. The son of a wealthy Bavarian lawyer, Schad was born in 1894 and fled to Switzerland in 1915 to avoid military service. There, he became involved with the Dadaists, attending their legendary Cabaret Voltaire in Zürich, before moving to Italy and adopting the Neue Sachlichkeit (New Objectivity) style that replaced expressionism as Germany's dominant Modernist form in the mid-1920s.

Painted in 1927, the *Self-Portrait* is Schad's most famous work. It is noted for his suspicion and hostility, and the disconnection between him and his 'model', but her identity has long been a mystery. It is not his then wife, Marcella Arcangeli, an Italian medical professor's daughter whom he married in 1923. Schad claimed that he saw her in a stationery shop in Vienna, where he lived from 1925 to 1927, but the remarkable find of two diaries from 1926 and 1927, by a 'transvestite' known only as 'Heike', a hostess in Berlin's El Dorado nightclub who worked as a maid at Magnus Hirschfeld's Institute of Sexual Science, has radically changed perceptions of Schad's work. They were recovered from an attic in Nice, near Hirschfeld's home after his exile from Germany. Along with Schad's letters to Dadaist friends, recently discovered by art scholars, they explain how Heike came to be the woman in the portrait, and provide a fascinating insight into gender-variant life in the Weimar Republic.

ON FRIDAY, 4 February 1927, Heike went to the El Dorado, a gay club in Berlin which had just moved to Schöneberg, opposite the Scala Variety Theatre. The following day, she wrote:

> *At the El Dorado last night, with Dora and the girls. I got my hair done like Asta Nielsen in* Joyless Street, *and I wore my long black dress with the beads that Marie got for my birthday. Conrad [Veidt] was there, getting drunk with Marlene [Dietrich] before her act.*
>
> *I went on-stage and introduced Marlene. A man at the front kept staring at me. I saw him go to the bar and buy some chips for a dance. As I stepped*

down, he grabbed my hands, told me he'd just moved to Berlin, took me to the bar and bought a bottle of absinthe. 'You're the most beautiful woman I've ever seen,' he told me. 'Listen,' I said, 'I'm the third sex.'

'That might be Dr Hirschfeld's line,' he yelled, 'but you transcend *sex!' He invited me to his studio in Vienna to model for him. I said I wanted to be in the movies but Conrad told me it could never happen. 'Ignore that two-bit somnambulist! Once they see my portrait, no director could resist you! As far as the pictures are concerned – you are a woman!'*

We danced. He kept staring into my eyes, smiling. I tried to kiss him. 'I'm married,' he said. He gave me a card with his address, told me to write to him and then left. Dora asked what happened. 'Nothing,' I said.

AFTER WORK on Friday, 25 February, Heike arranged to meet Schad. She thought they would go for dinner and then to the theatre, with her diaries detailing her dreams of leaving her domestic service to become an actress, but Schad's note to Richard Huelsenbeck, posted earlier that week, suggests that he never intended to meet her in public.

Welt-Dada,

Went to El Dorado to find The Model – Heike. She – he – is Uranian – an invert – but thinks I'll make her the new Pola Negri – will take her to a hotel – see what transpires.

Heike's diary for Tuesday, 1 March, gives her side of their encounter in Berlin's Hotel Adlon.

I got to the Adlon at 5 p.m. From Morning to Midnight *by Georg Kaiser was on at the Neues Schauspielhaus, and I asked if we could go. 'I need the time to paint you,' said Christian. I saw that his easel was already set up. He drew the curtains. 'Take off your clothes and lie on the bed,' he told me. 'Would anyone cast me if I was famous for being naked?' I asked.*

'How do you think Garbo got on Joyless Street?' *he replied, laughing. 'Take off your clothes and lie down.' He glared at me as I removed my hat. He stared at my hair-line, then caught my eyes. I turned around and took off my blouse, and then my shoes and skirt, and started to pull down my stockings. 'Keep them on,' he said. I turned back to him. 'Just the stockings.' I took off my bra and the inserts, and he just stared at me as I put them on the floor. Then I removed my drawers and lay on the bed.*

He looked at my penis. I thought he was going to be one of those men who vomits, but he just stood there, breathing heavily. 'I thought you said we transcend sex.' Silence. 'The Doctor says we're more beautiful than other women, because we have to –' He threw me onto the bed. 'Enough about Hirschfeld!' He kissed me. I thought he was going to kill me, he was so coarse and so rough – he just wouldn't stop. Finally, he got tired.

'I know what you're thinking,' he said, looking at my sex again. 'I can't.'

'Why not?'

'They'll send me to prison!' He looked into my eyes. 'I'm not an invert!'

'No, you're not,' I said. 'I'm a woman, and as soon as Dr Abraham gets there with Dora, I'll be complete.' He laughed. 'You're all the same, aren't you? Hirschfeld, Abraham – you just let them own you!' I stroked his hand. 'Are you jealous of them?' I said. He turned me over and screwed me harder than I'd ever been screwed. I screamed. 'Be quiet,' he whispered. 'Someone might hear.' Then he stopped and shoved my face into the pillow. I sat up and looked at him. He slapped me hard on the cheek. He sat with his back to me.

'My wife . . . my son . . .'

I stared at the wall.

'I'm sorry,' he said.

'I'll talk to Conrad and Marlene,' I replied. 'They'll introduce me to Pabst and Lang. I'll start with bit parts but they'll see, and once they do, I'll pay for your art, I'll –'

'Shut up, you idiot!' he said. 'They might make films about freaks but they don't cast them!'

'I thought you liked freaks,' I said, reminding him that Marie had seen him at the Onkel Pelle.

'Not when they seduce me!' he yelled. He stood over me. 'Should I leave?' I asked. He nodded. 'I'll go,' I said. 'Just don't hit me again.' He didn't move. 'I'll put on my clothes, just let me out!'

Silence.

'What about the portrait?' I asked.

'I can do it from memory,' he said.

He went and stood by the window. I got dressed and went to the door. 'Goodbye, then.' He looked at me and then turned back. I heard him open the curtains as I left.

Soon after, Schad painted his *Self-Portrait*. It was premiered in a group exhibition of Neue Sachlichkeit artists at the Neues Haus des Vereins Berliner Künstler, although we know that Heike was not invited. Schad sent her a letter, dated Monday, 3 October 1927, quoted in Heike's diary two days later.

> *Heike,*
>
> *The exhibition opened at the Neues Haus tonight – sorry you weren't there, and about the Adlon, but nobody can know that you were the woman in the portrait – I hope you understand. Marcella and I are finished – perhaps I will see you at the El Dorado.*
>
> *Christian.*

The *Self-Portrait* immediately caught the attention of critics, who cited it as one of Schad's most arresting works. In one of his first pieces for the influential politics and arts periodical *Die Weltbühne*, journalist and psychologist Rudolf Arnheim drew a comparison with another of Schad's works, which has assumed a new dimension since the discovery of Heike's diaries.

> *The* Self-Portrait with Model *is outstanding, with Christian Schad including himself amongst the dilettantes, bohemians, degenerates and freaks who populate his world. With the decadent city as a backdrop, Schad is in the foreground, wearing just a transparent shirt which serves only to highlight his nakedness. The artist stares at the viewer, as if he has personally intruded on Schad's clandestine moment of intimacy, his face filled with revulsion,*

heightened by the narcissus that points towards him, coming from the near-naked woman behind him. He blocks her midriff, perhaps protecting her modesty, or maybe hiding something from the intruder. Unwomanly despite her round breasts, she wears nothing but a black ribbon around her wrist and a red stocking, looking away from the artist, stunned, if not scared. They both look alone: there are just a few inches, yet the distance is huge, and it is impossible not to wonder if Schad's self-disgust and the scar on her cheek are connected.

The 'model' is unnamed, but she bears a strik-ing resemblance to the transvestite in Count St. Genois d'Anneaucourt, *which depicts an aris-tocrat caught between his public image and his desires, and between virtue and vice. The Count stands in the centre, ambivalent, seemingly hoping that the viewer will help solve his dilemma: the demure, respectable woman to his right, or the tall invert to his left, his cheeks plastered in rouge, his huge frame barely covered by the transparent red dress that exposes his backside? Either way, the transvestite's resemblance to the 'woman' in the* Self-Portrait *is noticeable, although Schad claims that the model was chosen through a chance encounter in Vienna.*

Heike saw the *Self-Portrait* later that week, recording her thoughts in the final entry of the recovered diaries.

Went to the Neues Haus to see Christian's exhibi-tion. I was alone – none of the girls could make it – and as soon as I got there, a group of society women stared at me, and then went back to the paintings. Of course they were fawning over the one of the dandy who wants to have sex with the hostess from the El Dorado but can't because it's not respectable. 'So brave!' they kept saying. 'So bold!'

I decided to find the picture of me, even though Dora told me not to. I should have listened to her. I'd tried not to expect anything, but hoped he might have tried to bring out something of me – something to show Marlene or Conrad, or even the girls – but then I saw the Self-Portrait with Model.

I stared at it. Some woman glanced at me like I was dirt, looked back at the painting and then walked away. He'd made a very good likeness of himself, but he'd brought my hairline down and changed the style, made my nose bigger and given me breasts. He knew how much I wished mine were like that! Of course, they were there because he doesn't want anyone to find out how much he likes the third sex, and in the picture, he was blocking me from the waist down. He remembered my stocking though – he was so desperate for me to keep it on – and he added a flower. The gallery attendant said, 'It's a narcissus. It represents vanity.' Then I noticed the scar on my cheek – the attendant just shook his head when I asked what it meant. A man said they were common in southern Italy – jealous husbands put them on their wives.

I could feel the tears coming. I ran back to the institute and wept, and told Dora that I never wanted to see Christian or his painting again.

In the summer of 1932, Schad had another encounter with Heike – almost certainly his last. We know this from another letter to Huelsenbeck, dated Sunday, 7 August.

Welt-Dada,

I promised myself I'd never go again, but last night I found myself in the El Dorado. It's been five years, but I'd only been there ten minutes when who comes on stage but Heike, from my Portrait. *She wore this glittering red dress, almost transparent, and I felt scared. As she got down, I called her. She recognised me and tried to run to the bar. I grabbed her wrist.*

'I won't hurt you.'

She looked at me, trembling. A couple of the inverts came over. 'I'm fine,' she said, and sat with me. I thought about when you said that being with her would be the perfect Dada gesture because she was so spectacularly ugly in the Portrait, *but I was stunned at how good she looked – just like when I first met her.*

'You look incredible,' I told her. She thanked me. 'I can't believe that Marlene is in Hollywood and you're still here.'

'You were right,' she said. 'They don't cast freaks.'

Silence.

'Did Dr Hirschfeld . . .'

'Dr Abraham got there with Dora,' she said. 'I'm fourth in line. Next year, they hope, if things calm down.'

'Which things?'

'Adolf Hitler says that Dr Hirschfeld is the most dangerous man in Germany,' she told me. 'And if he gets in . . .'

'My career is finished,' I said.

'Your career and my life!' she shouted. 'The club, the surgery, the institute, everything!' Silence. 'I might die on the operating table, anyway, like Lili.' She took a draw on a cigarette. 'That might not be so bad.'

'You don't need surgery,' I said. 'You're beautiful as it is.'

'If that's so, why did you cover me?' she asked. 'It wasn't a mistake – I could tell from that scar you put on my face.'

'I was breaking up with Marcella,' I told her. 'I didn't want to hurt her any more by letting her know I'd been with you.'

'The Count's shameful secret,' she said. 'Your shameful secret.'

'She's dead,' I said. 'Drowned. There's no need to stay here. Come away with me.'

'Where can I go?'

She started crying. I held her hand and I was sorry. She went back to her friends. I doubt I'll ever see her again. Will paint to work out how I feel about this. Let's talk soon.

Christian.

In October 1932, Franz von Papen, the right-wing chancellor of the republic, banned same-sex couples from dancing together in public, effectively killing the clubs in which Heike worked. The Nazis came to power three months later, and as well as stepping up the attacks on Germany's LGBT population, they resolved to destroy its Modernist culture.

Perhaps surprisingly, Schad was not targeted, and unlike many of his Dadaist associates and Neue Sachlichkeit contemporaries whose works featured in the notorious Degenerate Art Exhibition, he stayed in Berlin, being allowed to submit to the Great German Art Exhibition of 1934. He remarried in 1947, five years after meeting the young actress Bettina Mittelstädt. In 1943, his studio was destroyed in a bombing raid, and when he resumed painting in the 1950s, his style had become kitsch. He died in Stuttgart in 1982, aged eighty-seven.

After Schad's letter, we know no more about Heike. The Nazis raided Hirschfeld's institute on 6 May 1933, seizing its records and burning its library before repurposing the building and making the El Dorado into the SA's headquarters. Dora Richter had already tried to flee Germany but failed, and was never seen again after the attack.

We can only assume that Heike disappeared with her.

Reciprocity and Resilience in the Anthropocene Dying

Shirley Geok-lin Lim

Shirley Geok-lin Lim won the Commonwealth Poetry Prize in 1980, the first for a woman and an Asian; placed second for the *Asia Week* short story competition and won two American Book awards for co-editing *The Forbidden Stitch* and *Among the White Moon Faces*. She has published ten poetry collections and three short story collections, three novels, *The Shirley Lim Collection* and two critical studies, as well as edited/co-edited numerous literary and critical anthologies. She received the Multi-Ethnic Literature of the United States and Feminist Press Lifetime Achievement awards, and University of California Santa Barbara Faculty Research Lecture Award. Learn more at lim.english.ucsb.edu.

I am still figuring out the answer to this question: How *do* we come back stronger when we are each, individually, beset by childhood trauma, hunger, sexual assault, race-gender-religious-linguistic discrimination, marginalization and erasure, dispossession, exile – just a few examples of the forces that result in nasty, brutish and short lives for so many women – but, also, when we are collectively threatened by social and political corruption, autocracy, tyranny and various planetary catastrophes?

I can only begin to work toward an answer from my own personal experience. How we women 'come back stronger' is only through having to first suffer self-doubt, unease, questions and struggle – whether internal or communal. Women are molded by the constraints of societies where we are still objectified, subordinated and stereotyped according to gender roles, with everything stacked unequally against us. But it is precisely the renegotiations and compromises we are forced to make that enable us to come back stronger – *if* we are so resolved.

One of the first times I spoke up as a feminist in the United States, I publicly admitted my uneasiness about the invitations that white feminists offered me to present and publish my creative and academic work. My struggle then rose from how they composed their invitation, identifying me as an 'Asian woman' whose voice was valued for its added diverse attribute: a token to amplify 'Anglo-American feminism'. In a 1992 essay, 'Reciprocity and Resistance: Asian Women in Anglo-American Feminism', I addressed my confused mingling of sentiments. I was grateful for the opportunities offered, and this gave rise to a strong impulse toward reciprocity – to explicitly return a favor to these feminists. And yet I also felt a countering resistance toward these Anglo-American feminists, at being so singularly identified and tokenized.

These mixed feelings of gratitude and anger have troubled me from the moment I entered the United States as a Wien international scholar, and continued to trouble me as I underwent a series of paper transformations – from resident alien, to green-card holder, to immigrant and finally to citizen. This poem, found among some undated papers from that period, suggests my unease in a new land whose values I could not wholly share:

Shelter

Neither father nor mother followed
eastward to the West.
She did not think: bereft.
Did not figure: one, alone, single.
Strange bodies talked and schemed.
Strange avenues, skyscrapers dangled
in nightmare and dream.

Orphaned in America, the strange
grows old, a family
of fidgeters, forgetters, arranged
mismatched roommates. The tree
of life wobbles, uprooted again

and again, leans crooked
like the new country lines, drawn in sand,
in blood and profit.

Here's the geography of souls who
will believe only
what they can see, will only view
what they can touch. Be
only where they are not. Shelter
is your name, new land.
Homes left behind, mother and father
buried, only the grand
story of spirit rescues, even
as it shames our selfish heaven.

Almost forty years later, my understanding of 'reciprocity' has shifted. The charge to 'return the favor', when freely, deeply and authentically placed on oneself, is not coerced, and neither does it come in colors. Different kinds of reciprocities, obligations and responsibilities bind humans. The most profound of all is to Nature and the planet She inhabits – and which She has gifted us. We are, similarly, charged with returning the favor to other peoples, in the names of those who have parented, instructed and cared for us; returning the favor as feminists to feminists, across borders that separate us – national, racial, class, gender, sex, ableism, language, worship – all those many distinctions that can divide and wound.

Hence, my delight at the invitation to contribute to this anthology – particularly heightened by its transatlantic gambit in this appalling moment of America First policies – was immediately unalloyed. I remain delighted by the editors' support of charities across the ocean: womanist, feminist, human rights–based UK and US NGOs.

But on second thought, is my delight complacency? While this anthology encourages feminist voices across cultures and territories (the Feminist Press for over fifty years has acted as an empowering agent for women across continents and languages – see, for example, Florence Howe's anthologies of African, South Asian, Taiwanese and US LGBTQ+, multicultural and multiracial women), what is striking is the women erased from this gathering: absent as writers and voices, and also as readers. These absences include women not residing in the United States and the United Kingdom; that is, most of the nearly four billion women on planet earth. Also, more complicatedly, women in the US and UK whose tongues are not of the color anglophone will not appear here.

My concern over this silence of other-tongued feminists suggests the penance of the survivor. My childhood home languages were Malay (now renamed Bahasa Malaysia), which my mother spoke to chide and praise me, and Hokkien, a Nanyang (South China Sea) version of Fujianese: a Chinese dialect out of the Amoy region linguistically akin to Taiwanese, which was the only language my paternal grandfather, an illiterate merchant, spoke. My own access to British colonial educational superstructures erased my potential fluency in these original oralities, and the familial identities they would have endowed. The unequal relationship between English and 'native' tongues is still deployed in order to empower, or disempower, particular communities, and postcolonial debates over languages still make a lot of noise in Malaysian politics. This also explains my ongoing wavering over anglophone writing, and guilt over my own use of English. Indigenous peoples have suffered not simply whole tribal extinctions but, even when surviving against all odds, extinctions of their ways of living, their cultures and their languages. Linguistic records note the loss of indigenous languages, and scholars fear the increasing (if not total) disappearance of these languages over the coming decades.[1]

When I was belatedly introduced, in 1990, to Audre Lorde's comments delivered at the 1979 New York University Second Sex Conference,[2] I discovered a route leading out of my theoretical confusion. Counterintuitively, Lorde's critique of how feminists cannot dismantle the master's house with the master's tools unburdened me of the historical weight of linguistic guilt and debt. In making her fierce claim that difference should *matter*, and for the marginalized to be included in the central circle of US feminism, Lorde rejected the idea of showing gratitude for the token invitation to represent Black women and, with it, the niggling nudge to reciprocate; that is, to feel obligated in return. White feminist academics, she said caustically, were working within a patriarchal hierarchy of race, heterosexuality and class, leavened by trite gestures to include others she aptly named 'sister outsider[s]' – as in the title of her book in which the conference comments were published, years later.

Unacknowledged as part of the master's tools Lorde derided, however, was language. Lorde's essay wielded an English rhetoric, albeit one inflected and nuanced by generations of female commentaries and Black voices, by woman-to-woman keening, sharing and bonding. Her writing was a master's tool that *was* effectively dismantling the master's house, and its English-language force, wit, intelligence and edgy energy meant, for me, a liberation from the intellectualism of sterile apologia.

How, for me, could the master's house be dismantled, except by using this master's tool, the English language? English was the colonial tongue forced on Malaysian children, which in my adulthood I have determinedly appropriated and made my own. English, after all, is the power through which my voice is articulated, albeit sometimes unmusical, cracked, but nonetheless loud, clear and unmistaken. I have used English in expository prose, academic writing, life writing, fiction, poetry; in oral debates, presentations, etc.; in everyday exchanges; in monologues, streams of consciousness and dreams.

Ultimately, in my poetry, I have nodded toward women's strength being found in our inner core as individuals – the primacy of the 'happiness for a solitary' that is, as my recent unpublished poem below notes, the central importance of the individuals' ability to fulfill themselves.

Why I Walk Alone

May 24, 2020

because I am a social melancholic.
because I am a workaholic.
because walking is a way of working,
and because I work best alone.
because I love to talk
and because sometimes I must talk to myself.
because I dress down when I walk,
dressing down to my naked core.
because walking is a happiness for a solitary.
because pacing with two or three or more
is aggravating to soles.
because the breeze is lighter
without heavy human huffing,

and because steps are lighter
without heavy human sharing.
because I make bad decisions when I walk,
like running when lights turn orange.
because it is OK to kill myself but not you.
because I am more patient when I walk
and because I am impatient when I have to
    stop walking.
because walking is a dreamer's route
and it is impossible for a companion
to dream the same dream at the same moment
on the same route, wandering away
from madness, separation, despair, home.

But, as well as gesturing toward the importance of individual happiness, my poems also pay humble homage to Nature's capacities over humankind, as in this testimony to the annihilating power of an invisible aerosolized virus:

> 'how small we are/I am
> under the pan-shadow
> of this tiniest
> viral speck.'

Ode to Covid-19

November 2019–April 2020

Too little too late
    was not the white
        evening jasmine
on time late March
    profligate over the tall fence

shutting private
locked-downs from
   Main Street
America.

They'll fall through the weeks,
   the last fragrance
brown grit
on stepping stones,
so many just in time
   making way for
Easter lilies
blooming in grass
below climbers.

Never *unchartered waters,*
   unprecedented
      challenges.
Every spring
springs
unprecedented.
In nature the normal
   is always unprecedented
      ever the new normal.

The aged mortal
   is the normal
rage against the dying.
The moral
resignation
   resigned to the dying
of light in the sun's
   western fury
      streets emptied

darkening
with night as was
from the Beginning,

wordless,
agape at the speed
    Death leaps
human to human to human.
Before this power
    how small we are/I am
under the pan-shadow
of this tiniest
    viral speck.

And alternatively, countering the 'moral resignation' to dying, my imagination continues to grasp for women's collective activism. My poem 'The Laws', composed on the morning of the global women's marches against newly elected President Trump, found a means to resist the politics of patriarchal subjugation in the alignment of the laws of Nature with the laws of justice. I appropriate the style of English proverbs, to evoke a transcendence of Man's oppressive rule.

The Laws

January 21, 2017

Law of the stone:
I smash, I own.

Law of the flower:
Live for the hour.

Law of the bee:
No flight is free.

Law of the man:
I rule, I ban.

Law of the sun:
Above me, none.

Coming back stronger, however, cannot be the final goal for women. In the present Anthropocene, when all planetary life is threatened by human activity, my mixed feelings to reciprocity – having felt it as an unwanted obligation, something I must be grateful to white feminists for, for their invitation to present myself to their circle – shrink as if to rearrangement of the deck chairs while we are sinking, many of us locked down in our separate cabins, in life-preserving counter-Covid-19 isolationist cocoons.

Audre Lorde modeled a different salutary feminism, which foregrounds interlocking rather than autonomous positions, when she wrote:

> For women, the need and desire to nurture each other is not pathological but redemptive . . . Interdependency between women is the way to a freedom which allows the I to be, not in order to be used, but in order to be creative . . . Within the interdependence of mutual (nondominant) differences lies that security which enables us to descend into the chaos of knowledge and return with true visions of our future, along with the concomitant power to effect those changes which can bring that future into being . . . Without community there is no liberation, only the most vulnerable and temporary armistice between an individual and her oppression.

> But community must not mean a shedding of our differ-
> ences, nor the pathetic pretense that these differences do
> not exist.[3]

Women's interdependence, as Lorde lays it out, negotiating between *difference* and *community*, is a crucial aspect of women's complexity that knits us together and runs through our spines, one of the many complications to our lives we must negotiate and renegotiate, which, as I argued earlier, will help us come back stronger through this century's sequels of crises. I am especially struck by the question that stands unanswered in her essay: '[W]hat about interracial cooperation between feminists who don't love each other?'

The answer to this question is to regrade romantic love as only one aspect (although arguably an essential one) in not just human, but universal, kinship. Through anthropological space and time, kinship is a truth evolved into the shared DNA of humanistic imagination. Not the color of our skin, but the content of our character, as envisioned in Martin Luther King's 'I have a dream' speech. This means of survival is not of 'the fittest', but of what my final poem-example valorizes as 'akinship', a term I use to denote the intertwining of love, antipathy, hate, difference, sameness, presence and absence; which maps a way forward beyond ideology, sentiment, identity, choice, politics, and any division of 'us' and 'them', 'I' and 'it'.

In this essay, 'Reciprocity and Resilience', I am unembarrassed that I have come back stronger, with resources to invite others, to reach out to sister outsiders and to give back what I was able to seize and deploy. Resilience is that exponential multiplier when individual agency, hard-won, overlaps and credits feminist collective activism for its social power. The reductive Darwinian mantra of 'survival of the fittest' is left behind when we nurture the fragile fledglings that are near-extinct indigenous tongues – silenced, until now, by the master's anglophone bullhorn – and we do this through the survival of kinship.

William Wordsworth, desolated by human suffering and dying, wrote of the kinship imagination affords us when it creates the links between our most complex passions and the simplest manifestations of Nature:

> The clouds that gather round the setting sun
>   Do take a sober colouring from an eye
>   That hath kept watch o'er man's mortality;
>   Another race hath been, and other palms are won.
>   Thanks to the human heart by which we live,
>   Thanks to its tenderness, its joys, and fears,
>   To me the meanest flower that blows can give
>   Thoughts that do often lie too deep for tears.[4]

The final example poem produced below was composed as I looked to earth's historical extinctions to try to make sense of the present crises of multiple dyings – environments, species, languages, belief systems, economies, societies and more – crystallized in the juncture of the Covid-19 pandemic. The poem looks to life's resilience through its circular structure, Being, centered in the great cycle of existence of kinship: kinship of eons, extinctions, identities, particulars, single and collective.

Pandemic Akin[5]

May 27, 2020

the meanest flower is akin to me,
who's akin to a 100,000 and growing neighbors,
who're akin to 350,000 and growing extended family,
who're akin to six and a half billion distant cousins,
who're akin to billions of passenger pigeons,
who were akin to uncountable trilobites that sank into
    the Paleozoic waters,
from where the first web-footed fish crawled out,
akin to reptiles preying on the small warm-blooded,
who're akin to mammals suckling their just-born,
who're akin to me,
akin to the meanest flower.

What follows after we have 'come back' must be women who learn from our victimization and take from it the inner core of the survivalist (grit, independence, self-reliance and more). We acknowledge we have survived with the support, even love, of countless other women, both over the millennia, and in our individual life journeys – women who've stepped up as surrogate mothers, sisters and daughters, mentors, generous gatekeepers, as well as just and fair interlocutors, offering unconditional friendship. We keep in sight those who have passed like ships in the night, who have warned us of the rocks ahead that would wreck our voyage.

However, in order for generous reciprocity to operate, women need resilience, and that resilience is amassed, muscle by muscle, through others' reciprocity. We can learn from life itself, to see how life on earth has emerged and reemerged through many past extinctions. Similarly, our future as women depends on our resilience, which we can give to one another: the resilience of humankind, Nature and our planet.

NOTES

1. Around 7,000 indigenous languages still survive today, but linguists fear more than 90 per cent of these may be extinct by 2050. (Wikipedia, accessed July 20, 2020.)
2. Audre Lorde, 'The Master's Tools Will Never Dismantle the Master's House,' *This Bridge Called My Back*, eds. Cherrie Moraga and Gloria Anzaldúa, fourth edition (State University of New York Press, 2015), 94–97.
3. Lorde, 'The Master's Tools,' 95.
4. William Wordsworth, 'Ode: Intimations of Immortality from Recollections of Early Childhood,' first published in *Poems, in Two Volumes* (London: Longman, Hurst, Rees, and Orme, Paternoster-Row, 1807), lines 199–206.
5. The numbers of Americans and people all over the planet who tested positive and who died from Covid-19 appear as when this poem was composed on May 27, 2020. By the time the reader comes to this poem, those numbers will have radically increased, underscoring the pandemic as an out-of-control crisis.

Stories, Data, Data, Stories: Notes from the Middle

Jessica Moor

Jessica Moor grew up in South West London and studied English at Cambridge before completing a creative writing MA at Manchester University, where her dissertation was awarded the Creative Writing Prize for Fiction. Prior to this, she spent a year working in the violence against women and girls sector, and this experience inspired her first novel, *Keeper*. She was selected as one of the *Guardian*'s ten best debut novelists of 2020 and is currently working on her next book. Find her on Twitter @jessicammoor.

Beginning
The numbers seem to say it all began on the first of December 2019. Which seems rather neat. The first day of advent, the slip into a new decade, a moment of transition. But, anyone with a scrap of intellectual humility hastens to add, we don't actually know. Not for sure. People who understand data understand negative spaces. They pace out the measure of the gaps, attend to their shifting borders, defend the numbers from encroaching conjecture. Most people – including me – don't like gaps. We find them unnerving.

We fill them with stories.

Rather than look at the negative spaces and unknowns at the centre of this biblical-scale crisis, this Covid-19, the virus, the plague, these unprecedented times, this new normal, I prefer to remember when it began for me. I can make some sense of that, dating my story within this story from a moment in the early days of 2020, glancing at the headline of a BBC piece on my phone.

What is this mysterious disease coming out of Wuhan?

I hadn't heard of Wuhan, but it's a city of eleven million people. Considerably bigger than London, the centre of my universe, with its paltry 8,908,081 inhabitants.

Shows how much I know.

That was one beginning, a personal beginning.

In the shared story, the media story, in the beginning there was a wet market. What's a wet market? *Not sure*, says the media story with a shrug. Sounds exotic, though, right? Dangerous. A little unsanitary. Definitely foreign. Makes good copy. *We think it started in a wet market.*

We don't know for sure.

Then there was another beginning when the virus spread to Italy. I've been to Italy. A good story is often one that blends strange and familiar elements, so this caught my attention.

And then it all started happening very quickly. Then we went into lockdown. Something began, something ended.

Stories fill the gaps in data; data falls powerless at the feet of a good story. They're uneasy bedfellows. 'Where's the evidence?' we often ask, when what we really mean is *tell me a story that I can believe in.*

The problem is that our government and our media in the UK are largely made up of people like me, people who are often more interested in narrative than they are in reality. Boris Johnson saw the crisis as an opportunity to indulge in a pound-shop Churchill act. I currently live in Germany. The chancellor here is a woman. Much has been made of the way female heads of state have handled the pandemic. Angela Merkel is also a scientist, a Ph.D. in quantum chemistry. Her policies are based on data. She doesn't get to indulge in 1940s cosplay.

She knows the story of her country.

A tense relationship between stories and data is nothing new. We treat the two as if they're opposites. Yin and yang, logos and pathos, fact and fiction. But we all know that fiction can speak to a truth that facts alone cannot. Fiction without truth becomes agitprop, propaganda, dogma. Fake news.

I WROTE A novel that is and isn't a crime novel. It was published four days before the country went into lockdown, and I cried in the shower because this wasn't supposed to be how the story of my life as a published writer began.

I reminded myself to look at the data, to see how many people had died, to see how many people were suffering. To get a grip. To understand that I'm not actually the protagonist in all this.

It worked. Kind of.

The novel I wrote is about a young woman who dies. It's about a police investigation. It's about coercive control and domestic violence, and the women's refuges that support survivors and that are existentially threatened by funding cuts.

Where do you begin a story like that? I felt that to give a full account I'd need to go back to Adam and Eve, to the creation myth of men and women and what they really are. Why blame the devil when you could blame the woman who was deceived by him?

But you have to start somewhere. Most crime novels start with a dead body and go from there. I was suspicious of that. How could I unquestioningly follow a genre that so frequently treats dead women's bodies as entertainment fodder, as titillating props in the larger story of a maverick man's genius?

AUDRE LORDE put it best when she told us that 'the master's tools will never dismantle the master's house.' It's a dangerous game to tell women's stories using narrative structures invented by men, not least because subjective, personal stories are often posited as the only thing that women are capable of telling. Men are the custodians of hard facts, we're told. Men like things, women like people. I'd like to prove them wrong. I wish I wanted to be a statistician or an engineer, a solver of proper problems. I've been told that those things matter more than stories.

But I needed to trade in those kinds of stories because I needed to tell a narrative that isn't understood widely enough, even as it becomes part of our legislation. Coercive control became a crime in England and Wales in 2015, the first law of its kind in the entire world. I myself found it hard to understand, so I told myself a story.

Coercive control is sometimes referred to as 'intimate terrorism'. It's not just a crime against a person's body, but against her liberty – and I say 'her' because 95 per cent of the victims are female.[1] Coercive control is a pattern of behaviour. The manifestation of a desire to dominate, which borrows the costume jewellery of a culture that conflates possession with love.

It begins with the seeking of commitment, with love-bombing.

No. That won't do.

It begins with a history of abusive relationships.

Or, it begins with a history of family violence.

Not family violence. Male violence. It's important to call things by their true names.

It begins with a history of male violence against women.

And now we're back to Adam and Eve, or the invention of the plough, or evolved sexual competition. Pick your preferred explanation for the origins of patriarchy, I don't care. Just acknowledge that patriarchy exists, and you will see that coercive control is its logical conclusion. This is where we are, our starting point for future action: two women a week are killed by a partner or former partner in the UK.[2]

It matters where we choose to begin.

It became obvious, as soon as the country went into lockdown, that domestic abuse incidents and homicides were going to rise. Not everything is predictable, but that was. The story of the pandemic reached into another story, the story of domestic violence in the UK. The data started to rhyme, hospital deaths and domestic homicides. The lockdown continued, the death toll(s) went up and up. There I was, fretting over a story I'd made up, when real women were dying.

The data we gather on women and their experience is lousy. We know enough to know that we don't know enough – Caroline Criado Perez exposed that in her seminal work *Invisible Women*. Data on the relationship between women and the world largely doesn't exist, or if it does, it's often so flawed as to be useless.

When I worked in the domestic violence sector, I saw how front-line professionals relied on good data to make risk assessments. They knew, for example, that the risk to a woman's life skyrocketed if a partner had strangled her in the past, even if he wasn't otherwise violent. They knew that a woman's safety was further jeopardised during pregnancy and soon after birth. They knew that leaving was the most dangerous moment in the course of a violent relationship. They planned accordingly.

I came to understand, too, how bad data could be dangerous, just as a blunt knife is more dangerous than a sharp one. Local authorities with meagre funds and no understanding of power and control would make modest interventions and gather their own data, without thinking too much about what they were going to measure and whether it was a good metric. *Look*, they could say. *He used to beat her up three times a week. Now he only does it once a week. The numbers are going in the right direction. Progress.*

Bad metrics lead to bad decision-making. Trump didn't want the Covid-infected American passengers of the *Grand Princess*, a cruise ship, to disembark. He said, 'I don't need to have the numbers double because of one ship.'[3]

We don't just need any data. We need better data.

History is written by the victors, which is why it's mostly his story and not hers. Most stories, genres, histories, cultures were formed by men, and serve men's needs and interests. We need stories that serve women's experiences. We need better stories.

Middle

At the time of writing, on 13 July 2020, it seems like we're in the middle. Maybe the beginning of the end. At the time of writing, the UK has experienced 44,819 deaths from coronavirus. When I come to edit this essay, that number will have changed, and when it is published, it will have changed again. But this is where we are today, 13 July 2020. A snapshot, a moment in time, a data point. I suspect that when you read this, it will seem very different. This essay is just one data point of many in a period that will, with telling, become a story.

I'm a lifelong reader, a humanities graduate, a peddler of stories. I'm useless at statistics. Big numbers scare me. I like to shoehorn all my life experience into the safe confines of a three-act structure.

There's a value to storytelling. It makes communication possible. It gives shape to experience. It brings people together and gives them a shared sense of who they are and how they came to be there.

There's a cost too. I'm an author. I have authority. I impose my view of the world onto you with relatively little humility, and there's no one to check whether I'm using that power for good or evil. And if there were, who would it be? Stuff gets left out. A false sense of inevitability kicks in. We fail to pay attention to what really is if it doesn't fit with our idea of what should be, particularly when we're bored and could do with the pace to pick up.

Middles can be interminable. There's supposed to be a climax somewhere towards the end of the middle, or the beginning of the end, but you often don't recognise the climax until it's already passed. 'We're in the middle of a global pandemic,' I say several times a day, sometimes to console, sometimes for gallows humour, sometimes in disbelief. *When you're going through hell, keep going.* We're in the middle of a crisis; the crisis will pass; order will be restored. That story might be true if you live, say, in the UK. Less so if you're in Damascus. If your normal is violence and abuse of power, then the restoration of normality is nothing to aspire to.

The middle of a violent relationship is often the point at which the victim feels that she has lost touch with reality, that her every experience is filtered through the lens of her abuser. She might feel that she's lost herself, that she can't remember what life was like before. Her sense of who she is becomes eroded; she recedes to a background character in her own story. It seems that there is no way out.

When someone in a relationship is being physically abused, an average of thirty separate incidents of violence occur before the victim reports to the police. The old story says that this victim is passive, that she's masochistic. This media-friendly narrative blames drugs or alcohol or poverty itself. It works to absolve us, this story. It creates a false sense of inevitability.

But the statistics tell us otherwise. The statistics tell us that there is no such thing as a typical victim. The statistics tell us that domestic violence cuts across race and class. The statistics also tell us that leaving a violent partner is the moment of the most danger to a woman's life, so the safest thing she can do is stay.

Yet we're happy to write it off as a working-class problem, a problem for women who aren't sensible enough to save themselves, or who hail from cultures too hopelessly, backwardly patriarchal to know any better. We're also happy to deprive the women from those cultures of material assistance. The Domestic Abuse Bill has finally passed its third reading, without a key proposed amendment to provide support to women with no recourse to public funds.

A lot of people don't know that those who stay in refuges have to pay rent just like everyone else, and the way they pay that rent is by use of housing benefit. If you've got the wrong stamp in your passport, if the Home Office has decided that you don't have recourse to public funds, you're not entitled to universal credit (which includes housing benefit). So you're turned away from the refuge. You've got nowhere to go. That's that.

A lot of people weren't aware that this was the case. A lot of people, including our own Prime Minister, Boris Johnson.

'Hang on,' he said when being questioned by MPs at a Commons Liaison Committee. 'Why aren't they eligible for universal credit or employment support allowance or any of the other benefits?'

Why indeed?

Regardless of how we got here, the fact is that as of today, the law does nothing to help you if you're in that most desperate of situations. That is the case on 13 July 2020. This is a snapshot in time. We can change that story. Until we do, the story of this bill isn't over.

End

I've tried to keep the structure of this essay simple. Beginning, middle, end. But it's proved leakier than that, and I find myself jumping ahead, circling back, breaking off. Sometimes life is more a spiky graph than a smooth curve. In fact, that's the case more often than not. Yet we need to normalise those outliers, or we can't understand the narrative sweep, can't decipher what's going on. The stories clash against the statistics.

We're where we are because we didn't have the right data and we didn't have the right stories. We make advances because data is gathered and because narratives change.

But even though this essay is ending, the pandemic isn't, and neither is the story of violence against women.

There are generally two ways in which an abusive relationship can end. It can end, as the vast majority do, with the victim eventually leaving. Sounds neat, doesn't it? But it can take up to seven attempts before a victim can finally leave for good, can change her story from that of a victim to that of a survivor.

When a woman reports to the police, that's when the story begins to end. We'd like to think. But there are many barriers to reporting, which disproportionately impact marginalised women. A Black woman may have a harder time being believed. A Traveller woman may be seen as betraying her community. A woman with mental health problems caused by the abuse may be written off as crazy. Restraining orders are implemented, then broken. Perpetrators go to prison, then they get out. Fathers still get access to their kids.

Closure is necessary in stories, rare in life.

And sometimes the victim dies. We know that two women a week in the UK are killed by a partner or a former partner. That figure doesn't take into account the number of women who take their own lives to escape abusive relationships (an estimated thirty attempts per day, three of which are successful every week[4]).

In the month after lockdown began in the UK, sixteen women and girls were killed in suspected domestic homicides. This is too many. It was triple the number in the equivalent month of 2019.[5] But there are too many deaths every year, lockdown or no lockdown. Domestic violence may be exacerbated by lockdown, but it isn't caused by it. It is caused by people making the decision to abuse other people. It is caused by perpetrators believing that their perspective, their story, is the only one that matters.

Various powers seem to have decided that the pandemic needs to be over now. They act as if it's all a movie and the virus needs to familiarise itself with its part in the script. It's time for triumph now, right? Time for a summer holiday. But this is the moment when people like me need to shut up and listen to the scientists.

I don't yet know how the pandemic ends. Either we fall victim to the disease, or we will find a way to take control. The Oxford vaccine is looking promising, as of now. It seems to be the consensus that Covid-19 isn't over until a vaccine has been disseminated and the disease eradicated. Any number of deaths is too many.

But two women a week are killed by a partner or

former partner, and we're told that that's inevitable. Human nature.

We're so bad at saying 'we don't know.' But 'we don't know' is the source of all intellectual honesty, all creativity, all possibility. We don't actually know what human nature is, because humans are constantly in a process of becoming. Humans do things like eradicate smallpox and set up refuges, but they also do things like destroy the planet and inflict violence on one another.

We don't know when violence against women will end, but it's possible to believe that we can end it. Until 1992, there was no legal concept in the UK of a man raping his wife.[6] You can't rape your own property. It was inconceivable, until it wasn't.

Where is it written that every year a certain number of women must be killed by men who claim to love them? If I've learned anything from the pandemic, it is that no feature of life is so certain.

Proposing alternative stories is my best offering, but even if they weren't laced with pitfalls, stories alone wouldn't be enough. We need it all, hard power and soft, logos and pathos, fact and fiction.

We need better data. We need better stories.

NOTES

1. N8 Policing Research Partnership, 'Police Responses to Coercive Control,' June 2018. http://n8prp.org.uk/wp-content/uploads/2018/09/Police-responses-to-coercive-control.pdf.
2. Office for National Statistics, 'Domestic Abuse in England and Wales overview: November 2019,' November 2019. https://www.ons.gov.uk/peoplepopulationandcommunity/crimeandjustice/bulletins/domesticabuseinenglandandwalesoverview/november2019.

3. Gabriella Borter and Steve Gorman, 'Coronavirus Found on Cruise Ship as More U.S. States Report Cases,' Reuters, 6 March 2020. https://fr.reuters.com/article/worldNews/idAFKBN20T22W.

4. Sylvia Walby, *The Cost of Domestic Violence*, a report published by the Women & Equality Unit (September 2004). https://paladinservice.co.uk/wp-content/uploads/2013/07/cost_of_dv_research_summary-Walby-2004.pdf.

5. Amanda Taub and Jane Bradley, 'As Domestic Abuse Rises, U.K. Failings Leave Victims in Peril,' *New York Times*, 2 July 2020. https://www.nytimes.com/interactive/2020/07/02/world/europe/uk-coronavirus-domestic-abuse.html.

6. Following the case of 'R vs R' (1991) and ultimately outlined in the Sexual Offences Act 2003.

Connect

I'm with You and You're with Me

Fatima Bhutto

Fatima Bhutto was born in Kabul, Afghanistan, and grew up between Syria and Pakistan. She is the author of several books of fiction and non-fiction, most recently, the novel *The Runaways* and the non-fiction reportage on globalisation and pop culture, *New Kings of the World*.

In June 2020 Dennis Dalton, eighty-two years old, stood in Pioneer Square in downtown Portland and raised his right hand in the air. 'This hand shook the hand of both Malcolm X and Martin Luther King,' Dalton told the assembled crowd of African American pastors and protestors. It was the first time Dalton and his wife, Sharron, had been outside in the three months since lockdown. Their son had brought them groceries and handed them over; no one hugged anyone. No exceptions had been made; no one broke social distancing. Though Dalton had begun his life of protest marching for civil rights on the fringes of the Montgomery bus boycotts, taking to the streets against the war in Vietnam and America's myriad other occupations and invasions, and most recently in support of Occupy, he hadn't gone out this time. There was a pandemic going on and Dalton was asthmatic.

'You know I've given my life to studying Gandhi, more than Malcolm, more than King,' Dalton tells me over Zoom later. 'And Gandhi's greatness was, during Partition and during the last five months of his life, he made a series of speeches at his prayer meetings calling on the Hindu majority community to defend the Muslim minority community. He said at the time, you imagine you have human rights, but your rights are real only if you perform the duty, the obligation you face, and that duty is to protect the minority.'

Dalton is retired and now teaches classes on ethics and philosophy to students at a Portland public high school. It was in one of his online classes during lockdown that he was confronted with a student, a high-school senior, who told him she'd been tear-gassed by police at a protest and injured. 'I couldn't sit back and watch my own student be persecuted on the streets,' Dalton recalls. 'I joined the protests at that moment.'

'That day?' I ask, unsure.

'No, that moment.'

I FIRST MET Professor Dennis Dalton nineteen years ago, when he taught me political theory at Barnard College. We were studying Lao Tzu on the day 9/11 happened, after the towers fell and before Columbia University was closed down for the day and SWAT teams placed on our roofs. He taught us Plato, John Locke, Thoreau. In Political Theory II we studied Gandhi, Malcolm X and Emma Goldman, the Jewish anarchist and political activist. He showed us clips from *A Bronx Tale* to illustrate Machiavelli. He invited members of the nearby Harlem community to audit his classes for free; one of the elderly students who came was a lieutenant of Malcolm's, who had been with him when he was killed in the Audubon Ballroom on 21 February 1965.

At the beginning of each semester, Professor Dalton handed out a sheet we had to sign and return, promising we would not grow up to be lawyers. When his beloved granddaughter, then a young child, was bitten by the family dog – who was until then docile – Dalton stood in front of our class in tears and told us that though his granddaughter's ear had been torn, nearly ripped fully from her face, and the family was considering putting the dog down, he could not support them. He didn't believe in violence. No harm would come from his hands to another being, no matter what they had done. The dog was saved.

Dalton would end up being my thesis adviser; the friends I made in his class were a devoted set of disciples – all of us sitting in the first row, staying afterwards for the discussions Dalton convened twice a week, turning up at his office hours to ask one more question. We came together, and to Dalton, because we were in pain. A pain that he recognised and illuminated before soothing, speaking to us of other worlds in which it was possible to be freed from our anxieties.

It was during our finals for Political Theory II that I was struck by a vicious panic attack that began a frightened season in my life. I had studied hard for the exam and knew I would do well, but when my hands started shaking and my heart thrashed against my chest, I looked up at Professor Dalton and wondered if he would understand if I were to throw my blue exam booklet to the floor and run out of the classroom crying. He would understand, I thought, but I didn't want to let him down. I stayed and finished the exam even as the panic flooded warmly though my body and convinced me I was dying.

Professor Dalton was a guide and mentor during an uncertain time, and he changed my life and thinking in many ways. But it was Malcolm X and the study of his life and journey that affected me most deeply. Malcolm X, who, as James Baldwin said, knew that the Western world's relationship to us, all us non-whites, was one of plunder. Malcolm, who suffered violence from childhood, losing his father – murdered by white supremacists when he was just six years old, the age my own brother was when our father was killed in Pakistan. Malcolm, who dreamed of becoming a lawyer when he was a boy and was told no, Black boys couldn't be lawyers. Why didn't he – the smartest boy in the classroom – become a carpenter, his teacher suggested, why not work with his hands instead?

I love Malcolm for his truth and beauty. When asked, after leaving the Nation of Islam, what qualified him to be an independent political leader of any sort, Malcolm replied, 'I am not educated, nor am I an expert in any particular field. But I am sincere, and my sincerity is my credential.' Malcolm, who said to James Baldwin – another man I love for his deep truth and beauty – 'I'm the warrior of this revolution and you're the poet.' As the protests swelled across the world in summer 2020, I found myself thinking back in time, to my professor who brought Malcolm X to life in a college auditorium week after week. Where else could we travel during a global quarantine but the past?

I SHOULD HAVE been fine in lockdown. I've spent a great amount of life under some kind of quarantine, after all. After my father, a member of Parliament, was killed, I couldn't go anywhere except to school and back, shadowed by two trucks of armed Pakistan Rangers, a federal paramilitary organisation that the government insisted was there for my safety. I was fourteen years old. If I wanted to go to a friend's house, I had to give the Rangers plenty of notice so they could travel ahead to do a security check of the location. If the location was secure, the Rangers would surround the house, their Heckler & Koch automatic rifles in their hands, standing at the ready. I was allowed out for only two hours at a time, but given the scene the Rangers and I caused, I rarely went anywhere. My father had been killed by the state and now the state wanted to protect me. I learned how to be lonely from a young age. I had dogs and a telephone. I read, I wrote, I sat in solitude.

I have been preparing for this moment my whole life. Whether I'm going away for three days or a month, I take everything with me, in case I never come back. I have whittled down my shoulder bones carrying heavy bags, transporting my life back and forth across cities for years. This is how we'll have to live in a world of pandemics and lockdowns, moving hesitantly over a terrain of endless uncertainty. I should feel pleased to have had all this preparation and practice, but I don't.

In my adult life, I live alone, and loneliness has a different shape. I have a dog and I have my books and telephone and all my portals to the world far beyond my shifting borders, but I'm not the same person any longer. I miss the world. When the globe went into lockdown in March, I thought I would be wildly productive: Reading like in my teenage years! Writing thousands of words a day! Deep reflections and insights to follow! But mainly, I felt quiet and distracted. The acute isolation reminded me of my past. I worried about how I would live without being able to travel, to see people I love, to do all the things I had put off and avoided, thinking I had infinite time. I tried to remember what Susan Sontag said: 'Just wait until now becomes then, you'll see how happy we were,' but day by day, I felt a burning flame flickering down to the halo of blue light just before it fades, vanishing into nothing.

IN 1961, Dennis Dalton had returned from a year in India as a Fulbright scholar. He was beginning his master's degree in Indian political thought at the University of Chicago when he heard that Malcolm X would be speaking at a local mosque. He was curious to hear Malcolm, who was already known for his radical stance towards freedom – freedom at any cost, by all means necessary. Dalton was the only white person at the meeting that day. And though he was electrified by Malcolm, by his clear denunciation of the Vietnam War, Dalton had been intimidated by Malcolm's exclusivist rhetoric. He described white men as the devil and even as his words were carried by the power of their clarity and eloquence, Dalton felt uneasy. 'King didn't have the ferocity of Malcolm,' Dalton tells me, reflecting back to that day. 'He certainly had the charisma, he was immensely powerful as an orator, but there was a different chemistry about him. The chemistry of Malcolm was intense, so incredibly personal. King was of another style: aloof, imperial, deeply impressive – his voice was like listening to the angels.'

Uncomfortable as he was, Dalton waited till the event was over and went up to Malcolm afterwards. 'I said to him, "Malcolm, I am eager to help your movement against white racism in any way that I can."' He explained that he had recently returned from India and that he was considering returning to the subcontinent with the Peace Corps, which had just been founded. Dalton asked Malcolm X whether he had any advice on how to best use his time effectively with the Peace Corps. Malcolm gave the twenty-three-year-old Dalton a strange look. 'You know what Peace Corps means, boy? It means America getting a *piece* of the country.' Before Dalton could respond, Malcom X continued: 'You asked me what you can do for my movement, I'll tell you: you can do *nothing*.'

THE WEEKS BLEND into one another and time – already meaningless for a writer – becomes even more so. The arbitrary schedules we cling to with devotion and superstition mean less by the day. When the world is cruel to us, we endure by adapting ourselves to new ideas in order to survive. We persevere. But when life is cruel to others, it is so much harder to bear. What we are living through now seems unbearably cruel: that a minority of us can afford to lock down at home, lazing through the hours or even working from a comfortable desk with our guarantees of food and shelter undisturbed, while more than half the world, if forced to lock down, will starve to death.

The cruelty of the world comes in infinite sizes; we did not need a pandemic to know this. One summer, I saw a man at a fountain in a public park of a rich European city. He was dressed in jeans and a T-shirt and he ran his wrists and hands through the water, cupping it in his palms and splashing it over his face, rubbing his wet fingers behind his ears. I watched him for a moment, thinking he was a Muslim doing his ablutions. I wanted to see where he was going to pray in the park, but he kept washing and after waiting a moment, I moved on, but as I did so, I saw a toothbrush and a tube of squeezed toothpaste in the back pocket of his jeans. He wasn't doing his ablutions – he was homeless. He was bathing himself.

In lockdown, I sit at my computer on a desk stacked with books and notepads and wonder, what does any of this matter? My schedules, my writing, my suffocating feelings and assumptions of myself. My imagination that I alone endure daily catastrophes, personal and impersonal.

Nothing, I suspect. It doesn't matter at all.

THE SECOND AND final time that Professor Dalton met Malcolm X was four years later in 1965, on a rainy day in London. Dalton was working towards a Ph.D. at the School of Oriental and African Studies, where I did my master's, when Malcolm came to speak at the nearby London School of Economics (LSE). 'He was there speaking to end the war in Vietnam,' Dalton tells me. 'Malcolm had seen the immorality of the war early on. He immediately opposed it, four years before King. I was drawn to Malcolm still for that reason: because I was intensely opposed to war and was immensely disappointed that King had not opposed it.'

By the time Malcolm and King had been killed, as James Baldwin would write in *Esquire*, 'there was practically no difference between them.' But on that rainy day, small gaps still remained between the great men, and Dalton remembers being moved by Malcolm's anti-war speech. Once more, he waited till the event had ended and approached Malcolm. 'Malcolm,' Dalton intoned in his gravelly voice, 'we've met before – you won't remember this – in Chicago. But I want again to offer whatever assistance I can. We are both together in this cause to stop American imperialism abroad.' Thinking back to that last meeting, Dalton paused. 'His demeanour towards me had changed entirely. He reached out his hand and said, "Brother, if we can do anything together to stop American colonialism and racism, then we're together. I'm with you and you're with me."'

The world was aflame, Professor Dalton tells me. 1968 was on the horizon and Malcolm anticipated the danger ahead. He was a true prophet; he saw the conflagration coming. 'Malcolm was a man who searched for truth.' I watch my professor speaking through the small square of a Zoom window. 'And it was a truth attained through immense struggle.' The journey: this is what Dalton taught his students in that university classroom so many years ago. The beauty and the wonder of life is there in the process, in the stumbling and the becoming.

'If Gandhi, killed when he was seventy-eight years old, if he had been killed when he was thirty-nine, like Malcolm was, we wouldn't know Gandhi today.' Dalton shakes his head sadly. Malcolm was moving fast in this period of time. Ten days after his speech at LSE, he would be killed. But then, less than two weeks before he was taken from us, under that rainy English sky, Dalton reminisces, he was magnificent.

AS LOCKDOWN IN spring becomes lockdown in summer, as the world feels further and further away, and cruelty and trouble fester, I lose the heart and energy to dial in to other times. But I wonder often about my professor. One day when we speak on Zoom – where his screen name is 'Dennis (he/him)' – I ask him about the first day he broke quarantine to join his high-school students in Pioneer Courthouse Square, the day he made that speech about Malcolm.

They were all wearing T-shirts – Dalton's had a photo of the only meeting between King and Malcolm, on the steps of the Capitol in 1964, where both men had come to listen to a Senate hearing on ending segregation – but the police were out in riot gear. Standing with his teenage students, Dalton joined in the protest call-outs. 'There's no riot here,' they shouted, 'why riot gear?' They stood at the barricades and shouted 'Quit your job! Quit your job!' at the police dressed in turtle-shells and helmets.

Professor Dalton extended his hand to a police officer and told him a story about Thoreau. In 1848, when told he would be jailed for the refusal to pay his poll tax in resistance to his country's war with Mexico and the ugly sanction of slavery, Thoreau replied to the town sheriff, his friend Sam Staples, that jail or not, he would not pay his tax. 'I have no choice in that case,' Staples responded. 'I have to arrest you.' 'You do have a choice,' Thoreau reminded his old friend. 'You could resign your office.'

'And you too,' Professor Dalton said kindly to the police officer, 'also have a choice. You can quit your job.' The police officer was predictably unimpressed. 'But Professor Dalton,' I ask, 'wouldn't lawyers have been useful then – at these protests where high-school students are being tear-gassed?' Dalton nods at me through his screen. 'Yes, I suppose so.' And then he pauses. 'But remember, when Thoreau was arrested, he didn't say, "Call my lawyer." When Gandhi was arrested, he never said, "Call my lawyer." And he was one.'

Portland will become ugly later in the summer. In July, federal agents without insignia, in full camo, their faces covered, will pull protestors from the streets and force them into unmarked vans. I see video footage of stun grenades and tear gas fired into crowds of young people, a flashing of light before the thunder-clap of the grenade. Every time I ask Professor Dalton if he is still going to the protests, he says yes. He is standing at the barricades. He is there on day forty-five, day fifty, day fifty-nine. He hasn't been tear-gassed or beaten, he assures me, but he is not afraid. He doesn't promise any of us that he will stay home. I think of what Malcolm said of himself: 'I live like a man who is dead already.' Malcolm's beauty is that he was a fearless man. A free man.

Professor Dalton calls on Zoom one evening; it's early in Portland and he was protesting the night before. He is tired but Sharron, his wife, hands him the sign he was carrying at the protest to show me. 'Malcolm urged us ALL to protest Racism,' it reads.

United We Stand
Kate Mosse

Kate Mosse is the international bestselling author of eight novels and short story collections – including *Labyrinth*, *The Burning Chambers* and *The Winter Ghosts* – four works of non-fiction and essays, and three plays. Her books have sold over eight million copies worldwide and been published in thirty-eight languages. She writes historical fiction putting women's lives back at the heart of history and celebrating under-heard female voices. *The City of Tears* – the second in her No. 1 bestselling The Burning Chambers series – was published worldwide in January 2021 and her non-fiction book about being a carer, *An Extra Pair of Hands*, will publish in June to coincide with Carers Week in the UK. In September 2021, her adaptation of her Gothic thriller *The Taxidermist's Daughter* will be staged at Chichester Festival Theatre. A member of the Executive Committee of Women of the World, she is the founder director of the Women's Prize for Fiction, the world's largest annual celebration of women's creativity, which celebrated its twenty-fifth anniversary in 2020. A Fellow of the Royal Society of Literature and a visiting professor in contemporary fiction and creative writing at the University of Chichester, Kate was awarded an OBE in 2013 for services to literature and women.

Connect with Kate via facebook.com/KateMosseAuthor, @katemosse on Twitter and find out more at katemosse.co.uk.

No doubt, these seem like dark days. All over the world, there's evidence of women's rights being rolled back, evidence of systemic racism and inequality and misogyny; of governments gaslighting and despising their citizens; of a handful of self-absorbed boy-men in Silicon Valley washing their hands of democratic accountability; of how the interests of the few are being put before the well-being of the many; of unkindness and untruth on what seems like an epic scale. We are living through history, and we know it, and the confinement of lockdown has given many of us time to reflect, to consider, to regret and to mourn the passing of our familiar lives.

Though the pressures are unique to each of us and our challenges are different, many of us have also spent too much time in our own heads this past year. Sleepless nights and wild dreams, becalmed and yet restless. Sweet tea and Marmite toast at a quarter past three in the morning. Long walks in the afternoon.

As a woman rising sixty, who has lived most of her life in the same patch of southern England, I remember the optimism and sisterhood of the women's marches of my younger years – Reclaim the Night, Greenham Common, Anti-Apartheid, the Right to Choose, Women Against Pit Closures, Clause 28 – though, looking back, I realise these comings-together were nowhere near as inclusive as they should have been. Too many women were left out. All the same, it's hard not to be dispirited realising how many of the things we walked and fought for, and which seemed, then, secure, are now being challenged, stolen, withdrawn and eroded the world over. The pandemic is cynically being used as an excuse to diminish women's opportunities and liberties. Time and again, history has shown us how women's needs – particularly those of Black women and women of colour – never are put first.

And yet . . .

These are powerful days, too, and should be – can be – days of hope; for the old system – comforting as it might have been for many – was a collapsing system. All the iniquities that are so starkly being laid bare today have been here all along – racism, prejudice, poverty, inequality, misogyny, the despoiling of the earth, corporate greed, lack of access to education, the lack of childcare or appropriate care for older citizens, fears for our health or for those we love, fear of violence in the home or the street, the wanton destruction of whole industries, and the collapse of public trust. Women's lives change radically from one century to the next, and in different cultures and communities, sometimes for the better and sometimes for the worse. Three steps forward, two steps back. We must be vigilant to protect those gains, of course. But we also owe it to ourselves to find the courage to hope, to look back over our shoulders with pride at the road already travelled, to acknowledge our mistakes, then face forward and embrace change. To hold on tight to our idealism and our optimism.

And we owe it to those pioneering women in whose footsteps we walk to acknowledge that, in part thanks to the introspection and the consequences of a worldwide pandemic, voices previously unheard or under-heard or under-supported are taking centre stage and, with it, increasing our wider understanding and driving change.

Out of crisis is coming the possibility of a new dialogue – 'the dream of a common language,' as the American poet, essayist and activist Adrienne Rich put it – and it is for every one of us to work to foster a new kind of genuinely inclusive, genuinely listening, genuinely hopeful feminism.

While the big moments of history are happening on our screens, large and small, while people march for their rights and for those of others, while those who are at the forefront of active change are to be applauded and championed, we must not forget also to acknowledge that sometimes the most significant change comes from the smallest of actions – the everyday actions, the actions that seep into life at every level and create a different common consciousness. Stealth feminism, if you like.

Being oneself matters, not only with regards to what you are able to do in terms of your age, your circumstances, your responsibilities, your passions, your power, your privilege, your country or region of residence – but also your character. You might be the one on the stage with a megaphone or linking arms at the front of the march, or you might be working behind the scenes or supporting incognito from a hidden space.

The quiet revolutionaries, the hidden activists, matter just as much as the visible leaders.

It is our multifarious voices raised in a common song, it is all of us standing shoulder to shoulder with girls and women of all ages, that makes for sustained and enduring change.

So, speaking only as myself (a white middle-class heterosexual Englishwoman of a certain age; a feminist, a writer and interviewer, a mother, a wife, a bereaved daughter, a

carer to my brilliant ninety-year-old mother-in-law; someone who's often been the only woman in a room of men,
someone who's spent forty years campaigning at the feminist rock face, thirty years championing first women writers
and now the rights of older women and carers), here are a
few lockdown thoughts about tiny acts of everyday sisterhood, written in a spirit of hope.

Make Space at the Table

If you're asked to take part in something – a talk, a conference, a meeting, a panel event – and you cannot do it,
never put the phone down without recommending another
woman. Allied to this, if you are inclined to say yes, always
ask if there is another woman on the panel, and if there is
a Black woman or a woman of colour, a younger voice or
an older one. If not, ask why. Use your invitation to do your
best to make room for others. And, yes, that sometimes
might mean standing yourself down.

Challenge the Status Quo

Misogyny, racism, ageism and prejudice thrive on being
presented as both historic and normal – the assertion still
prevalent in our educational system and certain parts of the
media, for example, that there were no people of colour in
Britain before the mid twentieth century; or that it is 'just
how it is' that there are more men named Dave and Steve
leading major companies than all the female and ethnic
minority CEOs put together; or that girls 'cannot' code or
be astronauts . . . Society is constructed to suit middle-aged,
middle-class white men, not women. But *we* are the majority. Don't be afraid to comment on sexism or absence of

diversity and call it out, if you're in a position to do so. One voice can easily become two, can become four . . .

Be a Good Ally

Each of us will have a different primary priority – climate change, abortion rights, indigenous land rights, eradicating Female Genital Mutilation, fighting persecution on grounds of ethnicity or skin colour, discrimination on the grounds of faith or nationality, issues around pornography, combating online abuse, eating disorders, the right to live freely whatever your sexuality or gender identification, issues about addiction, disability rights, the right to vote, the right to an education, to be safe from violence and sexual harassment, the rights of older women, the rights of refugees, environmental activism, the gender pay gap, the ethnicity pay gap, inequalities in medical provision – and this will, in part, depend on our own lived experiences, luck, our relative privilege, our backgrounds, our genetics, our opportunities, where we live, the political systems that control our quotidian lives, the systematic barriers put in our way. But we should try to be allies. Patriarchy deliberately sets women against women in order to divert attention from its own sins. It is possible for each of us to campaign for what we believe in while also respecting those whose motivating priorities are different.

Learn to Listen

Women come in all shapes and sizes, all ages, all colours, all definitions, all countries of birth or residence, all personal histories. So why assume women can, do or should think the same?

~ We are allowed to disagree with one another. Men – so often presented as the neutral voice, the status quo ante – are given permission to be themselves, to differ one from the other without being accused of letting other men down. You don't have to agree with everything a particular woman says to also acknowledge the good she has achieved in the world. Diversity of opinion is to be welcomed, not feared. The tribalism of all or nothing, you're either 'for me in everything or against me,' is a masculinist way of looking at things, a fundamentalist and repressive way of looking at things. In part thanks to lockdown and a lack of face-to-face engagement, much-reasoned discussion and debate is being drowned out by a 'who shouts loudest wins' philosophy. Constructive debate, entered into seriously and with good intent, is healthy. Even if our views do not align, we can respect another woman's right to see things differently. Listen and agree, or agree to differ – and always be vigilant about the workings of a system that wants us divided and thrives on our division. Don't do patriarchy's job for it.

~ Trust your own experiences, of course, but also turn away from the mirror and look for other women's realities. Listen to other women and believe them – older women, younger women, women of different ethnicities, of different faiths and values, to women you don't agree with as well as those to whom you are naturally drawn. This is how things change . . .

Words and Deeds

Language is a weapon: language is a way to exclude and it's a way to empower. Different generations use different language to describe themselves and others, and we should listen and learn from one another. Women's stories and lives and histories have always been subsumed and vanished and sacrificed to a partial version of history where our names do not appear. Women of my generation and others – particularly older women, whose voices are so little heard and who are so often dismissed – are still engaged in fighting this fight: to be seen for who they are, not someone's wife or mother, partner, carer or secretary, but their own unique selves. Ask how someone would like to be addressed and respect that.

The Personal Is Still Political

The personal always was – and remains – political.

~ If you see injustice or inequality or prejudice, try to do something. For example, if you see a woman being verbally abused on a train, start talking to her so she knows she's not alone, or stand between her and her aggressor. Of course, you have to read the situation and it takes courage to help, but let's try never to look away if another woman or girl needs support. There are rarely any perfect solutions or perfect outcomes, but doing something is better than doing nothing.

~ The silencing of girls' and women's voices begins, for many, at home, then is reinforced at school, at church, in the street, in the supermarket, in the workplace. Without systemic change, girls' and women's opportunities will remain limited by personal experience, and this is why legislation matters. We can – and should – make changes in our own personal spheres, but without fairness under the law – and without those laws being upheld – things will not improve for the better. If you have privilege, acknowledge it, but then campaign to change those laws or strictures that are clearly unjust.

~ Raise feminist sons, brothers, nephews, grandsons as well as daughters (sisters, nieces . . .).

~ We all make mistakes. It's better to try, fail and try again than to be bullied into silence or inactivity. Social media is being used to bully and intimidate women, particularly young women. Every repressive state and ideology uses censorship and suppresses freedom of speech to silence its opponents. Censorship only ever benefits the status quo. Stand by those who are vilified because of their courage in speaking out. In the face of misogynist dog-whistle politics, rising intolerance and macho populism, it's surely better to campaign positively to bring about the changes you want to see. Not everyone will agree with what you're doing or how, and you might not succeed. But your voice matters; your actions matter.

Equal Pay for Work of Equal Value

It is feminist to value your time and skills, and to expect them to be monetised appropriately. Of course it's important, too, to donate your time (if you can afford it) to those causes that most matter to you, where you can make a difference, but in the world of work it is fair to expect to be paid appropriately. The gender pay gap, despite legislation, refuses to shrink, and the devaluing of work traditionally undertaken by women – particularly Black women, women of colour and differently abled women – continues without consequence. Lockdown and the fallout of Covid-19 have exacerbated this issue. In March 2020, there were some 8.8 million unpaid carers in the UK, the vast majority of them women. By the age of fifty-nine, it's been estimated by CarersUK, a woman has a fifty-fifty chance of being a carer. Now the figures have become even starker.

Divided We Fall

Patriarchy is not about individual men (or rather, not only) so much as systems and vested interests. It was never truly ideological, but rather about self-interest, about power, about keeping advantage and reducing opposition, about the benefiting of one (tiny) group at the expense of all others.

- It is in the interests of the patriarchal status quo to set women against women. So, if you're tempted to attack another woman, ask yourself first if you have also called to account men who propound the same views.
- Patriarchy holds women to higher standards and encourages women to judge one another harshly – by weight, looks, achievements, opinions, marital status, material possessions. But guilt and anger are destructive, paralysing emotions, unless they lead to action, to change. Be the best version of yourself. That's all any of us can do.
- Patriarchy belittles, demeans and ignores older women. It intentionally makes older women invisible whilst valuing the soi-disant wisdom of older men. So, without sacrificing our contemporary values, isn't it our job as feminists to respect the campaigning women who've gone before us, even if some of their views and attitudes do not chime with ours? Our battles are not necessarily their battles, but we are in a continuation of change. We walk in the footsteps of others – so we should read

the work of previous generations worldwide, respect the causes for which they fought, learn their histories, honour their names. Remember, every gain made for women has come as the result of other women refusing to accept the status quo. It's come from mobilising, from talking, from debating, from marching, from persuading, from suffering . . . everything from (limited) suffrage in 1918, the Abortion Act 1967, the Equal Pay Act 1970, the Race Relations Act 1976, legislation against marital rape in 2003, the Equality Act 2010, the Marriage (Same Sex Couples) Act 2013 and many, many more besides. All rights can be eroded or taken away, and without knowing how these rights were won, and at what cost, we leave ourselves unarmed and vulnerable when they come under attack.

United We Stand
We should aspire to stand for and with and beside other women.

~ We should stand shoulder to shoulder, old and young. We should be positive about what women have achieved, while accepting there is still a way to go. We should listen to those whose lived experiences are different from our own. We should speak up for others when that's what we are asked to do; otherwise we should get out of the way and create opportunities for others.
~ Learn, celebrate, remember, champion, share the names of every woman or girl you admire, in history or in the present day. Arm yourself with facts and data, so whenever someone attempts to say 'women can't do' this or 'women have never done' that, you will always have a

rebuttal – equal-rights campaigners, suffragettes, nurses, sportswomen, poets, novelists, composers, climate activists, lawyers, abolitionists, warrior queens, religious leaders, politicians, engineers, astronauts, artists, playwrights, doctors, the list is endless. Make your own roll-call and share it: a truly inclusive, wide-ranging feminism, where everyone has her voice.

~ Most of all, we should travel hopefully and with optimism. Believe we have the power to change the world for the better.

We are many. We are strong. United we stand.

– July 2020

Return to the Heart
Sarah Eagle Heart

Sarah Eagle Heart is an Emmy-winning social justice storyteller, activist, media strategist and producer focused on advocacy on behalf of Indigenous peoples. She is co-founder and CEO of the Return to the Heart Foundation, investing in innovative Indigenous women–led initiatives. She has a background working with tribal, corporate and non-profit organizations, and her creative projects are rooted in her worldview as an Oglala Lakota, raised on Pine Ridge Indian Reservation, supporting narrative change for healing and impact. Her self-help memoir, *Warrior Princesses Strike Back*, is forthcoming.

Recently I appeared on *The BIG We* podcast with two African American women, Anasa Troutman and Kristen Adele Calhoun. Anasa lives in Oakland, California, and Kristen lives in Accra, Ghana. Kristen decided to stay in Ghana after a fellowship and during Covid-19 to reconnect with her African roots. We were asked, 'What does the future look like?' Anasa said, 'I truly don't know.' Kristen said, 'Everyone should leave America. I have no hope for the future because the American foundation was built on white supremacy . . . It's never going to change.' I said, 'I'm not going anywhere. These lands hold stories of my Lakota ancestors, our ceremonial origins, and our star knowledge. Our spirit is reflected in sacred sites . . . I know exactly what I want the future to look like. It is a returning of traditional Indigenous values and knowledge; it's a returning to the heart.'

I understand Kristen's perspective though. I saw the heart center reflected in Ghana during the Year of Return in August 2019, when over half a million people from the diaspora answered the call to journey home four centuries after the first enslaved Africans reached Jamestown, Virginia. We were only a handful of non–African Americans traveling with the NAACP delegation returning to Cape Coast Castle to remember and reconnect. In the WhatsApp group of mostly elders, they shared their sadness and excitement of returning home to find their tribal roots in photos. They were beautiful, but it was their sadness that overwhelmed me as we traveled to Cape Coast Castle. I thought to myself, *What would've become of me if I didn't have my tribal roots as an Oglala Lakota? I would've been lost.*

I understood how being immersed in my Lakota worldview was essential to my own healing and survival as a Lakota woman. I am protected by sage and sweetgrass prayers. I had been blessed to know intimately protocols and nuances of the Lakota value system, also known as Wolakota. According to Sinte Gleska University, the following are the definitions for seven Lakota values:

~ Woc'ekiya (praying): finding spirituality by communicating with your higher power, this communication between you and Tunkasila (the Great Spirit/God/the Creator) without going through another person or spirit.
~ Wa o' hola (respect): for yourself, higher power, family, community and all life.
~ Wa on'sila (caring and compassion): for one another, especially the family, the old ones, the young ones, the orphans, the ones in mourning, the sick ones and the ones working for the people.
~ Wowijke (honesty and truth): with yourself, higher power and others with sincerity.
~ Wawokiye (generosity and caring): helping without expecting anything in return; giving from the heart.
~ Wah'wala (humility): we have a spirit; we are not better or less than others.
~ Woksape (wisdom): with practice and knowledge comes wisdom.

I know exactly how fortunate I am to have grown up in my poor rural tribal community, raised by my grandmothers and extended family in rural South Dakota. These values were demonstrated in action when I was a little girl growing up on the prairie. I never felt alone, even after our single mother was left with a post-traumatic head injury due to a car accident. She didn't remember having children and struggled with short-term memory loss, as well as ongoing addictions in her attempts to self-medicate. In crisis, our extended family did not hesitate to care for my twin sister and me.

Our family didn't have much financially, but we were rich in Lakota culture and values. We had an idyllic childhood shuffled between our loving grandmas, uncles and aunties. I vividly remember walking through the tall grass as children holding hands with our auntie, with my small brown fingers brushing the grass tops as we raced to the gate in the countryside. We danced at the powwows and prayed at sun dances with our aunties. I felt peace and happiness surrounded by my oyate (tribe) as I entered the circle to dance under the watchful eyes of my tiwahe (extended family) to the sound of drumming. Our eagle plumes fluttered in the wind, signifying we had our Lakota names, and our beaded dance outfits were made by our grandmother and aunties, demonstrating their love and honoring us as their Lakota daughters. Our exterior traditional dance clothing tied us to our family, and correspondingly our actions reflected our tiwahe and oyate.

The rural isolation allowed for a deep connection to Tunkasila through reflection and prayers of Mitakuye Oyasin ('We are all connected'). This is not an 'ancient Indian saying'; it is our amen. Through this prayer, I was conditioned to think and act collectively and holistically for my people. The unspoken rule was that to be a good Lakota and relative was to 'help the people' in whatever way you are called to do. This interpretation came after attending numerous sun-dance ceremonies (fasting, dancing and praying for four days), naming ceremonies (receiving a Lakota name), inipi (sweat lodge) ceremonies and powwows (dance celebrations and contests).

The knowledge of my responsibility came from observing my grandmas, aunties and uncles, who always supported one another for giveaway and honoring ceremonies, despite their own financial challenges. I observed the behavior of demonstrating respect and honor in action, as extended family and friends came to support my sons while they sun danced (even though this might be the only time I see them all year). For a decade, they came annually to honor our family and my sons' physical sacrifice with their presence. Throughout the years, we butchered buffaloes with our grandma to make baba (dried buffalo meat) soup and wasna (dried buffalo and chokecherries) for ceremonies. As I got older and traveled, I realized that this life was rare. I understood how my upbringing in an Indigenous worldview of collectivity was unusual in this patriarchal American society. This is why I understand why Kristen had chosen to live in her original African tribal community to learn their worldview.

On the road to Cape Coast Castle, the busyness of Ghana stoplights rushed with Africans carrying colorful items for sale on their heads: toys, chips, candy and bags of purified water. I gazed, eyes riveted by the elegance of the women; even with the heavily dusty traffic, I could see their ancestors' pride and regalness and I watched as our African American companions must have thought to themselves,

This could've been me. We passed various scenes of ocean shores and forests, as well as different types of housing, and were told you could differentiate tribes by the straw roofs, as many had migrated.

We arrived at Cape Coast Castle and danced off the buses to a crowd of people parading down the street to celebratory African music. I felt at home in that African circle, dancing to the drum in my white outfit selected to honor the return of my new friends. We entered into a large room with the African tribal leaders, both men and women, seated onstage in a single line. We proceeded to flow in a single line to greet each leader by shaking their hands, and they gifted us medicine to drape around our necks for protection prior to going into Cape Coast Castle. Even this ceremonial act is similar to the traditional Lakota ways. Lakota people often greet their leaders in the same fashion and protect themselves with sage. When the African tribal leaders saw us, they smiled and said they knew we were Native American. They held up their fists, saying, 'Keep up the fight!' I thought to myself how funny it was that they knew we were still fighting for treaty rights, while many in America are still ignorant to our struggles. I felt incredibly honored to receive this gift of medicine and smiled when the African tribal leader asked for a selfie.

However, notwithstanding similarities, I am often told by well-meaning Americans that Indigenous peoples are descendants of Africa or descendants of those that crossed the Bering Strait. In those moments, I tell them we are descendants of the Buffalo People that emerged from Wind Cave, and we learned our spirituality from the White Buffalo Calf Woman.

Lakota people have prayed for the people and Unci Maka (Mother Earth) for generations. The sun dance was one of the ceremonies brought by the White Buffalo Calf Woman to the Lakota people who were starving. According to our oral stories, two men were scouting for buffaloes and saw a woman appear dressed in white. One had bad thoughts about her and he disintegrated into a pile of bones. The other recognized that she was wakan (sacred), and she told him to return to his people and prepare for her return in four days. She then appeared as a buffalo calf, changing colors in the four cardinal colors of red, black, yellow and white. The White Buffalo Calf Woman shared the sacred pipe and seven ceremonies, including the sun-dance ceremony, vision-quest and sweat-lodge ceremonies. And so, the buffalo is considered our mediator on earth and the chanunpa (sacred pipe) is the gift.

Every year during the summer, sun dances are held by plains tribes, including Cheyenne, Arapaho, Crow, Blackfeet, Plains Cree and Wind River Shoshone, and many other tribes have also adopted this ceremony. Sun dancers fast between four and seven days, dance and pray from sunrise to sunset for four days, and they may offer themselves through the piercing of the flesh. In 1934, the sun dance was outlawed and went underground. Because of this history, to be invited to attend is rare and an honor; the ceremonial space is protected fiercely. To force your version of history upon us is to deny our presence as the first people of these lands and our sacred knowledge passed down through oral storytelling.

The final chapter of our visit to Cape Coast Castle started with a heaviness I felt come upon me as I walked into the white structure with cannons facing the ocean. We followed a guide down into dark holes with only a few beams of light shining. The dark holes led to quarters deep down flights of stairs to holding cells. The walls held handmade scratch marks, and when I looked up, I saw holes where we were told the guns were pointed at the slaves chained closely together. We were taken to another slave quarter without any light, from where unruly slaves did not return. I waited outside, somehow knowing the darkness would overwhelm me, and when our companions emerged crying, I knew I was right not to enter. Finally, we were taken to the Door of No Return, which opened to white waves crashing on the shore. It would've been beautiful if you didn't know the true history of the stolen people.

The history of Indigenous peoples in America is also of stolen people from the Indian Boarding School era, when over 500 schools across the country were government funded and administered by churches from the late 1800s to 1970s. The sole purpose and slogan was 'Kill the Indian, Save the Man.' Our children were stolen to become 'civilized' by removing all parts of them that were Indigenous, from clothing to language to hair cuttings, that took the strength of our connection to Tunkasila and our families. Yet thankfully our Lakota parents and grandparents returned to their families close by, who held on to their ceremonies and language underground. Not all tribes were as fortunate to hold on to their traditional ways, but the Lakota people fought for their spirituality and traditions.

We now know the tribes that did resist colonization also held on to protective factors – conditions and attributes that helped us to survive. In 2016, I commissioned the Native youth report *The Indigenous Lifecourse* while CEO of Native Americans in Philanthropy. As part of this research, I worked with Indigenous scholars who identified a series of protective factors that safeguarded Indigenous youth. I believe these factors support cultural identity and perseverance against all odds for all Indigenous peoples, including the descendants of Africa. They are:

~ Cultural connection and connectedness: knowing who you are by having access to traditional knowledge.
~ Family connectedness: a significant predictor of wellness in terms of physical health and mental well-being.
~ Community control: over land, natural resources and Indigenous institutions (governance and ancestral courts). This enables sustainable economies, self-governance and relationships with land in accordance with our 'original instructions'.
~ Spirituality and ceremonies: healing at multiple levels is necessary – from the child (micro level) to their environment (macro level).
~ Extended kin bonds and networks: networking is an ancestral practice that must be protected and restored.
~ Healthy traditional food: access to Native ancestral diets and food habits.
~ Youth self-efficacy: developing capacities that promote confidence and competence.

Returning to the heart means returning to 'original instructions'. Original instructions are defined in *The Indigenous Lifecourse* as including 'many diverse teaching, lessons, and ethics expressed in the origin stories and oral traditions of Indigenous peoples.' As the report notes, Indigenous cultures 'think primarily in terms of space and Western Europeans think in terms of time. [Indigenous peoples] understand the world and the meaning of life in terms of nature, and nature and space are linked to thought and experience. This world view [is centered on] concepts of "natural cycles" – seasons, harvesting cycles, moon patterns, etc.' Therefore, Indigenous peoples 'see their responsibility as living in harmonious and balanced relation with all creation, including other tribes and racial/ethnic communities.' This is the opposite of the Western worldview, which is focused on 'temporal concepts of progress, development, and colonization.'

The future is now and returning to the heart is not rocket science, but it is an undoing of colonized behavior of hierarchy and patriarchal societies and systems. It is an undoing of the impatience of American society, unwilling to listen to the truth with humility and to respect one another with compassion. It is giving generously to those in need, without expectation of receiving anything in return. It is returning to healthy ways that give us time to heal, reflect and pray in nature. Returning to the heart is the answer to our ancestors' prayers.

Fifty-Nine Questions
Jenny Sealey

Jenny Sealey has been Graeae Theatre Company's artistic director since 1997. She has pioneered a new theatrical language and
aesthetics of artistic access, experimenting with bilingual BSL and
English, pre-recorded BSL, creative captioning and in-ear/live-audio
description methods. Her theatre credits encompass new writing
and extant texts, all permeated with this 'aesthetic of access.'

Recently BBC Radio 4 aired Graeae/Naked Productions'
Bartholomew Abominations. Outdoor productions include a
contemporary opera for 14–18 NOW First World War centenary *This
Is Not for You* with disabled veterans.

In 2009, she was awarded an MBE in the Queen's Honours list.
Jenny co-directed the London 2012 Paralympics opening ceremony
alongside Bradley Hemmings. She also won the Liberty Human
Rights Arts Award.

Learn more about Jenny's current work at graeae.org, and
wmv.org.uk/declarations-of-the-vagina.

Why is our PM such a superlative knob?

How do you update Zoom?

My son updates me weekly on his latest conspiracy theories. Are there any truths in them?

Do I really need all this cheese?

Has our local Sainsbury's really run out of white wine? (It has.)

Is this the government's way of locking us away so they can plot and plan while we are caught up in our bewilderment, trying to understand this Covid-19 thing?

Are my team OK working from home? Have they got everything they need?

How do I pin an interpreter? My eyes are so tired watching signers in little squares.

How can I be an artistic director when I can't direct anything?

Why am I crying? Is it because I am doing the ironing? Why am I only ironing the top half of my dresses?

What is happening with Brexit in all this?

What the hell is going to happen to adult social care in all this? The cuts have been ongoing since 2012.

Why did I cry on a Zoom with extremely prestigious people from the arts on it? Why could I not hold it all together? I couldn't – I felt wretched knowing that I probably won't see half of my team back in the Graeae HQ until March next year because they are shielding (following the advice of scientists, not the government).

Why am I so crap at IT? All I had to do was click on the three dots on the interpreter square and they zoom out to full screen. Wonderful.

Why were we told to start wearing masks on 24 July and not the twenty-third?

Why does no one in the mainstream world know or acknowledge that two in three people who have died from coronavirus were disabled? That disabled womxn are more susceptible than disabled men?

Why am I crying?

Why do I feel so intimidated on this arts-sector Zoom?

Why has it taken until a fucking pandemic to be asked to take a seat at the table?

Am I drinking too much?

Why am I not having any creative ideas? Everyone is talking about the new big idea and I don't have one idea in my head ... Not one ... Except when I am asking if it is possible that all the theatres that have not given so much as a nod to real diversity, inclusion and accessibility should not deserve a look in with the Arts Council recovery money. That is my big idea – a theatre world which is truly ethically, aesthetically and practically diverse in the broadest sense of the word and not just in lip-service tick-boxing.

Why do I bow down and dare not speak when someone mentions they went to Cambridge? This happened on an unconscious-bias training course. It is one of my many unconscious biases.

I am reading an article by an African American Deaf man on Deaf white privilege. Why is it something we white Deaf have not properly considered?

Black artists are saying, time and time again, that they are not represented within the arts world. I display (to myself) that horrid white-fragility defensiveness and then I ask the question: 'Please, can you guide me to get this right?'

Can my exercise teacher (on Zoom) see me when we do lying-on-the-floor exercises? Because if it is one that hurts or is too hard, I have a wee rest.

Why in 2020 am I having to remind the arts sector that it is not 'diversity and disabled people', 'Black Lives Matter and disabled people', 'LGBTQIA+ and disabled people'? For your information, there are Black and brown and other ethnic-minorities Deaf and disabled people and, oh, guess what – gay, lesbian, non-binary, trans Deaf and disabled people. I would be rich if I got a pound for every time I have had to remind people of the intersectionality of our community.

Is it healthy to binge-watch *I May Destroy You*?

Why am I crying?

Am I beginning to look like a loaf of bread?

Is there any point in having an artistic director? This is a serious question.

Why did all the theatres furlough Learning and Participation teams first? Why did Graeae do that? Those teams are the bed-rock of theatre and crucial in keeping the arts alive and thriving, and they are the most glorious, inventive and resourceful people within an organisation.

Why am I feeling so fragile? I know I am so lucky to have a job.

This is a reminder that we are social animals and need three-dimensional communication, don't we?

Why don't I quite know who I am anymore?

I created this #WeShallNotBeRemoved Disability Arts Alliance with four other disabled people to ensure that we are not forgotten or removed from the arts agenda. We now have over six hundred members and did a truly fabulous disability arts takeover on Facebook and Twitter. I was beyond proud. I know I can make stuff happen, so why do I feel I have lost my voice in the midst of all this?

What else can we be doing for freelancers?

Do I really need to wear a bra today?

Why was my name not mentioned when a Deaf person asked in our new Covid-19 Deaf WhatsApp group to name all the Deaf directors? Why do I care so much?

Am I watching too much television? Is watching *Grand Designs* and Michael Portillo doing rail journeys a sign of my age?

Why am I not having any fucking ideas?? Why???

My head feels like a tangled ball of wool with the knitting needles stuck in it. I need to untangle and get knitting because my board will ask the question: Do we need an artistic director?

When can we hug people again?

Why don't my clothes fit me anymore? I do know the answer for this one – shop during the UNIQLO sale and buy the next size up.

Will we ever end ableism? We have to end ableism!

How come I am on first-name terms with the Amazon delivery driver? Did I need a garden chair, books, anti-ageing cream . . . a picture frame . . . some art materials?

How can I start feeling useful again?

What will the new norm be?

What sort of theatre will people want to go and see?

What are the conversations I should/need to be having? Probably answering the question above is a good start.

Who else should I be talking to?

When will I climb out of myself and look at the big picture?

Why is Dominic Cummings still in government?

Will we ever have any one as brilliant as Jacinda Ardern leading us?

Why, oh why did it take George Floyd's horrific death to re-ignite Black Lives Matter? This has been within the arts agenda for years . . . but as a paper document, a lip service, a duty. A Black woman CEO of a huge arts organisation said to us on a (small) arts Zoom: 'What are you [white people] going to sacrifice to let us in?' Her words are at the forefront of my mind. What am I going to sacrifice?

Am I drinking too much? Not if I take days off and keep it in moderation.

Why haven't I done a jigsaw or tidied my drawers?

How do I create a new model of best practice knowing that half my actors are shielding and half are not? I don't want to be the director who only works with the 'fittest'. There is already a sort of 'fitness' issue within Graeae, due to the ableism within the arts world and the 'show must go on' and all that. I don't want this problem exacerbated. The challenge is to create a glorious mash-up of live, recorded and livestreaming to ensure real equality and inclusiveness in the finished product.

Am I going to actually try out any drawing and use my art materials?

In my current fragility and imposter mode, how can I embrace the incredible skills of the people I work with and be brave enough to share my lack of ideas, to ask them to fill the gaps and make something awesome?

Stern question to self: Jenny – are you a glass half-empty or half-full sort of woman? I am actually, usually, very much a glass overflowing . . .

IN THE MORASS of Covid-19 questioning and feelings of diminishing use and purpose, my counterbalance has been to give daily thanks.

Thank you for:

~ My job, my health; being locked down by the sea with a lovely kind man who makes too much bread (and whose clothes still fit him – bastard).
~ Those moments of looking out to sea on rough windy days, during my daily walk. It's a humbling reminder of just how little we are in the grandest scheme of things.
~ Zoom. So that we have remained connected to family and friends. (Although my family are so crap at Zoom . . . all talking over one another, walking around the house while chatting – i.e. zero Deaf-awareness – but I am used to it. Nice seeing their faces.)

Heartfelt thanks to:

~ The Graeae massive who have remained extraordinarily creative, resourceful and brilliant. How wonderful it is to be part of a team who genuinely care for one another. Thank you for the millions of quizzes, pictures of cats and silly GIFs you have posted in our team WhatsApp, and thank you for our Friday drinks.
~ My sign language interpreter team, who have been on every single Zoom with me – you are gold dust!
~ The #WeShallNotBeRemoved Disability Arts Alliance for coming together and presenting a united front to end ableism. This is a huge purpose and a daily reminder of the battles we have yet to fight.
~ The Zooms – the Big Cheese one, WOW, Blue Skies and the others – that I have been invited on. Thank you for the profound learning I have had from listening to other people's perspectives, their openness and generosity of spirit.

- My Where's My Vagina? theatre group of fifty womxn, sharing the pandemic together, and the wonderful vulva-shaped bread and cake pictures on our WhatsApp group.
- To Arts Council, who have shown real leadership and guidance, and those funders who gave Graeae and Disability Arts Alliance rescue grants.
- My friends, whom I treasure with all my heart – the Zooms with womxn I have known since I was three and the many others who have held together through all this (especially those on the front line and in womxn refuges).

And a thank you to my son Jonah (age twenty-six), who was alone during this pandemic and struggled somewhat, but volunteered, taking medicines to people and being part of the neighbourhood, ensuring people were OK. He is probably the best production I have ever done. Proud mum.

These are just some of the thanks . . . I've still not got any ideas as such, but as I'm writing this, a few things are forming in my wee mind. So, my final thank you is for the opportunity to write for this anthology.

Are We Kinder Now?

Helen Lederer

Award-winning comedian Helen Lederer is probably best known for her role as Catriona in *Absolutely Fabulous*, alongside Jennifer Saunders. She is a comedy writer with an extensive portfolio that includes writing and performing her own material as a stand-up comedian, a writer for radio and a comedy novelist. Her novel, *Losing It*, was nominated for the Wodehouse comedy literary prize. At the time of writing, she is working on her memoir.

Helen is also the founder of Comedy Women in Print, a literary prize she set up to celebrate and support female comedy writers. You can find out more at comedywomeninprint.co.uk. and helenlederer.co.uk.

Before lockdown, I was a hustler.

I would pull on the same old black jacket and the slightly too-trendy boots (diamanté eyelets) to zigzag across town to meet well-intentioned people in posh bars, offices and hotels. No matter how old, hungover or despondent I felt, there was always something hopeful about meeting a new person in a fancy bar with velvet sofas . . . It was like a drug. I was in the second year of running a literary comedy prize for women, and I couldn't fail – it would waste the previous five years of banging on about it.

When I'd finished my first comedy novel, *Losing It*, I looked around – rather hopefully – for a prize to win, and discovered there weren't any for witty female authors. I knew there were prizes for women authors, because I'd been a judge on one; and I knew there were prizes for comedy novels, because *Losing It* had been nominated for the Bollinger Everyman Wodehouse Prize. But a prize for both didn't exist.

Ideas are concepts based on thought. Not everyone acts on them.

I had my first idea aged ten. It was to have a fête in our back garden. I even wrote to George Harrison to suggest he might like to open it. As it turned out, George was busy – or at least that was what the secretary of The Beatles' fan club explained in her reply – but lots of other people came.

I'd learned that an idea can become a reality. Did this make me overly cocky? Maybe a little.

My second idea was less successful. I'd had an epiphany while waiting for a friend on the South Bank in London one January. I was having a coffee in the National Theatre bar downstairs and feeling somewhat inspired. I visualised writing a comedy set in a TV studio, with actual food on-stage. Too easily, I was given a great venue at the Edinburgh festival, and although I'd like to blame the Assembly Rooms for their belief in me, it's probably best to blame myself for what came next. I cast Miranda Hart as the floor manager. I wanted a break from the exposure of stand-up comedy, but writing and acting in my own play ended up more exposing for me, as it turned out. It was kindly suggested I didn't read the reviews.

On the plus side, it was the first time I'd canvassed for sponsorship, and, at my request, Cath Kidston very kindly provided the wipe-down PVC material for spilt food for free. This was very needed. Suffice to say I shan't be doing comedy with food again.

My third idea was when I set up Comedy Women in Print, the first prize for witty women authors.

The belief in what I was selling had to be so strong, I almost had to question its authenticity at times. But I was determined to create a platform for other women writers who were either already successful or looking to get published.

Was this altruism or bitterness? Or both?

When I began as a writer and comedian in the 1980s, there were very few women on the circuit. Agents and television commissioners were already championing a few successful women (three or four), but that was it. The top posts had been taken. Market forces created a culture of competitiveness and limited a sense of community. I craved the easy camaraderie I saw all around me. Maybe I was too much of a loner. Comedians are outsiders, after all – which can be annoying if you are one. Everyone thinks they're an outsider now·. . . I might have to up my game.

My bitterness and sense of injustice at the 'one or maybe two funny women at a time' culture has not lessened with age, but I had my doubts. Was I hiding behind this prize as an escape from my own disappointment about work? Or was I genuinely angry? And if so, was I angry because I had failed at my career and this was a distraction that could flex my ego in a different way?

Questions like these don't have to get answered, but I find them useful when I feel like giving myself a hard time. Comedians like that sort of thing.

As I discovered, setting up a prize and making sure it is legal and functioning took me to another planet of people management, social-media dependence and humongous admin. I had no idea how to do it, so I survived on the enthusiasm of others. No money for me and not much money for anyone else.

In the summer of 2018, bestselling novelist Marian Keyes had gone on record about the lack of female winners in the Wodehouse prize. A pal told me to message her on Twitter, so I plucked up courage to ask for her support. A couple of respected women influencers had already 'passed' on my request to come on board, which made me doubt myself and cringe at my own naive enthusiasm as well as – I'm sure – my badly phrased request. To my surprise and delight, Marian gave her endorsement, and this gave my prize a remarkably swift credibility.

But I understand how showbiz works. No one will take a risk until they see other people join in.

This dependence on others reduced me to a fawning and feeble wreck. The very famous would say no, the relatively famous would say yes, although 'maybe not this year', and the not-famous-at-all would ask to do it.

I know I have also been that person who hasn't replied to emails, and have said no to some requests – but mostly I try to say yes. Doesn't this make me desperate? Or one of the not-famous-at-all?

Being turned down felt personal, because it was personal. Worse, my abilities to manage people have never been good. My emails are streams of consciousness with bad typos, and I can alarm those who aren't prepared for instinctive communication. Losing talented people was hard. But despite this, year two was looking good.

By this point I had fifteen comedic and clever celebrities in place, two volunteers plus one paid admin person, and the Groucho Club was going to host our judging meetings and winner event for free, as long as I paid for the croissants and booze.

And then came lockdown.

No longer could I race around town, buying people drinks and taking part in panel discussions where I plugged the prize, in between the occasional paid jobs.

The actualisation of being part of something depends on other people's perceptions. And it was suddenly no longer possible to network, or feel important, or indeed make other people feel important.

Bit by bit the loneliness and silence of my 'idea' began to show itself. The prize was only able to feature in the real world. I needed the sparkle. I needed visibility. Zoom meetings didn't offer those.

I lost my power. The black jacket gathered dust and I stayed at home. In leggings.

But so did other people. Bit by bit, we saw fewer celebrities on chat shows. The last time I saw a pair of veneers was when I caught sight of my own, and there was something refreshing and reassuring about this. Focus was, quite rightly, on the things that mattered.

Catching sight of my old Uber bills brought shame. How could I have raced around London in a taxi? Who cared about sparkly hair slides? What did clothes matter, in the scheme of things? I soon forgot what it felt like to carry, let alone covet, a handbag.

And there was the naughty schadenfreude of not having to be taunted by other people's success. I didn't have to worry I was hiding behind a prize to make a difference – at least not for a while. So I focused on carrying on with the prize in lockdown. I had to work out who we needed to be in bed with. Who believed in us? Who would sponsor us? We needed new tricks.

And then my daughter, who lives in Ibiza, caught the virus. She didn't tell me until she was better, and this was doubly painful. The thought of her being ill, abroad, without me, was harsh. I had trained myself to not worry about the things I couldn't control for quite a few years, especially while she was travelling, but it wasn't easy. Images of made-up disasters were never far away and when I got the call to say how ill she'd been, I felt helpless and inadequate. Of course, I wanted the details but when she gave them to me, I felt worse. The social side of making sense of the disease wasn't straightforward and I wanted to be there to protect her.

She recovered. We spoke more. It drew us closer. New friends would come and sit in the garden. Community became healing; it became essential. It staved off the loneliness and ennui.

Judging meetings for the prize took place on a Zoom call instead of at the Groucho Club, and, to my surprise, they felt focused and connected. Despite not knowing one another, all the women judges spoke out with passion and commitment. Where there were differing views, there was also respect and generosity to one another, in order to get to the best result. They had all given up their time to read so many books, all for free, and yet here they were sharing their perceptions and findings with such care and respect – it was quite wonderful.

Since this is a comedy prize, the differing views were inevitably marked and intense, but this was also a wake-up call. There are good women out there, being funny and supporting others and wanting visibility. Some were more gregarious and extroverted than others, and the joy of being amongst such a genuine range of presentation filled my heart with hope. We recognised one another.

The logistics of making an online film of a winner's event on a shoe-string budget were relentless, challenging and worth it. To have experienced the prize before lockdown, where we all acted out our parts in an assumed way – where status and money defined our behaviours – and then to have ended the prize with such genuine warmth and commitment, was humbling. The universality of our situation made us feel less threatened and find more in common but above all, cherish the importance of the wit that is amongst us.

With more space to reflect on who we are, what drives us, what we have and haven't achieved, lockdown has been both cruel and illuminating. It's also been practical. If there are no places to sell our wares, we have to reconfigure how to be meaningful. With the removal of status and the hier-archical hamster wheel of aspiration, we are free to be the best we can be.

We can't do that on our own.

Reaching out to others is part of survival. Connection increases serotonin while competing activates anxiety. I should know.

The successful funny author mocks the world we live in. This is so the reader may feel safe – or at least not alone – and connected through recognition. What is uncomfortable can be made comfortable. If lockdown has shown us how to recognise one another, then surely kindness will follow.

And when we go back to 'normal' (whatever that may mean) I hope we can hold on to those moments of connection and seek them out – despite the temptation to resume the aspiring hamster wheel.

Give Them Their Flowers

Yomi Adegoke

in conversation with Feminist Book Society

Yomi Adegoke is a multi award–winning journalist and author. She writes about race, feminism, popular culture and how they intersect, as well as class and politics. She has worked at ITN, Channel 4 News and The Pool as a senior writer, and freelanced for *Vogue*, the *Guardian* and the *Independent*, amongst others. She was listed as one of most influential people in London by the *Evening Standard* and was also named as a 'frontline pioneer' bringing the fight to 'a new generation' by the same publication. She was awarded journalist of the year by the Woman in Africa awards, named a Marie Claire Future Shaper and was awarded the Groucho Maverick for her first book, written with co-author Elizabeth Uviebinené, *Slay in Your Lane: The Black Girl Bible*.

What has your experience of lockdown been like, and how has it altered your creative and writing habits?

The first two weeks – maybe even three – I spent every single day Googling 'When will coronavirus end?' Then I simply wrote 'When will this end?' because I just knew that the internet knew what I was talking about.

I live with my sister; my mum lives ten minutes up the road, and stays here all the time. My sister is immunocompromised, my mum is over sixty and I have adult-onset asthma, so we are still taking extra precautions, still self-isolating, still trying to avoid journeys unless they're absolutely crucial.

But I have enjoyed it. (I mean, as much as you can enjoy a lockdown in the middle of a global pandemic.) I feel very lucky that I've been able to take the time to do different things, like writing fiction and making ceramics. So as lockdown eases, it's definitely strange that everyone else is getting on with life, even though I can't, for safety purposes – but I'm not upset about it. I have been forced to be more productive than I ever have in my life.

In your *Guardian* column Reality Checked, back in May, you wrote that 'reality TV may be one of the few

winners during the coronavirus pandemic,' given 'we are all cooped up indoors, just like the contestants.' Now that lockdown eases, are there any other lessons from reality TV that you're going to take forward with you?

I've never felt more empathetic towards the meltdowns, and never felt more understanding of characters who, upon first glance, appear completely unreasonable. Normally when I'm with my family it's been by choice, not because I have no other option. It's been a long time since I've lived in these circumstances.

When I've watched things like *Big Brother* or *Geordie Shore* or *Love Island*, and people have stormed off to a smoking area and acted like it was so difficult, I've thought, 'What was so hard about being cooped up in a mansion?' But now I completely understand how difficult it is to adapt to other people's idiosyncrasies and behaviours; how difficult it can be to be pushed into a situation with people, when you have that freedom of leaving taken away.

So what I'm going to be taking outside is a bit more patience, and an understanding that we've all really been through it these past few months. I'm going to try and have a longer tether. I'll be a bit less judgemental, less quick to dismiss people. This whole time has been eye-opening.

As Covid-19 hit in the UK, some feminist arguments and action appeared temporarily silent or suspended. Have you perceived that in your life and work?

Absolutely. Nothing speaks to it more than the fact that I used to write the woman's column in the *Guardian*. But unfortunately, that's had to be pulled (at the moment, it's on pause) because cuts have had to be made, and the industry itself has shrunk. I've been given a column on reality TV as that's what people are engaging with right now. A lot of amazing publications have just disappeared entirely. It was one of the first ways that I noticed it. Because, obviously, it's not the case that people don't want to talk about women's issues, but people engage with what they want to engage with online, so if that's going to be reality TV rather than women's issues, then that becomes the media priority.

There have been blind spots in conversations about lockdown or quarantine. Initially, the only kind of issues that people saw in the media were 'How are we going to work?,' 'Where are we going to drink?' or 'How are we supposed to socialise?'

Yet after the first couple of weeks, the conversation shifted to the fact that lockdown for many people is a literal lockdown. For victims of domestic violence, or victims of child abuse, it's a completely different situation. That's why I try to be cautious and aware of the fact that my lockdown experiences were different to those of many women. For a lot of people, it's been a very traumatic time. It took a while for us to get into that conversation about how it will affect victims of domestic violence, or those who use school as a refuge.

What do you think got us to that conversation?

When statistics revealed that domestic violence had surged in lockdown, I started to see a lot of discourse around the reality of the situation, and people started trying to look at what lockdown meant for different disenfranchised groups.

But prior to that, lockdown and quarantine conversation was shaped by the media, which is predominantly posh and white men, and those kinds of lived realities were not necessarily within their remit. I don't think it's wrong for people to discuss their own lockdown situations which might be more straightforward than others. But I do think that the initial invisibility was due to a lack of voices in the media that considered how it affected different groups of people. It's amazing how the internet has democratised information, but it's also important that there's that rooting in real life.

Your 2018 book *Slay in Your Lane*, with Elizabeth Uviebinené, connected with a huge audience of engaged, shrewd Black women in the UK. How do you see that contributing to an ongoing conversation around Blackness and anti-racism?

I'm really proud of *Slay in Your Lane*. Elizabeth and I created a powerful body of work that spoke to certain conversations that weren't yet really being had in the mainstream. It is ludicrous to suggest that we were the first people to write about the Black British female experience in any meaningful way – there are so many books in the past five to ten years that have helped shape anti-racism conversation. But we helped bring the conversation to the mainstream, and I'm really proud of the fact that we weren't centring whiteness at all. *SIYL* was very much speaking directly to Black women. And we stay true to that. That was always our intention.

There's often pressure, even with a work of fiction, to write for the default (i.e. white) person in the UK, that you need to speak that language. We showed that Black women are not a monolith. We said, 'We want diversity within diversity.' And we want to clarify that, for Black women, success can look very different. There are many versions of success.

At the moment, there is a 'first culture' – a focus on 'the first person to do x, y, z . . .' But we want to give the flowers to the Black women who have allowed us to even be able to embody this space in the way that we can, whilst they can still smell them. We can see the influence of the book everywhere, but I feel like there's a real hesitancy to acknowledge that something came before. All of us are building on pre-existing work but that hesitancy is because of a culture that really focuses on youth.

With that sense of those who came before in mind, then, what is the feminist book that made you?

The book that changed my life was *Black Feminist Thought* by Patricia Hill Collins. I studied law at Warwick University, and took two external modules. One was 'Race', Difference and the Inclusive Society, and the other was Women in the Law. Between the two, I came to understand intersectionality as a concept. It radicalised me because it was my first understanding of racism on an academic level. Growing up, it was very difficult not to see racism simply as 'no Blacks, no dogs, no Irish', or as the Ku Klux Klan. I didn't think about it on a systemic level until that course, where a white lecturer called Peter Ratcliffe deconstructed institutional racism. One of the hard-hitting moments was when he spoke about the fact that Black people are given older medication, in terms of use-by date, in psychiatric hospitals. Somebody in the lecture asked, 'Why is that?' and he responded that it was essentially because of racism. There was no biological consensus on why this was. It was just because the medical industry, like pretty much every other industry in the West, is institutionally racist. It was terrifying. But somehow his words led me straight to additional content. The next day I remember reading *Black Feminist Thought* and, with every page, being completely gobsmacked at how much it was articulating everything that I knew. I knew it on a biological level but couldn't, till then, articulate it, because I was never in a space where I had needed to intellectualise it.

For me, it always comes back to reality TV. Unpacking concepts like these is why I love reality TV so much. I've always been obsessed; I've always watched with no irony. I remember watching when Kate Lawler was the first female winner of *Big Brother*. I remember caring, but not *really* caring. Then the first Black winner of *The Apprentice* was Tim Campbell, and I did know it mattered; but the level of protectiveness I felt for Makosi on *Big Brother* was so much higher, because she was Black and she was a woman. I knew everything Makosi did was going to be more scrutinised. I wasn't able to articulate this.

Reading Patricia Hill Collins helped me name these issues. I remember reading and thinking, 'I knew all of this.' I knew it on a gut level; I knew it as a feeling, but I had never spoken about misogynoir as a specific concept. So, that book completely changed my life. I felt I'd been asleep my entire life until I read it. I just saw the world. I just couldn't go back after that.

Ping . . .

A short story by
Rosanna Amaka

Rosanna Amaka is the author of the novel *The Book of Echoes*. She began writing the novel over twenty years ago, to give voice to the South London community in which she grew up. Its depiction of unimaginable pain redeemed by love and hope was also inspired by a wish to understand the impact of history on present-day lives. It was shortlisted for the HWA Debut Crown. She is currently working on her second novel.

I woke up this morning. Opened my eyes. Listened. Could not hear a sound. Not the birds singing in the trees, nor the foxes prowling around my food bin, or the neighbours thumping about next door, or children screeching while playing in the garden downstairs. It frightened me.

I lay for a while, just listening. Pure silence. No planes. Nothing. I haven't heard silence like that before; not in all the years I've lived in this flat, or even all the years I've been alive. All thirty-nine of them. I thought I had seen a thing or two, and each time I thought, *Surely it can't get any worse.*

And so I lie here in my bed remembering the fear I felt after 9/11, after Goldman Sachs almost went to the wall and Woolworths went bankrupt, after the London terrorist attacks when I stopped taking the tube. I thought those were bad. But this, here, is a different kind of something I never thought I would live to see.

I keep listening, begin to wonder; so push myself out of bed, go to the window, draw back the curtains. The sky above is grey; it coats everything. The gardens below grimace back at me. The neat fences, the shrubs, the trees are washed in gloom. The block of flats at the end looks almost derelict with stillness. There is no movement. Nothing sways, not even the trees. The wind seems to have gone away.

So I run into the corridor, through the living room, to the front window and look out. The rows of terraced houses still stand and cars line either side of the road, parked as if asleep. There is no one walking on the pavements; no one driving by. It is eerie.

And so, the questions get louder in my head. *What if . . . what if this isn't a virus?*

I look up and down the street. There are no neighbours twitching at their curtains, no signs of life.

What if . . . what if everyone is dead?

The thoughts take over. *What if . . . what if it's nuclear? What if they lied? What if it's Chernobyl? And everyone is dead in their beds?*

I run to the phone, pick it up. Dial. It rings, keeps ringing. *Everyone is dead! I'm sure everyone is dead.*

'Hello?'

I breathe out. 'Mum?'

'Yes, dear.'

'You OK?'

'Yes, dear, we haven't gone outside; everything is fine. Well, apart from my arthritis. And your dad getting on my last nerve.'

'Well, as long as you're OK.'

'Your brother phoned.'

'And?'

'Well, you know him. He was supposed to get our prescriptions. But he can't make it.'

'Again?'

'It's difficult for him. He has responsibilities, kids to look after.'

I hear the unspoken words between us. *Go on, say it: 'Unlike you.'* But she doesn't.

'Please, could you get them for us?'

'But, Mum, he has a car, mine's broken down . . .'

'I'm telling you, the arthritis is paining me today.'

'OK, Mum.'

'Oh, can you bring toilet paper?'

'Of course, Mum. See you later.'

I put the landline down, wonder whether I should phone my brother and have a go at him, but then a few texts start pinging through on my mobile. I pick it up and scroll through them. Someone has added me to a Covid-19 WhatsApp group. I can see Jackie, my best friend since school, has responded. Then the pings are coming good and fast. My brother posts something.

'Oh, well,' I say, looking at the screen and feeling a little silly. 'So no one's dead, then.'

I WALK UP and down the aisles of several supermarkets. I've never seen it like this before; it's like I'm walking around the film set of some dystopian movie. They've stripped the shelves bare. No pasta, no canned goods, no toilet paper. I laugh. Is this for real? This has to be a joke. I notice in the distance a packet of pasta and toilet roll left on the middle shelf in the biscuit aisle, rush to get it, but an old lady beats me to it. I smile at her. She scowls back.

OK, lady, keep your wig on, I think.

I don't get it. What is it about toilet paper? I understand the pasta and the canned goods, but toilet paper? Why has everyone in the world gone crazy for toilet paper? Is there some inexplicable link between a stockpile of toilet paper in your house and this virus? Does someone know something I don't? Is it like in the Bible, when the Israelites were told to put a sign on the door, and so if you have enough toilet paper in your place then the virus just passes you by?

I head to my parents with their prescriptions, but now it seems they've run out of all sorts and I have to head back out again. Finally get the toilet paper at a corner shop. Five pounds for four rolls, can you believe it?

MY PHONE KEEPS pinging. My brother is the worst; he's constantly sending out stuff on WhatsApp. I don't get it: He's got time for that, but not to get Mum and Dad's prescriptions?

Two Mondays ago, when I left work, all I kept thinking was: *Everyone has to calm the F down*. As for calling it a pandemic . . . *Surely Spain and Italy do not make a pandemic*, I thought.

That morning I sat in my boss's office opposite him, the microaggressions implicit on his face and in his words, the desk between us while he went on about my expenses, trying to undermine me in every which way, snidely seeming to accuse me of something or other, but never quite getting to the point. It wasn't the first time he had me in his office; last time, he almost accused me of making up my sales figures, until I got the paperwork together and he had to shut up.

I wasn't sure whether it was the fact that I was female and had outperformed his mate (whom he had brought into the sales team to show us so-called girls, which included the men, how to do things) that had upset him. Or if it was my Blackness that he didn't like. Could be both? I caught him once or twice giving me a real sideways glance as we left work, saw him through my rearview mirror looking at me as I drove away in my brand-new second-hand convertible Merc with leather seats. I bought it out of the money my Auntie Jane, my mum's sister, left me in her will. In some ways we were very much alike. She never got married. She never had children. She always talked about wanting a convertible Mercedes, so I did it for her; for us. Sometimes, it felt like she was right there beside me when I let loose on the motorway on the way home. I could hear her squeal with delight when I pressed down on the pedal, just like she used to whenever I gave her a lift in my old car.

Last year just wasn't the best year for our family, so when I bought the Merc in January, it felt like a brand-new start. But as soon as they introduced my new boss to me, there was something about him that made me uncomfortable. I've learnt over the years to pay attention to that feeling; learnt the hard way.

'So, your expenses look in order,' he said with a smile.

I smiled back. But neither of our smiles reached our eyes.

'I will go, then.' And I got up.

'Oh, your company equipment. I just need to check that.'

I lifted my eyebrows.

'Just a new policy I'm implementing.'

'What, starting with me?'

'Might as well, you're here.'

I went to my desk and collected up the company equipment issued to me – the laptop, mobile, iPad and mini keyboard – and put it on his desk; he checked through each item, ticked it off on his paperwork as he went, and at the end he seemed somehow upset that all was in order. That's when I knew he was after me for something and wouldn't stop until he got me, so I handed in my notice the very next day. I left work on the Monday; taking account of holiday and overtime owed. I didn't want to end up in jail for something or other just because this man had it in for me. People don't joke with money, and I have a reputation to keep, can't afford for it to be spoiled by someone trying to suggest, even hinting at the possibility, that I'm not honest. Besides, I'm a good sales-person, the best they had, and I didn't need to put up with that sort of treatment, figured I could find another job. How was I to know then that the pandemic was going to shut down everything?

PING.

More texts come through. The flat is quiet. It magnifies the sound.

Sometimes, I leave the TV on just to hear human voices, but not this evening. I haven't spoken to anyone in two days, apart from checking in with Mum and Dad. Had an argument with my brother three days ago, so he's not speaking to me, and Jackie, my best friend, is tied up with home-schooling, working from home and trying to keep the peace with that moron of a husband. We used to speak almost every other day.

My brother is going on about 5G on WhatsApp. Can't believe he's got time for this nonsense, but not for Mum and Dad. He's a dickhead. Don't know why Angela married him. I start to read his text, but don't get what he's going on about, so I put the phone down and get on with surfing the internet, reposting some of Jackie's funny posts on Twitter, eating my dinner and trying to figure out how I'm going to pay my bills.

HEARD FROM SOME of my old colleagues today. Half of them are on furlough. I could kick myself. I'm an idiot. Shouldn't have handed in my notice. I would be on bloody furlough now if I hadn't. I'm such an effing idiot.

I continue scrolling through Twitter. Someone has posted a picture of the NHS staff that have died. It's beyond sad, and there are so many people of colour amongst them.

Ping.

More stuff posted on WhatsApp; it's an audio. I press play.

Some woman speaks out from the phone. 'Listen, we are in a terrible state here in Spain. We didn't listen to the authorities in Italy,' she says. 'Hundreds and hundreds of people are dying daily . . . There are no beds in the hospitals now . . . This virus lives on plastic for four days . . .'

It feels like she's screaming at me, and for the first time I am terrified. Four days, she said: four days it hangs about on plastic. I start to clean, from the front door all the way to the kitchen. I wash down all surfaces, spray bleach on all the plastic bags, wipe down all the handles, the doors, scrubbing as much as I can. I keep cleaning until I can't clean anymore. I am exhausted, but when at last I get undressed and into my bed, I can't sleep, and suddenly I can't seem to breathe without heaving the air into my lungs. *Do I have it?* I lie awake wondering. *Am I going to die?* I force the air in and watch my chest expand. I keep coughing every now and then. A dry cough. *Isn't this a symptom? I've got it. I'm going to die.* I lie in bed, looking up at the ceiling, and wonder who's going to find me here. *Who's going to know if I don't make it through the night?* I keep staring at the ceiling, trying to keep awake, to keep alive. I cry because I feel so alone. I have no job, no man, no children, no one. I keep on crying because I wish I had someone to call my own. Then I remember Tony, my ex, and cry even more, 'cause he just didn't want to fight for us anymore, and I keep crying until I fall asleep.

It is morning. I open one eye, then the other. There is light peeking through my bedroom curtains. I lie there for a while. It's another day. I'm still alive.

TODAY WAS NOT a good day.

Four hundred died today. The numbers keep climbing. Is there no end to this?

Had to drop off my parents' shopping on foot; my car is still broken down because the garage is closed. My brother now claims that he's got the virus so can't help, as his whole household is in isolation.

Jackie is going crazy. I heard it in her voice when I spoke to her four days ago. She had to rush off the phone 'cause one of her kids was jumping off the coffee table. Wish we could speak like we used to, but she just doesn't seem to have the time.

I need someone to help me sort out the mess in my head. Just can't seem to sleep.

Spent hours online trying to get my parents a home-delivery slot, was there till 3 a.m., had to give up in the end. So, I woke early this morning, dressed up like I was wearing a burqa, covering my entire body except my eyes; they say this virus is killing people of colour, got to protect myself.

Queued for almost an hour before I could get into the shops. Got the shopping to Mum and Dad's, then realised I forgot the milk, so had to go back and join the queue again. It took me two hours to unpack and sanitise it all for them.

I am so tired.

SHIT. Nine hundred today. Is this going to keep going until we are all dead?

Mum phoned last week, crying about a friend of hers from her old church, and her son, who both died. She's really upset; can only attend the funeral via Zoom. I think it's today. Apart from comforting Mum, I haven't spoken to anyone in over a week. Haven't even bathed. I can smell myself, but just can't seem to get myself together. Everything seems pointless.

I search the internet for more information. I don't get it. Why are Germany's figures so low? Why are Greece's even lower? I think they said on the news that New York was being hit bad. And what's going to happen when it starts hitting countries in Africa, Asia, like it has here? I worry about my extended family abroad. God help us.

It's Thursday evening, eight o'clock. I take my wooden spoon and a saucepan out of the kitchen drawers, go to my sitting-room window and lean out. I want to scream, shout. But I don't. Instead, I join the rest of the street and bang gently on my pan for the NHS. I feel the wind against my skin as I hang out the window. I had almost forgotten what it felt like.

God, I miss talking. Miss spending pointless hours on the phone talking. I miss Jackie.

TODAY WAS A bad day.

I watched a man get killed. Watched as a white cop squeezed the life out of another human being with his knee. A Black guy, who could have been my brother.

I didn't mean to watch it. It was a mistake. I was on Twitter scrolling, as you do. Saw a tweet about police brutality. Clicked on the video. Before I knew it, I was watching as a policeman squeezed the life out of a human being. A living, breathing, human being. I can't stop crying. It brings up so much of my mother's brother's death. It stirs up so many of the things I have buried inside.

I am tired. So, so tired.

Twitter is going crazy. Can't seem to get a word in edge-ways. Everyone seems to be yelling. My head hurts. It hurts so much.

I can't seem to make it to my bed. Curl up right there on the sofa, and I hug my laptop.

This world is so bloody wicked.

THERE IS A march today.

Jackie called me earlier, all riled up, said we had to go.

Was online the night before, couldn't believe my old boss was on the company website spouting on about Black Lives Matter; that bloody corporate vulture. Hypocrite. Yes, that racist, sexist corporate vulture was on there, preaching about the way forward on Black Lives Matter. I told Jackie about it.

'Well, we're going on that march and after we're done there, we're going to march on your old office. Let everybody know what a bloody hypocrite he bloody is,' she said over the phone. 'Shouldn't be allowed to get away with it, after what he did.'

Been lucky with food-delivery slots for myself and my parents recently, so haven't been out of the house in weeks. I'm a little apprehensive, but it will be OK.

I push myself up from the sofa, wipe the dribble from my face; my computer falls to the ground. I pick it up, check it and look at the time. 'Shit!' Jackie will be waiting for me.

I sniff myself. I stink, but it's too late to shower. Jackie is waiting.

I pick up my bag and my mask and head to the front door. When I get there, I put my hand on it to open it. But my hand trembles. I am scared. I manage to open the door but can't seem to walk out. I try again, but my legs are trembling too. I am scared to go outside. I feel a tear on my cheek.

I take the phone out of my pocket and dial. She answers.

'Jackie.'

'Yes.'

'I can't get out my flat. Where are you?'

'At the bus stop, waiting for you. What do you mean, you can't get out?'

'I can't seem to walk out. I'm scared, Jackie. I'm really scared.'

'I'll be right there.'

It took Jackie some time to coax me out.

TODAY WAS A good day.

Slept in, woke up, opened one eye, then the other, saw bright sunlight slip between the gap in my curtains. Lay there. Listened. Heard the birds sing, and children playing in the garden downstairs. Today, I opened my front door and went outside for a walk, straight after breakfast, saw the different shades of hedge green in front gardens, smelt the sweetness of the summer roses in bloom as I went by.

Today, I sold my car to my brother. He came by, kicked a couple of tyres, looked inside, said he could fix it himself. At least Auntie Jane's spirit can still get her rides. Don't need to worry about the bills for a while.

Today, I stayed away from my phone, my computer, my television. Did not surf the internet, go on Twitter or watch the news. Took an old cloth from my kitchen cupboard, laid it on the front door-step and sat down. Watched people pass on by, heard the cars as they drove past.

Today, I heard a car door slam close by, looked up, and there she was, standing on the front path. 'What you doing here?' I asked.

'Getting a break from the madness of my kids. Some me time,' said Jackie as she opened up a chair and set it on the front path.

I laughed, leaned back, stretched my legs out in front, felt a light breeze on my skin.

And we sat and talked and laughed, like we used to. God, I missed it.

'I missed you,' I said to her.

'I missed you too. Love you, girlfriend.'

I smiled, looked up at the blue sky, then at her. 'I love you too.'

Today, I took a break. The troubles will still be there for me to fight tomorrow.

Trans Rights Are Women's Rights Are Trans Rights

Fox Fisher

Fox Fisher (honorary doctorate and MA in sequential design) is an award-winning artist, author, filmmaker and trans rights campaigner living in the UK. Fox is a co-founder of Trans Pride, Brighton and director of the My Genderation project, making over 100 short films for TV, online and festivals. Fox is also adviser to All About Trans, facilitating interactions with the mainstream media. Fox was artist-in-residence for Homotopia Festival, 2020. *Trans Pride: A Colouring Book* and *Trans Survival Workbook* are Fox's third and fourth books. You can follow them @theFoxFisher.

Back in the 1970s, women marched for their rights under the banner 'biology is not destiny'. They were protesting the oppressive gender expectations and fundamentalist ideas of sex placed upon them because of their bodies. Since then, we've come a long way. From what was often focused solely on civil rights and the perspectives of white middle-class women, the fight for a more just society based on feminist principles has expanded. Black feminists, disabled feminists, queer feminists and brown queer trans feminists like myself have carved our paths and started telling our own stories, bringing us into a new area of feminism and feminist politics.

But as under- or misrepresented groups inch closer to a more equal and equitable society, the push-back has often become even greater. In modern times, we are seeing a surge in extreme anti-equality rhetoric, legislation and violence against minorities. This is clearly illustrated, at the time of writing (summer 2020), with the current civil conflict in the US, in the wake of the ceaseless and abhorrent police brutality and systematic discrimination against people of colour. Under the current presidential administration, reproductive rights have also been stripped, as well as some fundamental protections for queer people, such as anti-discrimination laws and access to health care.

In Europe, a similar trend is rising. Anti-queer sentiments

have been festering, with several parts of Poland being branded as a 'no LGBT zone', and their newly elected president, Andrzej Duda, making it one of his priorities to strip back rights allowing queer people to adopt and get married. Poland has also seen a surge of hate crimes and anti-queer rhetoric, leaving the community there frightened and isolated. The country has withdrawn from the European treaty on preventing and combating violence against women. In Hungary, Prime Minister Viktor Orbán has now banned transgender people from legally changing their IDs. This happened in the middle of a global pandemic. The Prime Minister has since moved on to stripping away women's rights.

Are we noticing a pattern here? We can see the trends quite clearly, and it's a worrying and horrifying thought that this is being allowed to happen. Political forces opposing queer rights are usually known for their right-wing extremism and conservative values.

This rise in anti-equality rhetoric has reached far and wide, and has formed many unusual alliances. In the UK, there has been a long and contentious battle, with conservative, right-wing forces and alleged feminist groups teaming up to advocate against equality for transgender people. While many of these so-called feminist groups claim to be fighting for women's rights, their sole focus seems to be opposing those of transgender people.

In London, where I was born, anti-trans protesters forced themselves in front of the Pride March in 2018, carrying hateful banners. It took over forty minutes for them to be removed as they marched in front of thousands of people. Their message was confusing for those who were already geared up to be cheering the start of the Pride March but were instead met with hostility and hate.

The alliances of 'feminist' anti-trans groups are often in blatant contradiction with what they claim to stand for. Many align themselves with alt-right conservative parties, politicians or think-tanks that have directly voted or advocated against abortion rights, anti-discrimination laws, and same-sex marriage and adoption. These groups are the first to celebrate the stripping away of transgender rights and thank those right-wing politicians who do – who, in turn, often move on to attacking women's rights, immigration rights and anti-discrimination protections, as illustrated in the US, Poland and Hungary.

The most recent rise in anti-trans sentiments in the UK came in 2016, when the government announced that they would be reforming the Gender Recognition Act 2004, a law that allows transgender people to change their birth certificates. At present, the law requires trans people to 'prove' they have been living as themselves for a minimum of two years. They must also be given a diagnosis of gender dysphoria from a medical professional, hand in large amounts of paperwork and pay £140 to have their applications reviewed by a panel of people they will never meet in person.

In line with progress being made in countries across Europe and beyond, such as Iceland, Malta, Denmark, Norway, Argentina, Portugal and Ireland, the British government announced they would be looking into simplifying this process, allowing people to change their birth certificates via a statutory declaration signed by a solicitor. This would make the process much more streamlined, and health care professionals would no longer be needed in this purely legal process. In countries that have passed similar or even more progressive laws, this has been highly beneficial for trans people, who can now access legal gender recognition and name changes at earlier stages in their transitions, making it easier for them to participate in society as themselves – both socially and legally.

This simple and straightforward change became a vehicle for strong anti-trans sentiments in the UK, and for the past four years the British media has been fuelling the fire of what has been so often described as a 'bitter culture war'. The false narrative spun is that transgender rights are in direct opposition with the safety of women and girls; that if transgender people are afforded the rights to change their legal gender more easily, violent men will exploit these laws in order to access women's spaces and abuse them, i.e. in bathrooms, toilets, prisons, women's shelters and other facilities or services that are single-sex spaces.

Daily, the British media pumps out articles, columns or news pieces that both trivialise and uphold this narrative – despite the lack of factual evidence of this danger being real. This is particularly frustrating for many queer people, given that in 1988 the government put in place Section 28, which banned 'promoting the teaching of the acceptability of homosexuality' in schools – with dire and detrimental effects on myself and my generation. This lack of support for people dealing with sexuality and gender issues still casts a shadow now. I have witnessed how it affected my peers and friendship groups, and I still carry that trauma. With not enough support or a safety net for anyone dealing with their gender identity or sexuality, it manifested in recklessness, self-harm or even death by suicide.

This law was not repealed until 2003, and marks a dark part of the UK's treatment of queer people. While gay rights have improved considerably in the UK, public concerns that kids might be influenced or assaulted by gay people in single-sex spaces are now being repeated in the discussions around trans people, where they are accused of 'grooming' children and influencing them with their 'gender ideology'.

In countries where more progressive laws about legal gender recognition have been put in place, there have been no such issues. Transgender people in the UK have already been using single-sex spaces in accordance with their gender identity for decades, and this right was solidified in the Equality Act 2010. I remember how anxious I was the first time I used the toilets, and, eventually, I realised it was no big deal. You're just there to do your business, like everyone else. (Although I once tried a shared urinal with a stand-to-pee and got really pee shy. Now I always use a stall.)

No one I know has ever been asked to show their birth certificate to use single-sex services or facilities. Trans people are already active service users of places like rape crisis centres, swimming pools and gyms. This is confirmed by service users across the UK – places that have long been inclusive and understanding of the fact that transgender people are particularly vulnerable to violence and discrimination. Research by Stonewall shows that transgender women are at an increased risk of domestic violence and sexual abuse – and are in much need of the same support as other women. We live in an unequal society where men certainly don't need to pretend to be women in order to abuse them. Nine out of ten women in the UK, as reported by Women's Aid, are abused by someone they already know. The myth of the abusive man in a frock pretending to be a woman is exactly that: a myth.

This has not stopped the UK government from trying to follow in the footsteps of Hungary and Poland though, with Liz Truss, minister for women and equalities, announcing recently that they would be restricting trans people's access to single-sex spaces, barring those who have not had genital surgery from using spaces in accordance with their gender identity.

How these restrictions were to be enforced remains a mystery, as the only way to know someone's genitals is to literally look down people's pants. Unless the government was planning to have a guard inspect every single person accessing bathrooms, locker rooms and other services – which surely everyone can agree is a gross invasion of privacy – it will be impossible. Transgender people are already using these spaces without having undergone genital surgery, so these 'concerns' are simply being used to whip up fear against them.

Essentially, this whole 'debate' has always been about excluding transgender people, under the guise of 'concern' and 'biology'. These arguments, especially the one about biology, are rarely put forward as mere observations about biological classification, but rather as a point to try to exclude, discriminate and justify bigotry. Much in line with this discourse, the Trump US presidential administration published a memo on how federally funded homeless shelters could spot a transgender person based on physical appearance.

In a speech on the 17th of December 2020, Truss claimed she would be focusing on 'conservative values' based on 'freedom, choice, opportunity, and individual humanity and dignity' rather than 'the narrow focus on protected characteristics' in the Equality Act 2010 – the UK's most comprehensive equality legislation.

She also said she wanted to turn away from 'fashionable' issues of gender, sexuality and race, only to follow that up with an article in the *Daily Mail*, where she compared equality issues to 'jumping on the woke bandwagon' – while ignoring real issues of poverty and disadvantage, effectively pitting the working class against queer rights and black rights. She also doubled down on her position on single-sex spaces, saying we have failed to 'defend the single-sex spaces that were won by the hard work of women over generations.'

Meanwhile, transgender people in the UK are suffering from the consequences of an increasingly hostile society. Hate crimes against transgender people have risen exponentially across the world, with black transgender women being at the highest risk of violence and murder simply for being who they are.

It should be clear to anyone who aligns themselves with feminist values that the fight for transgender equality is a feminist cause. Much as those in the 1970s for whom a slogan was 'biology is not destiny', transgender people now fight to be freed from oppressive gender expectations placed upon them purely because of their physical characteristics.

They suffer by the same oppressive standards in terms of reproductive rights, gender expectations and violence as cisgender people, on top of the relentless transphobia they face at every turn. To exclude transgender people from conversations that affect them or spaces that they require access to will inevitably only enforce the same oppressive binary that we have all fought against for a millennium.

It is important that we constantly challenge ourselves so we do not find ourselves on the wrong side of history. Finding allies in right-wing ideology and ultra-conservative values is a red flag all of us should recognise.

TRANSGENDER EQUALITY will never come at the cost of other people's rights or freedom, just like same-sex marriage or equal pay does not come at the cost of others. What it does mean is that we have to be willing to grant trans people the same rights that everybody else has. Equality often feels like oppression when our privilege is challenged and others access the same rights we have always been afforded.

Transgender people come in all shapes and sizes, and belong to various other minorities across the spectrum. They are as diverse, nuanced, complex and different as any other social group, and they are just trying to live their lives as best they can. As a feminist movement, we have to be able to recognise the struggles of others and not find ourselves in opposition of progress.

In the words of Audre Lorde: 'The master's tools will never dismantle the master's house.'

Liberation is not placing the same shackles that were placed upon us onto others, but breaking the system altogether.

Our Sisterhood

Melissa Cummings-Quarry and Natalie A. Carter, Founders of Black Girls Book Club

in conversation with Feminist Book Society

Melissa Cummings-Quarry and Natalie A. Carter met at secondary school in north-east London and bonded over their shared love of books (Zora Neale Hurston's *Their Eyes Were Watching God* and Alice Walker's *The Color Purple* remain firm favourites). Years later, Melissa, now a business development manager, and Natalie, a real estate lawyer, decided to channel that passion for reading and form the Black Girls Book Club (IG: bg_bookclub), a literature and social events platform that celebrates literature by Black female writers.

Now touted as one of the UK's top live literature events, Black Girls Book Club have hosted Bernardine Evaristo, Roxane Gay, Malorie Blackman, Afua Hirsch, Tayari Jones and Angie Thomas, and have been featured in media such as: *Vogue*, *Stylist*, BBC Radio, Buzzfeed, *Metro*, gal-dem, *Pride* and more. Melissa and Natalie were named as two of *The Bookseller*'s Rising Stars of 2019. Their debut book, *Grown*, is forthcoming.

I began to feel estranged and alienated from the huge group of white women who were celebrating the power of 'sisterhood'.

I could not understand why they did not notice 'absences' or care. When I confronted our teacher, she expressed regret and began to cry. I was not moved. I did not want sympathy, I wanted action.

– bell hooks

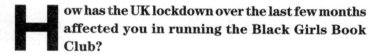 **ow has the UK lockdown over the last few months affected you in running the Black Girls Book Club?**

Melissa: Natalie and I founded Black Girls Book Club with one mission – to create a safe space where Black women could come together and celebrate life unapologetically. Not only that but it's an entire manifestation of our friendship. With that in mind we work from the perspective of giving people exactly what they need. 2019 seemed like a year of ambition and hard work. Many of our counterparts had secured book deals, new jobs and great opportunities. It was a great year and led to many successes for us. Our book club had run in excess of twenty events – with members coming from Tottenham to Toronto – resulting in over a thousand women coming through our door just to be a part of what we had created. 2019 culminated with the launch of our first literary festival – a month long soirée dedicated to the work of Black women writers with authors such as Emma Dabiri, Candice Carty-Williams, Dorothy Koomson, Bernardine Evaristo and Irenosen Okojie part of our line-up. As the festival closed we knew that we had to step back on Black Girls Book Club events and allow people to use 2020 as a cultural reset. We wanted to work on one or two events for the year but nothing too big. Instead, our focus would be on ourselves, the women who attend our book club and our debut book, *Grown*. However, we didn't realise that our reset would become an entire lockdown.

Natalie: There's a lot of pressure on this new generation to be constantly doing 'stuff' every day and to be 'making moves'. I think you do need to take a step back and dedicate your time to working on something to the highest quality and so we aim to have a spirit of excellence when it comes to Black Girls Book Club. What's underpinning our motivation and our work is that Black women deserve excellence. We recognised, especially after our literary festival, that to keep that level of excellence we had to naturally take a break and rest. Looking at what's happened with the pandemic and the lockdown, people have been forced to take a step back and pause.

What is the feminist issue that you think has affected you or will affect you as women and particularly as Black women?

Natalie: I'm in a very lucky position to work in the corporate world as a lawyer and so my employment hasn't been affected yet because capitalism still reigns, and my clients are still very active. My perception of feminist issues that impact Black women are not necessarily issues impacting me as an individual. My main concern is the wave of redundancies to come and how this will impact Black women. If we're talking about the prevalence of unconscious bias in the workplace and a double bind Black women face both as women and being Black, we should be concerned. The McGregor-Smith Review highlights the majority of BAME people, but I would say Black people, typically experience discrimination in the workplace. I'm concerned about how the unemployment rates will continue to rise for Black women as there's seemingly no policing of redundancies and how individuals are selected for redundancies. It's incredibly subjective. More importantly, from a basic health-care perspective, one thing that has been beneficial about the lockdown is that Black women have been so vocal about the poor health care given to Black women in the UK. A lot of that has focused around maternity care but it extends to the health care we receive in all areas. We see a situation where there will be a lot of cuts to the resources given to public services. As we already have those underlying issues with care we receive when we experience health problems, I just see the issues Black women are already facing being exacerbated and Black women being the victims of even poorer care from our national health system which already doesn't seem to serve us.

Melissa: My health has become a major issue and my main concern. Statistically, Black women are five times more likely to die in childbirth compared to their white counterparts. Five. Times. This isn't a socio-economic issue either. Money, class and network cannot save you. They blame it on things like a poor diet, lack of higher education, high blood pressure or the fact that many of us are frontline workers. But that explains nothing when, from Beyoncé to Serena Williams to my best friends, every Black woman knows a story or has had an experience where the health-care industry has ultimately failed them. Black women continue to suffer and be at risk.

Black people can't rely on a system that continues to fail them; where we are disregarded or dismissed; where our concerns are ignored by health-care professionals. I spend the majority of my time messaging my friends saying: *Have you got private health care? Have you sorted your life insurance? Do you have a will? Can you pay your bills?* I don't have time to worry about whether there's space for me at the table. Or if I can shatter the glass ceiling. I'm just trying to stay alive.

Natalie: Operating in a corporate world, we have heard about diversity and inclusion, women on boards and women in senior positions, but that's been one of my major gripes. When we've had these feminist conversations, they ultimately operate in a space that benefits white middle-class women. I don't understand why the feminism conversation, where it should have been active during lockdown, seems to have been sidestepped into a 'diversity and inclusion' conversation, because those two are not the same things. We have such a focus on having women on boards. I'm seeing mothers who can't feed their children and people who've been furloughed who don't know if their job has security. I'm sorry, but having women on boards won't fix these problems.

These are the kinds of issues where I feel feminism is not active.

Say if I'm a white middle-class woman right now, I have job security and I've not needed to take a mortgage break or ask my landlord to accept later rent payments because I don't need these things. Instead I'm going to start calling on feminism because I want to be promoted. Whereas if I'm a single parent, I'm the main breadwinner of my family, I'm working in a low-skilled job, that [promotion] isn't an option for me. That's where I feel feminism should be focusing – protecting Black women who don't have a secure income.

Do you feel like you have to work twice as hard as your white female counterparts to achieve where you are? Do you feel that itself can be a burden?

Melissa: Growing up I was taught that I was my only competition, so I try to make a point of avoiding comparing or considering my achievements, or lack thereof, in relation to my peers. Ultimately, I think it's harmful to centre whiteness. As a Black woman working in environments where very few people look like me, to continue to pit myself against others could ultimately be destructive to my self-esteem. Instead I centre me – I see myself as the standard.

Sometimes, the concept of 'Black excellence' can be so restrictive that it can feel like a burden – especially if you don't feel as though you are making the grade. It leads to feelings of imposter syndrome and you end up burning out.

It annoys me that often the onus is placed on the minoritised party to form answers that do little to centre the real issue – the systemic hurdles that continue to impact Black women's success. Visible Black women continue to be asked if we 'feel we have to work twice as hard' when instead those in positions of power should be asked 'why are Black women forced to work twice only to get half as far?'

Toni Morrison once said, 'Our lives have no meaning, no depth without the white gaze. And I have spent my entire writing life trying to make sure that the white gaze was not the dominant one in any of my books,' and I think that it's this sentiment that has been fundamental to the success of Black Girls Book Club. We centre Blackness. Black womanhood. Black stories. We avoid using the tools, language and process of an industry that has traditionally excluded us.

I'm sure many observers see two Black British West Indian girls with no connections or publishing background and wonder how we were able to disrupt the industry in the way we have. But our success wasn't borne from working twice as hard as our white female counterparts. We focused our energies instead on creating a platform where we were at the centre. When we open a door we kick it down so everyone else can come through. So, it's important to us that in our space it's twice as easy for Black women's voices to be heard. We want to amplify the success stories of the many Black women who could dare to have the audacity to dream of creating a space for Black women like us.

Natalie: I'm not a fan of respectability politics. This whole idea of working twice as hard as your white counterparts is damaging. Respectability politics is rooted in the principle that you can work your way out of your Blackness, which I disagree with, as you will always be Black. When talking to people about how hard to work, I encourage people to work smart. We need to be comfortable enough in our Blackness and comfortable enough in being authentically ourselves to have some ownership and say, we're not going to work twice as hard for half as much. My encouragement to young Black women is to think strategically – not to put limits on yourself or to obsess with saying that you work hard and that you're 'Team No Sleep'. You need sleep and rest, but what you need most is a spirit of excellence.

Melissa: Working to a particular level is the most important thing for me personally as I don't need anybody else to validate what I've done. I can't come and kill myself just because someone may be doing better than me. As far as I'm concerned, we are the standard. We set the tone and I don't need to look and see what anyone else is doing or has done. Ultimately, you have to gas your girlfriends up and be your own cheerleader.

Natalie: Working hard has to be rooted in the goals that you're trying to achieve and what's important to who you are. I posted on Instagram yesterday because it's seven years since I qualified as a lawyer. It's been a really tough last few months and I was just reflecting. But ultimately, I've done that work as part of a wider goal. I've had to reconcile that with myself. I agree with Melissa that there's no point going out there killing yourself to work hard, just to say that you did it.

Has the content and how you're working on your upcoming book *Grown* changed as a result of the pandemic and recent events with Black Lives Matter?

Melissa: As Black women, nothing's changed for us, the mission is exactly the same. I'm working exactly as I would have done but this moment has allowed me to be a bit more explicit, a lot more vocal. Writing this book was rooted in the realisation that often young Black girls aren't afforded the grace that is given to their white counterparts. They are seen as 'grown' and treated as such. Black girls in media are depicted as baby girls or big women. There is no in between. But we realised quite early on in the writing process that they are exposed to the realities of life every damn day. Whether it's when they walk into Tesco and are followed by security, or when they are punished for things their white friends get away with. It's even seen in instances where family members make remarks rooted in colourism. These girls see it, they live it.

Our book seeks to put a name and definition to the experience they face. We want to expose things, reaffirm what they are feeling and let them know that it isn't all in their heads. We want them to know that there is a sophisticated language out there that articulates and validates their experiences and that they aren't alone. Natalie and I had to wait until our mid-twenties to get the terminology to explain the feelings we felt. I don't want anyone to tell these young girls that what they're experiencing is not true. We want them to have the language to be able to advocate for themselves. *Grown* is for Black girls everywhere. We want them to know that every letter, every word, every thought was written with them in mind. I want them to see themselves in the pages. For them to also understand that we've been through it and so have other Black women. I couldn't see how the pandemic could have changed or impacted our writing and our purpose – we're Black women and this is just our life.

Natalie: We've had extensive numbers of Black people die of Covid-19, both in the UK and US, in disproportionate amounts. We're now going into a recession where we will see waves of redundancy and unemployment. Black women will be impacted; we're the ones that will bear the brunt of this. When you look back in history you see how long it takes for social change to take place. You will see what events will spark conversation and spark discussion, but if not sustained these events fade into the abyss. Ultimately, it's only been a few months since George Floyd was murdered but I'm not seeing people say Black Lives Matter with the same energy they were before. There's still police brutality in the UK and a countless number of injustices, which I won't go into because it's physically exhausting and these events are not being handled properly and there have been no changes put in place to stop these events from recurring. All these companies with their black squares, 'diversity and inclusion', and their statements. Nothing is *happening*. But the problem with institutional racism is that we get so used to it that we accept it as standard when we see the bare minimum effort made . . .

Melissa: [continues] . . . and people get excited, even by that.

For me, there's not going to be overall change. I think this is why I tend to look inward. Black women will do what we have always done. Get shit done. Lead change. We will focus on sisterhood, friendship, the community and children. But I don't think anyone else is going to follow suit. Already you can see that the majority of the public are sick and tired of us talking about our issues. That's why at times this movement still feels like a moment. All I know is that Natalie and I have each other; and we will continue to support each other and those who form part of our sisterhood.

What has caught your attention on social media during this time?

Melissa: There has been so much trauma, so I've used social media for laughter, to talk about the programmes I'm watching and for the joy of having random conversations. I have been quite active on social media because I don't want to confront what's actually going on.

Natalie: Melissa is stronger than me. There was a time when I would look at Twitter and every day there's a new racial injustice, there are new facts and figures, there's a new example of a Black woman being abused or British police brutality. For me, the most shocking and disgusting thing was the response that Marcus Rashford received for simply trying to make sure that working-class kids were still able to eat over the summer holidays, when it's clear that food poverty is an issue in this country. People now have a channel to spout hatred and their ignorance on a platform that everyone can see. It's highlighting something we've always believed – racism is always brewing under the surface and we now have evidence and proof.

Melissa: People think we're audacious to even still be here, to be successful, to dare to be excellent. Social media has shown me that people are just waiting to bring us down. Whether they're calling us angry Black women, saying our behaviour or attitude is aggressive, stereotyping us, putting limits on what we can do or ultimately deeming our contributions to society as redundant. When Maya Angelou says 'and still I rise,' I think a lot of people don't really get it. There's something very special about Black womanhood and something magical about Black sisterhood. It's galvanising. It's knowing that no matter what people say or what they do I have people around me who have my best interests at heart. I think that our sisterhood and the way in which we work together is our strength. Often minoritised people are seen as less than, depicted as struggling. But people fail to see the support that we have. The ways in which we care for one another.

Despite the fact that it seems that we are set up to fail and people think we're not going to make it, I have a lot of joy and a lot of happiness for Black women as I know that no matter what, we've got each other's backs and we're going to support one another. You might want to call it feminism. I don't. It's Black sisterhood. It's powerful. It's life-changing. It's the core of everything I do. I don't think I would be here if it wasn't for Natalie, my mum and the women around me.

For you, Natalie, is sisterhood how you also find strength?

Natalie: One hundred per cent. There's no way to describe when you go into an environment, and you see all white women and you see one Black woman there, and you smile at her and she smiles back; when you're working, especially in a corporate environment, and a Black woman comes in and you make eye contact, you can see her just breathe and know she will be all right as she hopefully has an ally in you and vice versa. When you're working in these environments where, typically, [Black women] haven't been supported or haven't received what they have required, despite the money they've been paid – that's what's important for me: it's the idea that, as Black women, we're just supporting one another.

What feminist book has inspired you?

Melissa: The book I always go back to is *Their Eyes Were Watching God* by Zora Neale Hurston. It was my first introduction to 'feminism'. I understood the concept of equality amongst the sexes. But that means nothing as a Black woman standing at the intersections of gender and race. Without giving it a name, Hurston showed me the meaning of independence, sexual autonomy and financial freedom. It was an awakening for me. She centred me in her feminism in a way that I hadn't encountered before. She dealt with experiences that seemed familiar. I felt seen. Prior to that I don't think I'd really considered my position in the world. But seeing a young Black woman be audacious. Push boundaries. Be comfortable in her own skin. It was truly a revelation. I believe reading it changed the course of my life. I became louder. More assertive. Sure of myself. That's the book I always go back to. When I need to centre myself and find my purpose. When I need to remind myself of who I am, this is the book I go to.

Natalie: I'm quite similar to Melissa in that I haven't really sat down and studied feminist texts. To me personally, it's always been about the stories, it's been important for me to read stories where Black women overcome and technically have everything up against them but still thrive and perform to excellence.

Two stories gave me comfort as a Black woman. *The Color Purple* by Alice Walker – Celie is one of my favourite kinds of characters; it's the watching her grow and what she goes through trying to be an independent woman, trying to raise her family and seeing how she's battered and bruised but still triumphs. And reading Maya Angelou's *I Know Why the Caged Bird Sings* gave me an idea of the progression of Black women and the story of coming from nothing and claiming a space for yourself.

If you asked me five years ago if I was a feminist, I would have said no. The version of mainstream feminism I was exposed to seemed to be crazy white women screaming off the top of their lungs about what is good for them. It didn't include me or the women around me, and I didn't see how it benefited me at the time as I was trying to survive, keep my head down and keep my job against all ends. Through developing an understanding of Black feminism and women, my perspective has completely changed and taking the chance to study womanism texts has changed my life. I would say the book that I was inspired by most recently has been *Hood Feminism* by Mikki Kendall. That book for me was phenomenal as it elegantly put my 'beef' with mainstream feminism into words. It says everything that needs to be said about feminism. You can't call yourself a feminist until you've read, understood and accepted it. It deals with the fact that feminism is not addressing the women at the bottom. Mainstream feminism for me is a glorified conservatism as the principles of conservatism are to preserve a certain position in society. Feminism, as far as I'm concerned, is trying to preserve the position of middle-class white women in society. Where you have people relying on public services, you need to eradicate the patriarchy from these services and the discrimination against poor women, Black women and women from ethnic minorities. *Hood Feminism* perfectly sets out a manifesto for feminism that needs to be adopted.

Show Up

This Is How You Come Back Stronger: Show Up

Dorothy Koomson

Dorothy Koomson is the award-winning author of sixteen books and several short stories. She wrote her first, unpublished novel when she was thirteen and she's been making up stories ever since. Her third novel, *My Best Friend's Girl*, was chosen for the Richard & Judy Book Club Summer Reads of 2006, and reached number two on the *Sunday Times* Bestseller List.

Her books *The Ice Cream Girls* and *The Rose Petal Beach* were shortlisted for the National Book Awards and a TV adaptation loosely based on *The Ice Cream Girls* appeared on ITV in 2013.

Dorothy has lived and worked in Leeds, London and Sydney, Australia, and is currently residing in Brighton on the South Coast of England.

Find out more at dorothykoomson.co.uk.

Dear White Feminist,

Congratulations if you've got this far.

I know some of you will have stopped reading after the second word in my greeting. And I know some of you will soon stop reading. And maybe you should. Because, honestly, you're not going to like what I'm about to write and some of you really haven't got the head space, gumption or willingness to read what I have to share with anything approximating an open mind.

Better to turn back now, to pretend you didn't see this bit and carry on with your life.

Still here? Oh, good, there may be hope for you yet.

About five years ago, something happened that was the tipping point in my mind about feminism. The details aren't important. What happened wasn't anything outlandish or new to me – it was simply the final straw in all the tons of straws that had been loaded onto this particular Black woman's back. And I was so angry, so incensed, I sat down and wrote you all a letter.

I poured out my feelings to you; my hurt and sadness and burning-hot rage went onto the page, marking and dampening and scorching it as I wrote. It was the only way I could find a sense of peace that would allow me to carry on without rocking up on every social media outlet and angrily calling out every single one of the white feminists (and those enabling them) who'd screwed me and other Black women over.

(By the way, I'm not going to preface anything I write with 'not all'. You're intelligent enough to be reading this book, so if you don't know that I am not talking about 'all' of anyone or anything, then you are most definitely part of the problem and you should probably stop reading now before you wilfully misinterpret whatever I say and give me a hard time over it.)

Do I sound snarky? Am I being a little rude? I honestly don't mean to be, but that's part of it, isn't it? The constant tone-policing of Black and brown people, women in particular. I've come a long way since my first letter five years ago, and I'm not going to speak to you in the strong terms I used back then, but I'm not going to soft-soap this either.

Simply, Dear White Feminist, I need you to think about standing up for those women who don't look like you.

That's it.

You seem to think furthering the cause of feminism is only about the issues that are pressing to you and those who are white like you. You act as though at best, the rest of us don't exist, and at worst, we don't deserve your support.

Before you start to protest about all the *wonderful* work you do, money you give and awareness you raise, I'm talking about standing up for Black women, brown women, Asian women and women of colour who *aren't* in different, often 'developing', countries. As laudable as your endeavours are in those arenas, they very often position you as Ms Generous Benefactor saving lesser mortals with your gentle-but-powerful way of being a (white) woman.

(Just checking in: Are you still here? If you are, are you reading with an open mind or have you been so spun out by anger and indignation that you're now hate-reading every single word? I hope it's the former, consider it might be the latter but suspect it might be a mix of the two. And that's cool. It says something that you're at least still reading, right?)

What I'm trying to say is, if you want to move forward with feminism, how about offering solidarity to the Black women and women of colour in the 'developed' countries you inhabit – you know, the ones who walk the same streets as you, who work in the same companies, who could essentially lead the same lives as you?

Before you insist that you already do that, let me assure you: You may think you do, but you don't. You simply don't. I'm often left wondering where are you when *we* need your backing and assistance and a full-on show of the might of sisterhood? I'm often left disappointed because you barely utter a peep when there's an outcry over something misogynistic *and* racist. I rarely, if ever, see you up in Twitter-arms or writing articles about Black women being verbally and physically abused on public transport, or Black girls being assaulted by white police officers, or Black colleagues having to tolerate sexist *and* racist jokes on a daily basis.

You're eerily quiet about those kinds of things. For example, you don't seem to notice that a Black politician who is constantly abused and derided online, even by those in her own party, might need defending and support, but you're front and centre as defenders when a white politician, who has a history of policies that cause nothing but harm to huge swathes of mainly disadvantaged people, has a couple of mean things said about her.

You simply don't show up for us, but you still want our support when some entitled, famous misogynist is horrible to you. You still want to do a flounce and have your acolytes tell off all non-white people when you're called out (sometimes even by other white people) on your casual racism. You still push the idea that the fight is against the patriarchy and nothing else.

If you don't understand where I'm coming from, maybe try this: the next time something terrible happens to you 'because you're a woman', double the feelings of outrage, hurt and humiliation you feel. In other words, think about how much worse it is to have something happen to you 'because you're a woman' *and* 'because you're Black/Asian/non-white ethnicity' too. And then add another truck-load of hurt onto *that* when you discover that the people who've been your mates, whose backs you've had in every situation imaginable when it comes to fighting the patriarchy, develop a sudden inability to even acknowledge you, let alone speak up for you. Once you're there, realise that this is how we Black women, Asian women, minority ethnic women feel, sometimes on a *daily* basis.

When the murder of George Floyd catapulted Black Lives Matter back into the headlines across the globe, you were deeply affected; your shock and horror was real and visceral. Your need to help was genuine and heartfelt. You seemed to suddenly be aware of all the things Black people had been telling you for years. But for many of us who inhabit the Black and brown bodies you now were so concerned about, we had all that trauma with an added element of distress on top of it all – *your* response.

With your horror and upset came either the need to declare yourself already a defender of all Black people when you blatantly hadn't been, or a sudden need to loudly and publicly confess your formerly racist mindset. It was through these confessions that I discovered that people

I had thought of as colleagues – writers and authors I'd admired – had never once picked up one of my books, because they were written by a Black woman. By me, a bestselling author who had gone out of her way to support their writing and books, whom they had met in many situations and had shared stages with as equals.

These revelations hit me hard because I realised how *monumentally stupid* I had been – I had shown up and supported these people while ignoring all the signs that had indicated these feminists would never support a woman who wasn't white like them. And no, it wasn't just me. So many other Black women told me similar stories about people from their industries and groups – colleagues and 'friends' who'd never really been there for them over the years, now having a public epiphany and declaring themselves cured of their racism and wanting to 'help' us.

And – like all the other Black women I spoke to – I sat and watched as these white feminists had their very public mea culpas met with understanding, support and congratulations on having seen that they were racist and had behaved in racist ways. Did any of those white women think to reject those supportive words and instead direct them to the people – like me – they had harmed? Did they think to say they didn't deserve to be coddled and that it wasn't all about them, it was instead about the people whose lives they now realised actually matter? Nope. Of course not.

Why not? Because, Dear White Feminist, you've become very used to thinking the world of feminism and injustice revolves around you, revolves around those you can help 'in Africa' or 'in Asia' or some other continent mostly inhabited by brown people; you don't tend to think about what it's like for the women you see every day. You don't think to consider the women who have to go through what you do in the same modern world you live in.

The thing is, the system is rigged to allow you to have your say, to have millions listen to you and raise a groundswell of support for you when things don't turn out right. Whereas the rest of us – we Black and brown people – we're just supposed to be strong, aren't we? Suck up our tears and be 'rocks'; remodulate our speech so we don't sound angry and aggressive; have a word with ourselves about being unapproachable to stop ourselves putting off those who might stand beside us if we weren't so *angry* all the time.

To be honest, having to write this five years after the last letter I wrote is more than slightly depressing. It breaks my heart a little at the same time that it hardens it. It makes me realise that, much as the world changes, the people in it stay the same unless they make a huge effort to alter their mindsets and behaviours. And there has been no incentive to change for you, has there?

Me? I am constantly coming up against barriers and situations that require me to change, twist myself, bend myself to try to come through in as close to one piece as possible.

So this is how we come back stronger: you, white feminist, you show up.

You call out your problematic faves when they're wrong. Publicly support Black, brown and other women who don't look like you even if you don't like their politics (you know you can readily do this when the woman is white).

Think before you unleash your supporters on those who pull you up.

Hell, simply put yourself in someone else's shoes for one moment and think how they feel.

Obviously, I can't make you change. I can't make you decide to show empathy and care for someone who isn't public and in vogue enough for you to notice them. I can't make you apologise to those you've hurt because your body without a racist bone in it has been behaving in quietly racist ways all these years. I can't make you turn away from all the soothing coos of support your fellow white feminists will cast your way. All I can do is ask you to show up for someone who isn't you, who isn't like you. Like we have been doing for you all these years.

Dear White Feminist, thank you for reading to the end. I know it won't have been easy. And I know I probably haven't changed a thing in your mind. But the next time you wonder how you can effect lasting change in the world, I hope you'll remember what I've said and you'll think, 'Yes, this is what I can do, and this is how I can make feminism stronger.'

Dorothy

Why Passivity Will No Longer Do

Mireille Cassandra Harper

Mireille Cassandra Harper is a writer, editor, sensitivity reader and PR consultant. She writes about arts and culture, as well as on societal and topical issues. She has contributed to the likes of British *Vogue*, *Nataal*, GUAP, Nation of Billions, *Clash* and more. As a PR and communications consultant, she works closely with grass-roots arts and culture organisations on creative, cultural and community-led projects. Mireille is also the author of *Timelines from Black History* and a contributor to *Timelines of Everyone*, and you can follow her @mireillecharper.

I t was those weeks in the wake of the Black Lives Matter protests. The tidal wave of anger following the murders of George Floyd, Ahmaud Arbery and Breonna Taylor had seeped down into something heavier: a shared anguish that extended across states, countries and continents. The collective grief was palpable.

One day in late July, sometime after the heights of that period, I was sitting on a rickety wooden stool in my living room, tuned in to yet another work video call. I would describe myself in that moment as downcast, exhausted, demotivated. Numb, even. It was an amalgamation of lockdown life in a small flat, the physical and mental effects of my newly hermit-like existence beginning to take their toll, and the constant, exhausting sight of Black people brutalised, abused and discarded – from the nameless faces of doctors who had died on the Covid-19 front line, broadcast across my screen as statistical casualties, to the frozen, blurred image of George Floyd lying incapacitated on concrete, with a police officer's knee digging into his neck.

Before the video call had started, I'd been having a phone conversation with a friend, during which we'd discussed the passivity of white people, from colleagues and friends, even from family members. We had vented, pouring out our anger, exasperation and sheer disappointment at those who had been silent in the face of racism and discrimination prior to this movement, but who had been the first to post black squares, quoting: 'I understand that I will never understand.' We hung up after I realised I'd lost track of time, and I was in fact due to be on the work call that second.

I'd taken a pause, braced myself for the inevitable words I was going to hear. And yet, I think, at that point, I was still hoping that I wouldn't be faced with the clichés. I sat, almost wordless, as the performance played out.

The furrowed brows, the shaking of the heads and the hands on hearts as each participant expressed their disgust at the treatment of Black people in the United States. The horror at the 'few' police officers whose 'cruel' and 'callous' behaviour were deemed to be singular characteristics of lone individuals; not symptomatic of a larger, more systemic evil. I let it unfold for a moment, my momentary silence communicating my disobedience to participate in the charade.

'Thank God it's not like that here.'

'Or at least not *as* bad.'

As if the rallying cry we had borne witness to across the world, for the past month, was a response to a one-time tragic event that would 'never happen here.'

It was for *this*, as well as the police brutality, the cold-blooded murder of Black civilians, and the videos documenting outright racist abuse, that hundreds of thousands of protesters were marching mile upon mile. It was this apathy, this passive response to the disregard for Black lives that had sparked this uprising.

Even after the protests, the social media posts and the videos of Black celebrities we'd all lauded for their strength now pouring out their long-held trauma, it was clear that while one pillar had been pulled down, another had risen up. This one would be more difficult to tear down than statues of slave traders.

To say there has been no change would not be correct. In the months that have followed, we have seen these proud displays of defiance result in changes to legal systems, increased scrutiny and critiquing of institutions that once garnered so much respect that no one dared challenge them. Some reputable organisations have apologised profusely, set in motion active steps to make amends and sped forward initiatives that were formerly 'too difficult to put in place now.'

But, at the same time, I've seen passivity played out on a global scale, as engagement and interest has dwindled, and so many of those who jumped at the chance to participate in a parade of solidarity have returned to indifference.

Even worse, allyship has been performed in the most warped of ways, as brands and corporations rush to plaster Black faces and bodies on their pages and products – as if 'representation' at surface level absolves them of any guilt from their exploitation of the same groups of people they suddenly feel inclined to promote their products to. Used as fodder, we see the same corporate machines continue their mission of dominating and dictating 'mainstream culture'. This is often through cultural appropriation, the theft of ideas, and the pulverisation of real diversity and originality.

I have been left wondering, on several occasions: How do we actually go about making tangible change while keeping our integrity? Is it even possible, in the world we live in? Can we really make a difference while operating under an oppressive system?

There is no simple answer to this, and it is clear that a revolution is not going to occur overnight, but the key is to first recognise how the world in which we live operates, and what role we play within it.

How are each of us, as individuals, contributing to the problems that exist in our society?

How are we responsible for upholding inequality and injustice?

If we are to step forward, out of this darkness and into the so-called light, it isn't going to come without sacrifice. We must all look at our actions – and our inactions – in order to bring about impactful and positive change. It simply isn't enough to feel *sad, disappointed and angry*. To just sit with our emotions and be passive and silent is, in the words of Desmond Tutu, 'to choose the side of the oppressor.'

In looking at ourselves, we must first interrogate our behaviours.

Do our actions reflect the morals and values we speak so loudly of?

For those of us sharing social media posts that talk about 'solidarity' and 'support': Where have we exercised these in an active and positive way?

In the spaces we occupy, what positions of privilege do we hold? What are we doing to share and give up that space?

IN A TIME where we are so focused on attention, engagement and clout, we must step back from the virtual façade and start focusing on what needs to be done in real life. Passivity is thinking that liking, sharing and posting a black square will make active change, yet in the face of outright racism and discrimination, choosing to remain silent. It is living in and reaping the financial and material benefits of the Western world, yet finding it 'exhausting' to address the history of these nations and how they acquired this wealth. It is regarding call-out culture as a crime, but failing to address why there are individuals who are so brazen to express offensive, derogatory and harmful comments in the first instance.

In this same vein, passivity is shouting 'solidarity!' but not self-educating, signing petitions, emailing MPs or doing any work that requires going beyond our social media feeds. It is the act of adorning ourselves in garments emblazoned with the word 'feminist', when those very items are made in sweat-shops, through the exploitation of predominantly women garment workers. It is declaring ourselves to be for the liberation of all women, but seemingly only supporting white able-bodied cis women. It is calling out brands one minute, yet purchasing their products the minute our payday money rolls in. It is the performance of showing solidarity, yet the failure to maintain integrity: the inability to follow through with positive action.

I don't want to see another '100 days on' video, as if three months of action following one of the most brutal documentations ever of an innocent man's death is enough to absolve the inhumanity of the system that caused George Floyd's death in the first instance. Obtaining the same material and capitalist gains that the white man has held throughout history is no affirmation of justice or equality, nor would that change the status quo. If this is our measure of progress, and we accept it as our lot, then we may as well accept defeat. I hope, not only for the next 100 days, but for the next 100 years – or as long as it takes – we continue to challenge, disrupt and question how we can all do better, and be better.

One thing is for certain: passivity will no longer do.

A Glorious Act of Rebellion

Lindsey Dryden

Lindsey Dryden (she/her) is an Emmy-winning film producer, director and writer. She is a founding member of FWD-Doc (Filmmakers With Disabilities) and Queer Producers Network, and runs an indie production company, Little By Little Films. Her film credits include *Unrest*, *Trans In America*, *Jackie Kay: One Person, Two Names*, *The Forgotten C* and *Lost and Sound*. She is the 2019 Simon Relph Memorial Bursary winner and a 2020 BFI Vision awardee and a full voting member of BAFTA. Find out more via lblfilms.com, @LBL_Films on Instagram and @Lindsey_Dryden on Twitter.

'm a filmmaker and writer because I believe that stories can change the world. More than anything, I want to tell stories that show people who have been derided, devalued, ignored and – frankly – underestimated by mainstream white, cis, hetero, ableist Western culture that they are valuable, adored and extraordinary. I hope my work will contribute to showing those of us who fall outside of that culture's patriarchal, heteronormative, racist, ableist ideals that we are seen and appreciated, and that we are so full of wonder and potential that society fears our magic.

My goal is always to create narratives that reveal the many possibilities for an incredible life, even – especially! – if you've been made to feel ugly or unimportant in the world. I hope my storytelling can help us break free from the heaviness of a capitalist culture that does everything possible to make us feel broken and unworthy, while offering us only consumerism as a salve. I believe that to create the lives of our choosing with integrity, self-acceptance and self-love in the face of capitalist dominance, racism, sexism, ableism, homophobia and transphobia is a glorious act of rebellion and a worthy lifelong endeavour.

So, this pandemic moment feels at once strange, painful, frightening and tentatively full of hope. Many of those in our societies who were already unsafe, mistreated or vulnerable are now even more so. The racist, sexist, homophobic, gender-normative and ableist structures that have long oppressed people are leaning even more heavily on their targets; this is what they are designed to do. And yet . . . there is courage everywhere. New conversations are being had, and old conversations (often by thinkers in marginalised communities) are being heard in new quarters.

We are so alone, yet so together. Many are demonstrating their care for others by wearing masks, keeping a distance and minimising movement; making difficult but effective compromises in a shared effort to protect one another from both acute illness and long-term effects. The notion that everyone has suddenly been able to slow down and reflect is a very privileged one, which ignores that millions are under more pressure than ever before. But thinkers, dreamers, workers, organisers and artists from those under-pressure communities are generously offering leadership and bold thinking to improve the ways we all live, and the ways we have been *allowed* to live by the systems around us. And some kind of collective dialogue does seem to be emerging, gathered around the idea that many of our existing labour and life structures just don't work. It is time to engage with the voices offering a brighter way forward. It is time for us to dream a new world.

The BFI Press Reset campaign that I've been involved in with a collection of brilliant D/deaf and disabled filmmaking talent in the UK (including Kyla Harris, David Proud, Melissa Johns, Jacqui Adeniji-Williams, Frankie Clarence and Sam Renke) speaks to the opportunity afoot for us to reckon with the arbitrary labour and social rules that we've been building for decades, and to reimagine a better, more inclusive reality. As *Under the Skin* actor Adam Pearson describes: 'Prior to the Covid-19 outbreak, as far as disability and inclusion was concerned, the [film] industry was very much broken. And now . . . it's pretty much broken for everyone. Welcome to our world.'

Far beyond the film industry, the pandemic is a 'welcome to our world' moment for many communities. It is revealing what it means to be excluded and diminished by the systems that we have intentionally created for work, pleasure, art, education, family, culture, travel. Those systems have always excluded *some* people; what does it feel like to now be one of the excluded?

From a queer and deaf point of view, it's been illuminating to watch as millions of people have had new, intimate and disquieting experiences of being locked out of the world they so easily inhabited before. Opportunities and spaces have been suddenly closed to people who until 2020 faced comparatively few barriers to living a full life. Many have encountered for the first time the heartbreak and frustration that others have long experienced, of being prevented from living the life they hope for: moving around freely, socialising, having relationships, working, getting into places and spaces of work and pleasure, accessing education, interacting safely with health care providers, moving through the streets without threat or risk, obtaining products and medicines when they're needed, enjoying arts and culture, making choices about how to spend time and feeling welcome to be in the world.

So, my question is this:

Could you bear to live the rest of your life like 2020 in lockdown: a lifetime of barriers that cause exclusion, isolation and missed opportunities?

And if you could not bear it, how could you let anyone else go through it again?

WE'RE TOLD THAT once Covid-19 is under control, the world can 'go back to normal.' But I don't want a return to 'normal'; I don't even want to consider it. I don't want to return to the way we lived before, when it was failing so many of us. By no means did we live tragic, unbearable lives; the opposite is true. But we *all* deserve better than the barriers and burdens that are placed disproportionately on people of colour, LGBTQ+ people, D/deaf and disabled folks, women and other marginalised communities. I don't want to return to a white-supremacist, ableist, sexist, homophobic and consumerist society in which the majority of people were struggling and many of us were told we were not worth including. Do you?

Now that the devastation of what it is to be excluded and marginalised because of circumstances entirely out of our control is clearer than ever before, how will we take steps to ensure that no one else is locked out again? How will you? How can we make certain that those with whom we've recently discovered shared vulnerabilities are not cast back into oblivion?

We have a genuine opportunity to change how we live, expand the categories of who we value and include, and conjure new lives and stories. Let's rebuild the world anew.

A Call to Action

Layla F. Saad

in conversation with
Feminist Book Society

Layla F. Saad is an East African, Arab, British Black Muslim woman who was born and grew up in the UK, and lives in Qatar. She is a *New York Times*– and *Sunday Times*–bestselling author, anti-racism educator, international speaker and podcast host on the topics of race, identity, leadership, personal transformation and social change. Her ground-breaking anti-racism education workbook *Me and White Supremacy* debuted on the *New York Times* and *USA Today* bestsellers lists.

We first came to know you through your 2017 essay 'I Need to Talk to Spiritual White Women about White Supremacy'. Since then you have written about your faith and how it intersects with your feminism. How has spirituality and religion supported you throughout the last few months?

It's the foundation of my life and of who I am. It informs how I do what I do, and why I do what I do, because as a Muslim woman – and as someone who is deeply spiritual – ideas of justice and equality are baked in to my belief system.

My parents are a great example of the living embodiment of the practices of Islam. They inspire me and my brothers. They built an orphanage for over a hundred orphans in Tanzania (where my mum's from). They taught us that everything you make, you're not going to take it with you once you're gone. So you must make your life meaningful. Make it mean something. And so having them as that example really informs *why* I do what I do, but it also informs how I do it as well.

What makes you hopeful about our immediate feminist future? And what about the long term?

What has always given me hope is the people who have come before us. Those who saw the status quo and chose to go in another direction, to insist on their full humanity. They chose to insist on demanding their rights, they chose to insist on speaking truth to power.

It wasn't any easier for them. In fact, it was harder for them than it is for us now, because we're in a different world now. I don't know if I could have drawn on the courage that they drew on. And so I draw from theirs now.

Today, my peers and leaders are speaking up and doing this work in the same environment of anti-Blackness, of sexism. And they still show up. There's so much evidence of the other side of humanity – capitalism, racism, sexism – yet we are all capable of great courage, of being caring, of being great self-listeners and of giving up privilege so that others may live more freely. Hope comes from the potential of the human spirit.

Bearing in mind the widespread commitment to the work you set out in *Me and White Supremacy*, do you think the resurgence in the Black Lives Matter movement would have happened without the pandemic?

I don't know that I could say whether it would have happened without it. But I do think that being at home, not being with each other, has created more space for many people to be able to say, 'Let me just sit my butt down and open this book right,' or 'Let me just sit down and learn something that I didn't know before.' Being indoors has created space in our minds.

I don't think that we can say that the pandemic has played no part in what's going on right now. But I also think it's important to note that it was long overdue and we shouldn't have had to wait for a pandemic for any of this to happen.

And even in the midst of the pandemic, Black people and brown people in the UK and US are fighting two pandemics: they're fighting Covid-19 and they're fighting racism. For those with white privilege, this should be at the forefront of their minds as they're using phrases about how the pandemic has been a 'great equaliser'.

So many people who read and love books are looking at racism and feminism from an intellectual perspective, and not digging deep into how it plays out in their life; and so not taking any action. While we saw all the protests, we saw companies and institutions being forced to reckon with racism that has always been there. This is a time when we're seeing that pairing of the two consciousnesses: the awareness and the action. It's my hope that this continues to play out.

What I have seen – in becoming aware of any '–ism' or any place in which you have privilege and realising, 'This is what it's like for those who don't have privilege in that area' – is that once you get that real understanding, you can't go back to before. And so it's my hope that as people are coming into a more conscious awareness, they can't go back to before, but that it continues to be paired with action.

What is the feminist book that made you?

The first one is *Sister Outsider* by Audre Lorde. Given my own understanding of myself, specifically as a straight Black woman, it was being able to hear from the voice of somebody who was a Black lesbian woman. That book really did make me; it's a book that I return to again and again. As a Black Muslim woman in the predominantly white publishing industry, with a very white-facing audience, it can be easy to lose yourself, and I really appreciate her writing on the importance of defining yourself *for* yourself, no matter what your outside environment looks like; as well as the importance of speaking up, seeking truth and not staying silent.

And the other one, which helped me more to understand things from historical and systemic contexts, is *Ain't I a Woman* by bell hooks. It gave me a very specific understanding of US history, in a feminist movement that I had no context for, and the relationship between white women and Black women; and Black women and Black men; and white women, white men and everybody else. It helped me to understand that, as someone who isn't a descendant of enslaved Africans of the Atlantic slave trade, while I may be able to relate with women and people of the African diaspora because we're Black, I don't have the shared experience of the specific context of US history to be able to know what that must feel like. And it gave me an understanding of how to observe things with a wider context, and how to ask questions about what's going on under the surface that you may not be aware of. I remember reading and thinking, 'Every white woman needs to read this!'

Do you have a call to action for readers of this book?

This moment has exposed to us how the most marginalised amongst us are impacted, and given us no more excuses.

The call for me is the same call it would have been before lockdown, which is to look towards the leadership of Black women and Black femmes, *of all backgrounds and experiences*. Throughout history, we are the people who've shown up consistently, for ourselves and for everybody else.

Support our bodies of work, uplift us, share them with other people. Support Black businesses, because – as we've seen through this pandemic – these are the people who slip through the cracks, even though we work so hard. And it shouldn't just be the people with bestselling books; it should be the people in your communities, at your jobs, in your work, at your schools, because they need the support and they're often doing that same level of work, but without that public recognition.

And so, what do you want us to let go of?

I specifically want Black women to let go of the need to work for everybody else – we should be able to rest. Other people should be picking up the mantle of all the work that we have created and put out into the world for the next generations and saying, 'Let's put this into practice.'

We've always been there, we're always going to be there. We continue in all areas across all industries to show up, despite sexism and despite racism, right? And we show up in excellence. We show up wanting to take everyone else along with us too. I just wish that other people would do the same for us that we do for them.

Survive and Rise

A Geometry of Stars
Catherine Cho

Catherine Cho works in publishing and is the author of *Inferno: A Memoir*. Originally from the United States, she's lived in New York and Hong Kong. She currently lives in London with her family. You can connect with Catherine on Twitter @Catkcho.

I have a scar on each hand, one just beneath my left ring finger and the other on my right index knuckle. They look like small stars, bursts of brightness under skin, a map of constellations across my hands.

I've tried ointments, vitamin E capsules, balms, but the scars have remained, and so I decided to leave them. They are reminders that some memories aren't dreams, that they are real.

I've heard that some scientists think of the universe like a sheet of paper. It was an astrophysicist named Koryo Miura who created an origami fold that is used in space exploration, a pattern of repeating parallelograms. It is considered a shape-memory fold, in that the paper remembers, and once unfurled can be returned to its folded state. I imagine that our lives are this way, neatly compressed only to expand and reveal the multitudes within.

As much as I would wish it, I do remember the man who gave me the scars on my hands. It would have been easy for me not to meet him. But we did meet; our paths crossed on a night in a New York summer. I was at a party I hadn't planned on going to. I was getting ready to leave, the music was too loud and the drinks were watered down. He was a friend of a friend. 'Stay,' he said. And he grinned like he knew every secret in the world.

He liked to laugh, and he laughed loudly and often. He

was always surrounded by friends – the first to open his wallet, the first to offer a drink. I took his generosity for kindness, his confidence for conviction.

I fell in love with the way he saw me, as something precious, to be treasured. Perhaps he saw me as something to own.

If I saw a hint of darkness, it was always momentary, and quickly hidden. And I was distracted by his promises, by his certainty, by what I thought was proof of his love.

We spent the summer going to parties, staying out until the sun came out, bright and glinting against the skyscrapers. He was only in New York for the summer, a work training program, and then he'd be going back to Hong Kong.

He asked me to move there with him, and I wondered what it would be like to live by the sea.

I would move to Hong Kong as he wished, half a year later, feeling like I was taking a dare, a leap into the unknown. I moved into his family's flat, a beautiful stone building with a view of the ocean. The sea was so still you couldn't tell where the sky began. I remember I would stand on the balcony, looking out at the horizon of pale blue – where there was only mist and the sound of soft waves.

The first time it happened, it was only a few weeks after I had moved. It began with an argument about something small. It was sudden, sharp. I had slapped him first, and there was a dash of a fist to the nose and lip, which split. There was the sound of glass breaking, a photo frame in the living room. His father held him back, grappling with him while I ran out of the apartment in slippers.

It was the middle of the night. I took a taxi to a friend's house. The expression on her face was grim. I remember holding a packet of frozen vegetables against my cheek.

The inside of my lip had swollen and turned dark. 'What will you do?' she'd asked me.

It took me a moment to realize she meant how I would leave. She didn't see that I was trying to figure out a way to forgive him. My mind was already twisting, finding reasons for why this had happened.

It was a stressful time. It was an accident. He hadn't meant it. I had hit him first.

I didn't sleep that night. I went over the events in my head, smoothing and unfolding them until I could see all the edges. I twisted the truth until it made sense to me, turning it over again until I could accept it, until I could hold it within me.

The next morning, his mother came to pick me up. She drove me to the pharmacy to pick up some concealer. We had roast duck and congee at his favourite restaurant. He held my hand between courses and topped up my beer. We laughed and smiled, and I tried not to notice the crack in the glass table and the way it distorted my reflection.

I DIDN'T KNOW it then, but that night was a lever – whatever mechanism that had been hidden was now broken and had released what was within.

In the months that would come later, I would think about those hours, the sleepless hours of wondering how to forgive, of trying to make sense of what had happened. It had been so difficult, that initial forgiveness. But afterwards, the forgiveness was simple. It came easily. It was a simple pattern we fell into. The slaps had escalated to punching, belts, a knife to the throat, a pillow against my face until I would faint, an airsoft pistol held at close range.

We moved out of his family's flat by the ocean to a

skyscraper apartment in the middle of the city. His parents thought it would help, but it didn't.

Sometimes the neighbours would stand in the hallway, but they never knocked, I could hear their breathing through the door, raised in annoyance. I imagined them standing with their hands on their hips, staring at our door, wondering if they knew on the other side that I was lying on the tiled floor.

'You look as though you've been hit by a truck,' a doctor said to me flatly when I told her I'd fallen down. I had shrugged to show my clumsiness. I had a fissure on one cheek, and she ordered a CT scan to check for further fractures.

I relayed this to him to see if he would react, but he looked bored, with no trace of guilt.

And so I swallowed my anger. My anger was a darkness, hidden, the way a bruise lies deep within a fruit.

I learned to fade into the night, to disappear. I would ride the wooden trams that went through Central, a fare paid just with a few coins. I'd rest my hand against the open windowsill, taking in the harbor breeze, looking at the soft pastel of lights, of the fluorescent signs. I'd eat mango ice in front of the storefronts and buy coconut sliced into moons. Sometimes I'd sleep on park benches, under the soft wet of misting fog.

I learned to stop asking friends for a place to stay; they didn't look sympathetic. Just annoyed. Bored. It was too predictable. It wasn't spoken, but wasn't I asking for it? Why didn't I just leave?

In public, we played our part. My face was never marked. I learned to wear sleeves that covered my arms, laughing when someone asked why I would wear long sleeves in a Hong Kong summer. We would walk through the streets of Lan Kwai Fong where crowds of partygoers spilled out onto the streets. We'd walk hand in hand, his slightly too tight around mine, and I'd watch him laugh with the friends who never seemed to notice or care. I'd look at his eyes to see if his face would turn, if there would be some warning for what was to come.

And then later, during the inevitable fight, I would stare at the curl of his mouth as he spat in my face and looked at me with all the hate there was in the world. And I wondered just how had it become like this.

Sometimes he would sob, in anger, in self-hate. Why did I make him like this? Why did I make him a monster? And I would find myself having to be the comforter, the power in my hands.

I did try to leave once. He cut up my passport into precise small squares. I sat with his mother at the American embassy, the pieces in a Ziploc bag. 'Well, it shows that he wants you to stay,' she said cheerfully. And I twisted my mind to accept the logic of that, a Möbius strip – no exit.

Perhaps we would have stayed this way indefinitely, preserved in a twisted loop.

Instead, I found out that he'd been texting an old girlfriend. Her name was saved under a guy's name. I remember seeing the constant flash on his phone, a single first name, no last name. It was as though something tore in that moment. This one truth meant that everything had to collapse beneath it.

This was not love.

It was so simple, but with that knowledge, I was released. I was free. The thought was exhilarating, desperate, like the first gasp of air after breaking through a surface.

We fought. I told him I was leaving, that I knew the truth. I remember he was stomping on my leg, turning it so he could find a strange angle. He locked me in the bathroom, and I sat staring at my reflections, repeating and fractured. And I wondered if I was going to be able to leave.

It lasted for several days, and I knew that I would have to leave quietly.

It was a summer night, a starless sky. I left with only my wallet and phone, wearing a slip dress and flimsy flip-flops. I'd made a show of taking off all my jewelry and putting it on the nightstand – the gleam of a necklace, rings, the twist of earrings. I told him I was going to go buy something from a shop downstairs. He shrugged.

I opened the door. I remember seeing the lines the door made across the hallway, the triangle of light, the promise of it. I didn't look behind me. I let the door close slowly, heavily behind me. I walked down the corridor and waited for the lift to come. I counted each moment, drawing out my breath to match my steps.

I walked into the night. I wanted to shout, to spread my arms, but I kept them still and close. I kept walking until I was sure no one would follow. I kept walking until I thought I would disappear. I wanted to dissolve, to scatter, but instead I folded the night within me and kept it close.

This was many years ago.

I think of those memories as something caught behind glass – separate and distorted, but always recognizable.

Sometimes I imagine there is a version of me who didn't make it out that night. That she stayed, folded within those doors, caught in the never-ending reflection of glass.

I try not to imagine this too often. Because then I can feel the darkness spread like a stain.

Instead, I look at the stars marked on my hands, and I think of constellations, of the universe unfolding in all its possibilities, so vast, so still – a geometry of stars.

Rise Stronger

Extract from chapter fifteen of
Rise: Life Lessons in Speaking Out, Standing Tall & Leading the Way

Gina Miller

Bloomberg described Gina Miller as an 'establishment wrecking ball', but her drive for transparency, scrutiny and integrity in public and corporate life as well as the UK Financial Services industry is about reform, fairness and social justice – not wrecking. Whilst Gina – a lawyer, speaker and author – became a household name for her legal challenges to preserve Parliament's sovereignty, she has been a respected activist for over thirty years, campaigning about modern-day slavery, discrimination and equality, domestic violence, and for those with special needs.

Most recently, in response to the Covid-19 pandemic, and an alarming increase in online scams and hate crime, much of it targeting women, children and the vulnerable, Gina has been and continues to campaign for Online regulation. She is calling on the UK Government to urgently bring the Online Harms Bill to Parliament in 2021 – and to impose a duty of care on technology firms, as well as establish an independent Online Harms Regulator. You can follow her at @thatginamiller.

Whilst the issue of domestic violence, one of the last social taboos, has come out from dark corners and is being openly acknowledged, debated and addressed by numerous stakeholders, there are still several myths and deep-rooted misconceptions. One is that victims of domestic abuse and coercive behaviour are either weak or uneducated or otherwise women who provoke men into being abusive, and 'Why don't women just leave?'

The truth is far more complex. When the person you love becomes your abuser, your home your place of torture, trust turns to terror and you are a victim of the systematic breaking of your confidence, personality, judgement and emotional stability, even the strongest of us can break. I wrote this chapter to reach out to so many women who are suffering, who need support, not judgement, and to let them know that they are not alone; that they can survive and rise again.

THINGS CHANGED WHEN we got married. It seemed to me as if, after two years of courtship, Jon felt he owned me. I'd moved away from my home, my friends and my support network.

The very things that he appeared to love me for, he was now determined to undermine and break. It was small things at first. Emotional abuse often begins like this: it is almost impossible for a victim to be able to point at a specific action and say, 'There. That is when it started. This is what's happening and it's wrong.' 'Coercive control' – I didn't know the term even existed. What I knew was I felt like a bad wife.

I was drowning in a world of alcohol, broken confidence, control, confusion.

At first, I would try to confront him, but he'd just laugh off the things he said as 'banter' or say I was being overly sensitive. Step by step, without my realising it was happening, I found myself cut off from everybody I loved. I didn't recognise it for what it was. Back then, emotional abuse wasn't talked about. I know that it happened, and I know that I survived it, but in truth I can't explain it. I look back and I don't recognise my weakness; I still can't recognise that Gina.

From the outside, we had a wonderful life. We lived in a rambling country house, with expensive furniture and a state-of-the-art kitchen. My husband was successful and charming in public. We didn't have to worry about money. I adored his three children – two sons and a daughter – who often came to stay with us. His youngest son was the same age as my daughter Lucy-Ann, and was just gorgeous.

But scratch the pretty surface and there was an ugly truth nestling beneath.

This is what I remember:

I remember the coldness of the floor.

I remember the hardness of the slate pressing against my side.

I remember the numbness, the absolute incomprehension that this could be happening to me.

This is what I do not remember:

I do not remember the pain.

I shut down. I floated out of myself. It was as if it were happening to someone else entirely. It's a way of coping. You simply can't process the emotion of a situation like that in the moment: you can't feel, you can only survive.

And for a while it works – even when I woke the next day and my ribs were so bruised that every time I breathed there was a sharp pain in my chest.

Why didn't I leave? Well, I felt guilt and tremendous shame at being a failure as a wife and mother. I didn't want to tell anyone what was going on in case they judged me negatively. Anyway – who would believe me?

It was not easy. I had lost who I was. I was losing a grip on myself, on who I thought I was. I compare it to drowning, falling deeper and deeper into the water towards the sea bed. I could still see the surface, and the dappled sky beyond it, but I could not reach it. Sometimes I felt I couldn't breathe, as if all the air was being squeezed out of me by an iron fist pushing down on my chest. I kept spiralling downwards.

My confidence dwindled to a point beyond zero. I tried to leave three times; every time, I went back because I believed it would be different. He promised it would be different, he promised he would drink less. A pattern of behaviour so many men and women suffering domestic abuse engage in.

Then, one day, it really was rock-bottom. Jon and I were having terrible rows once again. I woke up one morning with a terrible gash and pain on my back but could not remember what had happened the night before.

I went to Lucy-Ann's room and packed a small case with her clothes. I threw some things into an even smaller bag for me. I wasn't thinking beyond that moment of knowing I needed to get us out.

I took Lucy-Ann by the hand and rushed downstairs with the bags. I didn't take a single possession other than the most basic necessities. I stopped for a second and looked around at all the beautiful things which had adorned our supposedly picture-perfect life, and which I had spent hours choosing – the plush sofas, the crystal brandy glasses, the silver-framed photographs, the kitchen with its cold slate floor – none of it meant anything anymore. It was a mirage, a chimera, a hollow shell of something that had never really existed.

We ran outside and threw the bags into the back of my car and drove away from that house without a second glance. I was lucky because a woman I was friendly with nearby was about to go on a two-week holiday with her family. I called her; she offered me the use of her house while they were away. That's where Lucy-Ann and I stayed. No one knew where we were or what was happening, as I had shared very little with anyone. Sometimes the safest place is right under someone's nose.

After those two weeks were up, I didn't have anywhere to go. I didn't want to go to my family or friends because I thought he'd try to follow me there, and I didn't want to be a burden, for anyone to have to lie on my behalf or get involved. It's a fault of mine that I can be very proud – too ashamed to ask other people for help.

I tried to rent a flat for the two of us, but every time the estate agent asked for a permanent address, my bank account details, where I last lived, I was declined. I had no documents.

We stayed the odd night in a bed and breakfast. When I ran out of physical cash, Lucy-Ann and I slept in the car, with all our possessions stuffed into a couple of bags in the boot. More than once, we slept in a multi-storey car park.

Due to her special needs, the sounds of nightlife made Lucy-Ann frightened, so I bought earplugs to help her sleep. They seemed to work a little, but she mainly clung to me, burying her head into me to block out the noise, as well as keep warm.

It was at that point – one of the lowest ebbs of my life – that I thought to myself, *Gina, you just have to be strong, survive, rebuild for your daughter.* I needed every ounce of my energy to recover from this. And that meant I had to let go of everything and just look ahead.

It was the best decision I could have made.

Women find it so hard to let go. It's partly because we're conditioned to feel guilty about failure, even if that failure is not our fault. And it's also because, in a divorce scenario, we are often encouraged by lawyers and advisers to fight and get as much as possible, in terms of money, assets and physical possessions. But reliving moments of pain, the hurt, keeps the pain alive and the damage continues.

Holding on to a grudge, negative emotions, is a waste of time, effort and energy. If, like I did, you need to put yourself back together, then you need to refocus all the power you expend on hating someone into more positive efforts. Otherwise they still have a hold on you, they are still in control. Holding on to feelings of resentment or revenge is like sipping arsenic and expecting the other person to die. If you forgive, forget and forge forward, you can use your energy to strive, create and rebuild.

I'm not saying it's easy, but those nights sleeping in my little blue car in multi-storey car parks, when I would wake with a stiff neck and a ballooning panic in my chest, forced me to look at my situation honestly. To understand that I was the only one that could turn my life around. I knew I could survive. As the shackles of Jon's mental and physical abuse dropped away, I could breathe again, I could believe in myself again, I could find the strength to look after myself and my daughter. That sense of resilience is extremely important. I didn't need anything or anyone. I could walk out of the door and be OK, although I came to realise, I also needed to swallow my pride and ask for help.

In the end, out of desperation, I phoned Lucy-Ann's father, Adrian, and told him what had happened. I am forever grateful that Adrian listened and immediately offered to help. He said that there was a flat in the same block he lived in for rent in Tooting, South London. He said he would organise everything so that Lucy-Ann and I could live there, and we could split the childcare equally, so I could work.

I didn't ask Jon for anything. I didn't want his money or his possessions. I just wanted to be free, to become myself once again.

Lucy-Ann and I moved to Tooting. It was a good arrangement. She had a bedroom in my flat and a bedroom in Adrian's, and during the coming weeks and months as I set up my own business, if I had to work late or had dinner with friends or clients, or a networking event, Lucy-Ann could pop upstairs and stay with him.

I had not heard from or about Jon for years. Then I read an article in a trade publication in 2016 saying that he was to stand for the English Democrats, an anti-immigration political party, at the next general election. The article read:

[Jon] will stand in the Chippenham constituency of Wiltshire for the party, which proposes that 'no more so-called asylum seekers should be allowed into England' and pledges to withdraw the UK from the 1951 UN

Convention on Refugees. The party also opposes multi-culturalism, and pledges to close down all 'politically correct quangos.' 'We want English freedoms and values, not multiculturalism,' it states in an election leaflet. He outlined his support for the English Democrats, which was also campaigning for a separate Parliament for England. He was quoted as saying, 'They want to say cheerio to the Scots, the Welsh and the Irish – and hooray for that and let England pocket the stupid cash we keep sending across our borders.'

As I read the words, thoughts and memories started tumbling through my mind. This was my former husband. Had I ever really known him? The fog in my mind cleared as I recalled the racist names he called me, the arguments where he would tell me I would never be as clever as him because he was English and I was just a coloured woman who needed to know my place. That I should be grateful that he had taken me and my disabled daughter in, that most men wouldn't have been that charitable.

Slowly, step by step, brick by brick, I rebuilt my life and my shattered sense of self. There is a mistaken perception that only a certain type of person suffers from domestic violence: it can only happen to somebody who is weak or from a deprived background, who is so financially dependent on their spouse that leaving is impossible. There's a sense that it doesn't happen to people who've got money, are professionally successful, who live in a nice house. There's almost an unwillingness to believe it's true. In the months that followed my divorce, some of my closest confidants would say to me, 'But you were perfectly fine in public,' and 'We never saw any bruises.' There is a belief that strong women can't be victims. It appears to scare people to know that it can happen in their own back yard.

After many years of burying this period of my life, it has been upsetting to revisit it, to talk to others – friends and family – and hear their memories of a woman I do not recognise.

What I now realise is that I should not have let feelings of failure cripple me, that I should have reached out for help. But when you feel yourself drowning, you are too emotionally crippled to reach out for help, you feel trapped. I consider myself a strong woman, but this happened to me. And that is what I want anyone reading this to understand. Because if I can share, then hopefully other women in similarly damaged, toxic relationships will be less afraid to speak up, to reach out.

Sixteen years ago, domestic abuse was still a social taboo. Today, the myths are being dispelled, but there is still much more to do to build awareness of the signs, for women to find the courage to save themselves and their families.

To whoever is in a damaging relationship, I say: You are not weak, even when you think you are. You are special, you shine and that is what can attract men who feel the need to control or own you. You have more strength than you realise. Leaving is a lifeline to another better life.

Start by forgiving yourself, letting go of guilt – setting yourself free. Focus your energies on making a positive future.

It will not only be a liberation; it will also give a renewed depth to your resilience and confidence – knowing that having survived, anyone who attempts to bully or abuse you will not succeed in silencing you again.

It did for me.

Radical Acts

I Do Not Know
Stella Duffy

Stella Duffy is an award-winning writer with over seventy short stories, fifteen plays written and devised, and seventeen novels published in fifteen languages. She has worked in theatre for over thirty-five years as an actor, director, playwright and facilitator. She is the co-founder of the Fun Palaces campaign, supporting community cultural co-creation as a catalyst for local connection. In 2016, she was awarded the OBE for Services to the Arts.

do not know how we come back stronger.
I want to keep not knowing.

I want to embrace my uncertainty, the possibilities that not knowing offer us all.

I have been out for four decades, have lived and loved those politics.

I have worked in the arts trying to achieve equality and inclusion and I have been constantly disappointed that we didn't get there yet.

I have lived through two cancers and worked through both of them trying to make a difference.

I have lost five embryos, one after the other, because of cancer and chemotherapy and because planning and wanting and working towards does not always mean it happens.

I have written and talked and workshopped and speeched and keynoted and facilitated and taught and led and demanded and decided and agonised and strategised and planned and marched and called for and worked towards.

And we did not get there yet.

I want to sit in the sun and read a book.
I want to swim for the sake of it instead of counting lengths.
I want to walk in a forest and listen to the trees.
I want the ocean to hold me.
(The ocean always holds me.)

I have not given up my belief in equality and the vital need to work for this.
But I am a little more interested in talking to people I don't understand.

I am not choosing to stop the work I am passionate about.
But I am becoming more interested in other people's passions.

I am not ready to give up.
But I am ready to support others to step up and take my place, my places.

I do not know how we come back better.

I want to find out how to be here, now, and well.
I want to take the time that my activism and campaigning and action hasn't allowed.
I want to take that time and breathe.
I have a sense that in taking time, in breathing, in letting

be – even if just for a while – some new paths might show themselves.

At fifty-seven I am far less certain than I was at forty-seven, at thirty-seven, at twenty-seven.
I am welcoming this uncertainty.
Unlike all the other times, I am not running to plan, to sort, to fix.
Well, I am a little, but less.
Less.

There is so much still to do.

I want to understand my place as a white woman, able-bodied woman, a cis woman, and how I might be a better ally.
I want to understand my place as a queer woman, a working-class woman, a woman living with chronic pain, and to support others to better ally me.

And I have an idea that some of this is not 'work' at all.
It is sitting with.
It is allowing.
It is letting be.
It is being.

I want to sit in the middle of the labyrinth and trust that the way out will show itself.

I want to acknowledge that I am in the labyrinth, that I am swimming in the abyss and that being here is OK.
It can be uncomfortable, it can be painful, it can be difficult – and that is OK.

It can also be quiet and still and seem like nothing is happening.

I have a dream that in the nothing, from the nothing, there is a path.
Paths.
We are too many, too varied, too gloriously different for there to be one path.

I have a hope that if I can wait, and be still, and allow, then my path will show itself.
And your path will show itself.
And yours. And yours.
And that we can support each other on our paths, allowing their difference, welcoming our multiplicity.

Allowing the uncertainty, allowing the waiting, the quiet – maybe they are paths too.

It can all be different.
It can all be better.
We can all be different.
We can all be better.

I have no idea how we come back stronger.
I trust we can.
I believe it might take some quiet waiting.

Quiet waiting might be the hardest work I have ever done.
And it might be lovely.

The Wobbly Revolution

Francesca Martinez

Francesca Martinez is an award-winning wobbly comedian, writer and campaigner who has performed sell-out shows around the world. Her debut book, *What The **** Is Normal?!*, was published in 2014 to critical acclaim and was nominated for two National Book awards. Her first play, *All of Us* – in which she also stars – is directed by the legendary Ian Rickson (*Jerusalem*) and was due to open at the National Theatre in London in March 2020. The play will run at the Dorfman Theatre as soon as Covid-19 allows.

Brain-damaged. Disabled. Crippled. Handicapped. Abnormal. Spastic. Broken.

The world into which I was born used those words to describe me. Along with the ubiquitous 'What's wrong with you?', they combined to create an environment that was disempowering, negative and totally at odds with my own self-perception. Born into a loving family who showered me with affection, time and attention, I was confident, happy and as far away from those ugly words as you could get. My wobbliness was very much there, of course: I couldn't walk until I was three or manage anything fiddly like doing up buttons, cutting up food or picking up a glass of water. I still can't. But that was my 'normal' – neither good nor bad, just a set of circumstances I lived with in the same way most people accept they cannot fly or will never perform a pirouette with the Royal Ballet. I was in love with this wonderful thing called life, and bursting with a determination to make those around me laugh.

A chink in my armour began to form when I first became aware of those foreboding words. I struggled to see how those labels applied to me. Apparently, my brain – which was able to read books, conjure up vivid daydreams and craft witty jokes – was damaged. If you'd received it from Amazon, you'd send it back. I flinched when I first heard the words 'cerebral palsy'. I didn't know what they meant but they sure as hell didn't sound like me. I was Chess – funny and kind and happy and adventurous, with a head of unruly blonde ringlets – and those words were, well, Serious and Foreign. So, I decided to stuff them into a little box in my (damaged) brain, shut the lid and get on with the delicious task of living and loving and flirting with boys and squeezing as much fun into my days as humanly possible.

This strategy served me well, until high school forced me to prise open that box and plaster those words all over myself. It was excruciatingly clear that the world around me didn't give a damn about how I perceived myself or what was inside me. It was going to judge me on how I walked, how I talked and all the other ways that singled me out as An Alien. My resistance fell away in the face of such a unified onslaught from classmates and teachers alike, and my bubbly persona retreated under an increasingly heavy, grey cloud. I became my own worst enemy, judging myself to be unlovable, unattractive and abnormal. Throughout the years of bullying and isolation, my internal narrative sought to make peace with the unhappiness that now dominated my days and nights. Clearly, I was being treated as if I were unworthy of better because I *was* unworthy of better. The world had always viewed me that way. I had just stubbornly refused to believe it. I now embraced the words I had shunned. I embraced them with total acceptance. They defined me. This was my destiny. This was the truth.

The unhappiness generated by that decision, together with the cold treatment I encountered at school, was a fixture of my teens. Yes, there were moments of joy, especially during my five years on the BBC TV series *Grange Hill* – an experience that boosted my self-esteem, gifted me some much-needed friends and propelled me towards my dream of becoming an actor – but the insecurity still gnawed at me daily. It was hard to live in a world that defined me by what I couldn't do, and I didn't know how to make peace with it. How could I love myself when others saw me as faulty? I became increasingly resentful of my body. I began to experience a disconnection from myself, becoming a cynical observer who scrutinised my every move with a critical eye and a withering tongue. To the outside world, I was on the telly, leading a so-called glamorous life with glamorous people but I struggled privately with the cruel voices that plagued my thoughts.

Rock-bottoms have a habit of saving us. When I hit mine, drowning in a potent concoction of self-loathing and paranoia, I could hardly leave my house, and my body was wracked with pain. The resulting panic attack shook me to my core, and the reverberations lasted over a year. Finally, I opened up my heart to my family, something I'd been too scared and embarrassed to do. It was a profound relief to share the toxic thoughts I'd grappled with for so many years. I'd just turned twenty. Looking back, I was blooming and beautiful, a truth I was unable to appreciate at the time.

Eighteen months later, a conversation in a Soho pub changed my life. 'You are not disabled,' he said. 'That's just a word other human beings have made up to try to define you. You are perfectly you.' The words flew around my head like jittery bees. I was so hungry for those ideas, for their seeds to burrow down and take root in the arid desert of my brain. And boy, did they take root. That night, I lay in bed glowing. 'I am not disabled. Or broken. Or wrong. Or abnormal. I don't have to accept them. I won't. I am Francesca. I am perfectly me. I. Am. Perfectly. Me.'

As I said those four words over and over in my mind, the insidious weight that had crushed me for so long disappeared. I laughed out loud at my new-found lightness. The simplicity of the truth was startling. I could define myself whichever way I wanted. It was my choice. Mine alone! I laughed again. The high that I felt in that moment was intoxicating, beautiful, meaningful. As I drifted to sleep, it melted deep into my bones like warm sunshine, and has never left me.

The next morning I woke up transformed, listening to the bird-song outside as if for the first time. *I'm alive*, I thought. One by one, I ripped up those labels that had caused me nothing but pain. It was then that I decided to call my condition 'wobbly'. The word was accurate, non-judgemental and made me smile. Yes, there were people who would still use those other words to describe me, but they did not concern me, for I had no control over what they thought. The only person whose view of me I could influence was mine, so that was the only view that mattered. I promised myself there and then that I would never compare myself to anyone else again. I am perfectly me.

That mantra, repeated over six months, instilled in me a completely different way of seeing myself. I apologised to the limbs at which I had directed so much anger for not functioning 'properly'. My body worked every second to keep me alive. Without it, I would not be here. Humbled and full of gratitude, I now try to thank my wobbly body every day for giving me the gift of existence, for allowing me to be. These atoms of stardust could have been something else, like a Pot Noodle. I fell in love with my body on that March morning when I was twenty-one years old.

My battle to like myself had nothing to do with being wobbly and everything to do with living in a world that breeds self-loathing. Most girls and women (and boys and men) I meet feel negatively towards themselves, despite most of them being able-bodied, healthy, and, yes, young and beautiful. This negativity is a product of the culture we live in, a culture that fuels dissatisfaction with our bodies and lives. Instead of cultivating a perspective that focuses on the fact that we exist and ought to cherish our bodies for enabling us to live and love and create, we are encouraged to measure ourselves constantly against unrealistic 'aspirational' images that are impossible to live up to. We are bombarded with messages telling us that happiness and confidence are attained by becoming thinner, more beautiful, richer or more successful. A range of psychological studies show that the opposite is true: the more you align your happiness with material goals, the more likely you are to be unhappy. (For more on this, see the work of Tim Kasser.)

In my journey to claw back my self-worth, I had to reject many of society's definitions, goals and values, and replace them with healthier ones. If your value system doesn't serve your well-being, it's time to get a new one. This act of liberation is likely to transform your life for the better. And it won't involve a single transaction, purchase or retail outlet. And therein lies the problem: under capitalism, perpetual growth is required to avoid economic crisis. This growth requires perpetual consumption, so the mainstream value system keeps provoking feelings of inadequacy in us. Why? Because values that generate well-being for free threaten the culture of consumerism that sustains this growth. A system whose survival depends on people buying things they don't need doesn't want us realising that self-acceptance is the way to a fulfilled life. Contented people, rich in confidence and inner peace, spell disaster for an economic model that is structurally reliant on the never-ending expansion of production and consumption (of mostly junk for the mostly affluent). This system, with its addiction to exponential growth, is destroying the conditions for much of life on Earth.

These realisations laid the foundations of my political outlook. A system that manipulates human vulnerabilities in order to exploit them is not one that I can support. Many people ask me how we can create a world where disabled people are treated with dignity, respect and equality. I can't see how this can ever happen under our current brand of capitalism. We live in a world that reduces human beings to economic units, that ties someone's worth to how 'productive' they are, and this fosters a climate of division, competition and aspiration – qualities that are incompatible with the notion of an inclusive society for those with disabilities. The recent pandemic has shone a stark light on existing inequalities. In the UK, as I write, the Office for National Statistics reports that disabled people make up two-thirds of Covid-19 deaths.

Within this system, the experience for disabled people everywhere can be improved to a certain extent, such as with better access to buildings, more representation in the media and better legal protection against discrimination. These are valuable changes, but any changes that conflict with capitalism's obsession with human productivity are rarely achieved, and if they are, they rarely last. What progress can be made is firmly restricted to small gains that do not challenge its central mantra of 'make, make, make, buy, buy, buy.'

To acknowledge that someone who can't work because of their disability is still entitled to a dignified life is anti-capitalist. To believe that a person's worth should not be determined by their economic productivity is anti-capitalist. To believe that everyone – regardless of gender, race, religion, ability, sexuality, economic background – should have access to food, shelter, health care and education is anti-capitalist. To prioritise nourishing relationships and rewarding work over materialistic goals is anti-capitalist. To love ourselves and care for one another is anti-capitalist.

I believe that feminism faces similar restrictions under capitalism. Red lines determine which changes will be tolerated, which changes will be integrated into the existing model of capitalism and which ones are deemed too much of a threat. Demands such as increasing the percentage of women in high-level jobs and improving the visibility of women in the media are deemed acceptable, as are calls for more female politicians and heads of state. But what about the essential care work done largely by women, upon which the whole of society rests? Our system demands that it remains unpaid or, when it is commodified, undervalued. Capitalism thrives when it takes more from people, nature and the state than it gives back. It is fuelled by poverty because desperate workers are compliant workers, ready to sign exploitative contracts for want of a better alternative. Extracting value from the (mostly female) carers and nurturers of the world, who raise the young and look after the elderly, is fundamental to the health of capitalism. According to Oxfam, women and girls contribute 12.5 billion hours of unpaid care work *every day*. If the women of the world were to be paid what we are truly worth, the current system would be thrown into a deep destabilising crisis.

Parity in pay and representation between men and women at every level of society is achievable under capitalism. This parity would be a valuable step in the right direction but it would do nothing for the billions of women around the world, mostly from the Global South, who are exploited on the lower rungs of the economy. It would do nothing to halt the ongoing destruction of nature that will force hundreds of millions of women to flee their homes. It would do nothing for the economically vulnerable women forced into sex work in order to survive. The sad fact is that, although parity of pay and better representation are positive steps, they don't address the structural inequalities or the myriad complex and serious challenges created by climate change that blight so many female lives. Because of these uncomfortable truths, I do not think that genuine female solidarity is compatible with capitalism because the only aim of capitalism is to accumulate more capital. To a tiny minority, this logic is rather appealing. Today, the twenty-two richest men in the world own more wealth than all the women in Africa. The solution is not more female billionaires but the creation of a society in which no billionaires exist.

To fight for a world in which women and minority groups are treated as equals requires us to embrace one truth – that all people are human beings who are deserving of love, dignity and respect. My battle to tear off the disempowering labels that society slapped on me at birth, rendering me 'other', is the same battle faced by all oppressed groups: to emerge from behind a label and be seen as a real human being. How people are defined and categorised is a political choice. It's a choice that matters. You cannot dehumanise people without first assigning labels to them and turning those labels into terms of abuse. Words like 'refugee', 'immigrant' and 'disabled' serve to distract from the deeper reality that, despite perceived differences, said person is a human being like you and me.

A system that is wholly dependent on exploitation is deeply threatened by our humanising of one another, our care for one another and our unity. It survives because the tiny group who maintain power and wealth continually divide us, preventing us from realising our collective power and shared interests. A system that offers so little to the majority of people can only survive by scapegoating large sections of humanity – people of colour, women, disabled people, immigrants, refugees, single mothers, benefit claimants and, of course, those who publicly challenge its core logic. Division is the primary tool for fragmenting resistance. For this reason, capitalism can never embrace the values that underpin real equality: that human diversity is beautiful, that we learn and grow from it, that we have so much more in common than that which divides us, that we are one family sharing one home. These unifying truths are incompatible with the need to pit us against one another in order to continue the extraction of value from people and planet.

It's no accident that the most vilified politicians in recent times have been democratic socialists calling for a redistribution of wealth, and policies that would foster greater equality and well-being. Jeremy Corbyn and Bernie Sanders – both of whom would be labelled 'old white men' – posed a true threat to those in power with their progressive social policies and bold environmental plans. Their attempts to bring people together around this urgent and forward-thinking agenda kicked off a propaganda machine that went into overdrive to destroy any chance of systemic change.

The notion that more women in power will automatically lead to female emancipation is a superficial one. Naomi Klein refers to it in *No Is Not Enough* as 'trickle-down identity politics': 'Tweak the system just enough to change the genders, colors, and sexual orientation of some of the people at the top, and wait for the justice to trickle down to everyone else. And it turns out that trickle-down works about as well in the identity sphere as it does in the economic one.' In general, such a system grants real power only to those women who have already internalised its toxic values and destructive logic. Powerful women – from Margaret Thatcher to Hillary Clinton – are just as capable as men of promoting and defending a divisive brand of politics that is unsustainable, exploitative and harmful to women domestically and internationally.

I believe many people long for a world that embraces diversity, promotes healthy values over toxic ones, and prioritises the needs of people and planet over short-term profit. If we are to succeed in creating such a world, we are going to have to confront the fact that our current economic system is fundamentally opposed to it. We are often told that although capitalism is imperfect and flawed, it's the best option there is. But a system that thrives on personal dissatisfaction, endless consumption, mass exploitation, perpetual war, inequality and environmental devastation cannot be the best option. We can do better. We need to do better. Unless we make profound changes to the way we live, our happiness, well-being and futures will remain under threat.

As a wobbly woman, I face particular challenges which may lead me to have specific ideas about the kinds of changes I would like to see. The same goes for other disabled people, women, gay people, trans people, Black people, Jewish people, refugees, Palestinians and so on. Each partial identity brings with it certain experiences and prejudices that coalesce into certain demands. Beneath our different labels, however, we are just people, all striving to be seen for who we are, to have our talents recognised, our concerns addressed, our differences embraced.

We will only be able to trigger the deeper change we need if we focus on our common humanity and join the dots of our diverse struggles. Our fights may well differ in their details but most stem from the same destructive philosophy. Everyone, no matter what their label, will benefit from a world that celebrates human difference, diversity, cooperation and the beauty of nature. These values are the bed-rock of human progress. Join the Wobbly Revolution.

Introducing Myself
Radhika Sanghani

Radhika Sanghani is an award-winning journalist and author. She is the author of two novels, *Virgin* and *Not That Easy*, and her third novel, *30 Things I Love About Myself*, is forthcoming. She regularly writes features for the *Daily Telegraph*, *Daily Mail*, the *Guardian*, *Grazia*, *Glamour* and *Elle* magazine. She is an influential body-positive campaigner and founded #SideProfileSelfie, a movement to celebrate big noses, which has reached millions. She has given a TEDx talk on self-love, and regularly appears as a commentator on TV and radio news shows. You can connect with Radhika @radhikasanghani and via radhikasanghani.com.

ntroducing myself has always been hard. I never know exactly what to say and I often feel I put far more thought into it than most people do.

The first thing I say sounds simple enough: 'I'm Radhika.' Only I don't add in my surname, even in a professional setting. I'm not sure if this is because I don't think I'm important enough, or because my first name is complicated enough for people to remember without adding in the equally complicated surname 'Sanghani.'

Then there's the fact I have to decide how to say 'Radhika.' Do I anglicise it into 'Ra-dick-ah' (a pronunciation I made up for myself in primary school) or do I pronounce it the Indian way 'Ra-dhee-ka'? Making this decision involves me assessing the ethnicity of the person I'm introducing myself to. If they're not Indian, I choose the Western way, but if they are, I need to decide if they're Indian enough to handle it – or if they're so Indian they'll lecture me on not pronouncing my own name properly.

The next part – the hardest part – is saying what I do. This used to be so easy back when I was a student. It was even fairly easy when I became a full-time journalist at a newspaper. But it got complicated in my early twenties, when I became a published author and realised that creative writing was what I truly loved.

I wanted to start calling myself an author or a writer.

But imposter syndrome got in the way. Even when I'd written two novels, I didn't feel like a *proper* author because I still earned my living as a full-time journalist. And even though 'writer' was factually accurate for both journalism and my novels, it felt much more pretentious than saying 'journalist.' As a male colleague put it, 'When you introduce yourself as a writer, you sound like a dick.'

It took several years (and the help of author and vulnerability research professor Brené Brown's TED talks) before I was able to recognise that his opinion was irrelevant; he hadn't written any books, so why was I listening to him? I was ready to start owning my label as a writer.

Only now there was a new obstacle. I hadn't actually written anything creative since I published those books several years earlier. I was still a full-time journalist (albeit freelance) but I no longer wrote creatively in my spare time. So how could I call myself a writer when I'd stopped writing?

The moment I *finally* felt able to introduce myself as a writer was both poignant and short-lived. It happened at the start of 2020, when I was twenty-nine years old. I had just written another novel after a six-year gap, and my agent was in the process of selling it. I was officially writing again, and any hesitancy I had about calling myself a writer was quickly quashed by the universe; I was selected onto a programme called 'BBC Writersroom'. In every sense of the word, I was a writer. It was time to own it.

For a few months, I did, and it was amazing. Every time I said it, the imposter syndrome drifted further away. As I introduced myself, 'I'm Radhika (Ra-dhee-ka?) and I'm a writer,' I laid another brick in the foundation of my growing confidence – a foundation I knew I'd need when the wave of insecurity hit me.

But then – it suddenly stopped being true.

Coronavirus happened, we all went into lockdown, and I stopped writing. Again. I'd submitted my finished novel to my publishers, my BBC scheme had come to an end and, even though I knew I could create something new, my inspiration was gone. I'd lost my ability to create.

I did not even have any journalism to do. Commissioning editors weren't reaching out to freelancers, and there were no longer any emails in my inbox asking me to write articles. Nor was anybody answering my emails suggesting ideas. With absolutely zero warning or fanfare – and no suggestion of whether this would be temporary or permanent – my seven-year career as a journalist came to a crashing halt.

I had no idea how to feel. All my projects were over and, for the first time in my adult life, I had absolutely nothing to do. Nothing. No work. No ideas. I didn't even have any emails to reply to.

I panicked. I cried. I tried to invent projects. I pretended I was on school summer holidays, like when I was a child. I counted myself lucky for being able to manage the financial implications of what was happening. I felt sorry for myself for living alone and having no one whose shoulder I could cry on (physically – not on Zoom. Please no more Zoom).

But the worst part was that my identity crisis came back tenfold. I did not know how to call myself a writer, or even a journalist, when I wasn't doing any writing or journalism and had no idea what my future would look like. Admittedly, I had far less need to introduce myself to anyone now that I was spending 90 per cent of my time alone at home. But when I did meet people in the Sainsbury's queue, at my local café when it finally opened, and in my building's shared garden, I had no idea what to say.

I didn't feel I had a present-tense label. I definitely didn't seem to have an occupation. I didn't even have a social life. I turned thirty alone in early lockdown when we weren't allowed to go out. It was like that riddle of a tree falling in the middle of the forest: If there's no one to hear it fall, did it even make a sound? That's how I felt about being a human being.

As the days turned into weeks and the weeks turned into months, it got worse. I still had nothing to do. No writing. No inspiration. No journalism. Nothing that required productivity. I'd have days where I was happy enough sunbathing in the garden with neighbours-turned-new-friends, but then I'd panic. Was it OK to not be productive in any way? How long could I survive without earning more money? And if I wasn't doing anything with my time, what was even the point of me?

The questions became more and more convoluted – and more existential. Forget not being able to introduce myself as a writer; how could I keep introducing myself as Radhika? The Radhika I'd been for thirty years was different from the one I was now. The old Radhika *did* things. She worked, she saw her friends, she had adventures, she spoke to people, she left the house.

New Radhika did nothing. Sure, she fed herself. Showered. Read novels. Journaled. Went for walks. Had phone calls. Spoke to her neighbours once in a while. But she did not do anything *productive*. She certainly did not do anything that could merit an introduction title. 'Hi, I'm Radhika and I . . . do nothing.'

It did not help that people around me *were* doing things. Most of my friends were still working. Some were working and home-schooling children. Others were on furlough, or they were freelancers like me, suddenly bereft of work, but they were using the time to work on their personal projects or business ideas.

Why wasn't I? What was wrong with me? Why was I so unproductive?

A small part of me – the part that had been in therapy for several years – was aware that I was filtering my reality, catastrophising, overgeneralising, blaming, jumping to conclusions. I was doing the whole spectrum of cognitive distortions that led to things like anxiety, and the more I gave in to these thoughts, the worse it got.

Deep down, I knew that you could still define yourself as a writer or whatever you wanted to define yourself as, regardless of how long you'd been doing it for, how much you were paid, and how many breaks you took. Rationally, I understood I could introduce myself to people as whatever the fuck I wanted to.

But on an emotional level, I felt paralysed and stuck. All I wanted was something to *do*. A purpose, a job. Just something to give my life meaning and give me some kind of identity again. I didn't mind what. I just wanted to have a reason to wake up before midday and put on clean clothes.

I wanted a chance to be productive.

I wanted it so badly.

Only I didn't get what I wanted.

I got the opposite. Months of being unproductive, of doing nothing. Of mind-numbing quietness, of days that all blurred into one, of stillness.

I resisted it for a very long time. But then there came a point – a really low point with a lot of crying – when I realised I couldn't go on like I was. I had to stop craving productivity so much, and just accept my reality.

A reality where 2020 was the year of doing fuck-all.

SLOWLY, as I let my reality sink in, things started to change. Not externally – my life carried on in pretty much the same way as it had for weeks. But internally, I stopped feeling guilty about my lack of productivity.

I stopped panicking about trying to find something to do and started to enjoy how quiet things were. I deleted social media from my phone and realised that now I had no idea what anyone else was doing, I felt more relaxed about my own empty schedule.

The more time I spent doing nothing, the more I started to wonder how I'd survived before Covid-19. I'd done *so much* – had I even been OK? And why had I done it all – because I wanted to or because I felt I had to? Was it because I loved it, or because I was so desperate to be able to introduce myself to people in a way that made me sound successful?

MY EXISTENTIAL CRISIS did a full 180 and turned into something resembling an epiphany. I realised that throughout my life I'd been defining myself in relation to the external – to things outside of myself, be it my work (OK, mainly my work) or my relationship status, or even my friendship circles. But when all of that was taken away from me, I was left with the core of myself. The 'Radhika' without the job title that came after it.

I still had no idea who this new 'Radhika' was when she was not doing anything, when she was just being. But it didn't really matter. Because now I understood that she would always be worthy, whether she did anything or not.

The moment this really hit me was when my god-daughter Dana turned one in July 2020. I couldn't go to see her because she was in Spain, but from previous visits, I knew that she didn't do an awful lot. Sometimes she danced and smiled and had tantrums. But mainly she just ate, slept and did the basic mundane things of life – the exact same things I did during lockdown.

She is not productive. She does not do anything important. She does not have a fancy way to introduce herself. But I still love her with all my heart and, to quote *Love Actually*, to me she is perfect.

Which means I might be perfect too?

Society tells us that our worth and value comes from the way we look, the things we do, the way we live our lives. It's why I was so desperate to be able to introduce myself in a way that gave me worth in other people's eyes. But the more I thought about Dana, the more I realised this can't be true. Our worth comes from the fact we exist, and that's it.

I would be devastated if Dana ever grew up to define her worth through her appearance or how she earns her money, rather than her passions, her loves, her mistakes – the things that give her life.

Yet I've been doing the exact same thing to myself for so many years: judging myself through the eyes of others rather than choosing to live in my own lane; going along with a societal definition of success I don't even remember actively subscribing to rather than creating my own and, worst of all, believing I need to be productive to be worthy.

I'M WRITING THIS at the end of summer in 2020, and I already feel so different to how I did at the beginning of lockdown and at the beginning of this year. I have stopped agonising over the question of who I am and how to introduce myself. I've even stopped agonising over the fact that I've wasted so many years of my life and so many brain cells agonising over how to introduce myself – because accepting myself means accepting everything, even my anxiety.

And, I've finally worked out how to introduce myself. It's so simple and so complex all at the same time. I am Radhika – pronounced the way I feel like pronouncing it in the moment. I am me, and I am worthy. And I always will be, whether I do things, or whether I don't. My value is not attached to my productivity, or how others see me, or even how I see myself. It is just there and always will be.

I can introduce myself semantically in a multitude of different ways, and so long as I choose the one that works for me in that moment, then it will always be the right one. If I want to embrace my identity as a writer, then so be it. It doesn't matter if I last wrote in 2005 or last week, and it sure as hell doesn't matter if I earn a living from it or not.

But it's also OK if I want to introduce myself in a different way – by telling people that I teach yoga (something else I've let imposter syndrome stop me from owning), that I'm learning to cook (even though others might have learnt this years ago) or even that I spend most of my days just obsessing over how cute my cat is (I no longer care if people see me as a crazy cat lady).

I can choose whatever introduction I feel like and it will continue to change as I do. I have no idea what I'll be introducing myself as next year, or even tomorrow. But what I do know is that I will never again try to shove myself into a smaller socially appropriate box just so people don't think I'm a dick.

I'm me and now, finally, I can see that's good enough.

Empathy and Echo Chambers

Amelia Abraham

Amelia Abraham is a journalist and author from London. She is the author of *Queer Intentions: A (Personal) Journey Through LGBTQ+ Culture*. Her second book, *We Can Do Better Than This*, is an edited anthology on LGBTQ+ rights featuring over thirty writers, actors and performers, out in 2021 with Vintage. You can follow her @MillyAbraham.

One day in June 2020, two months into the UK's coronavirus-necessitated lockdown, I sat at my computer and read a now much-publicised blog post that author J. K. Rowling had written. The post outlines her stance on transgender rights. In it, she recalls her experiences of sexual assault and domestic violence, and how these experiences informed her concerns about what she deems 'controversial gender recognition plans' threatening the safety of cis women. She explains her belief that allowing people to self-determine their gender could lead to male-bodied people using single-sex spaces – and how she thinks this might put cis women in danger. Later, she expresses worry that many young women are transitioning because they are experiencing sexism, or because they're gay and have experienced homophobia. She believes that, for these people, transitioning could seem like a more appealing option than what they're already going through.

I'm a genderfluid cis white lesbian and, like most millennials, once ardently consumed each and every Harry Potter book with an enjoyment that was diametrically opposed to what I felt when I read Rowling's blog post: scared, tired and ultimately sad. Scared because of the impact that her words – which put women's rights at odds with trans rights – would inevitably have on trans people's well-being. Tired because I had seen the arguments J. K. Rowling was making so many times before. And sad because, as a person who has written and campaigned about why feminists should support trans rights and has friends who are trans activists, I felt when reading the post like we weren't getting anywhere. Or rather, we *can* make progress but then someone with a much bigger platform can come along and drastically set that progress back overnight.

On the one hand, J. K. Rowling's comments feel deeply personal to her; the blog post is 3,600 words long and reads like a very specific diary of radicalisation, detailing how what she had been reading and learning on Twitter led her to become 'a gender-critical feminist'. (I say 'specific' because most women I know who have experienced sexual assault at the hands of cis men don't link these experiences to transgender people's rights.) On the other hand, Rowling's words feel representative, bigger than her. At the time of posting, they reflected an established and ongoing 'debate' in the UK between a select group of self-described 'feminists', and trans people and their allies. They also reflected what was happening in America, where Trump had, since his election in 2016, either rolled back or attempted to roll back numerous transgender rights, including trans people's right to serve in the US military and trans people's right to access health care without discrimination. Rowling's words captured so much about the deepening inequalities and culture wars playing out in 2020.

The day after I read the blog post, I discussed it with someone I was interviewing, a gay and genderqueer musician called King Princess, who put all of this more articulately than I could: 'I think the problem right now is that people are failing to see beyond themselves,' she said. 'J. K. Rowling feels attacked and threatened by the presence of something that she isn't, which is the same type of attitude that causes and has systematically implemented racism and homophobia. She talks about how trans women will never understand cis women's experiences and it's like, OK, but cis women will never understand trans women's experiences . . . That's called identity! She sighed. 'I don't know why people feel they need to *be* something or they can't possibly relate to it.'

What this person was describing is a kind of crisis in empathy. It made me go back to a book I once read called *The Empathy Exams*. Its author, Leslie Jamison, sets out to explore what empathy means and how we can best use it. 'Empathy isn't just something that happens to us – a meteor shower of synapses firing across the brain – it's also a choice we make: to pay attention, to extend ourselves,' she writes. 'It's made of exertion, that dowdier cousin of impulse. Sometimes we care for one another because we know we should, or because it's asked for, but this doesn't make our caring hollow. The act of choosing simply means we've committed ourselves to a set of behaviors greater than the sum of our individual inclinations.'

AROUND THE SAME time J. K. Rowling published her blog post – a few weeks after the murder of George Floyd had sparked a new wave of global Black Lives Matter protests – I considered my own complicity in this crisis of empathy, the problem of people failing to make the effort to see beyond themselves. I was sitting in my friend's garden. I'd known her since college – a state comprehensive school with 2000 students where, as a mixed race person, she was one of very few people of colour. That evening in the garden, we talked for a long time about Black Lives Matter, structural racism and then about those years when we'd studied together and what that was like for her. As though reading my mind and the question that was privately passing through it, she told me, 'You were all racist.' In other words, whether or not I'd ever been guilty of microaggressions towards her was in some ways irrelevant. I participated in a system and culture that made her feel othered.

We weren't close friends but, to my shame, it was the first time I'd had a conversation with this person about what that experience was like for her. Like many other white people, for me George Floyd's murder had been a tipping point that made it impossible not to be thinking about and talking about racism daily, whereas my friend – whether directly or indirectly – had thought about and talked about racism daily for her entire life. In the liberal bubble in which we had existed during our college years, we – by which I mean my teenage self and my white friends – probably saw ourselves as 'colourblind'. No one was overtly racist, so we believed that we were not racist at all, and yet we held biases and made hurtful comments. We inherited this attitude from our parents, and it perpetuated itself within schools and colleges with almost exclusively white students and teachers in a rural part of Britain.

I may never fully unlearn the racist biases I have learned, but wish I had engaged more actively with this process sooner, and that in the future, parents and schools encourage conversations around race and privilege to happen earlier for others, along with encouraging anti-racist work. I didn't truly start considering my privileges until I moved to London at the age of eighteen, where exposure to more people from cultures and life backgrounds that were different from my own – as well as those people's patient explanations and confrontational jokes – were both educational and expansive. I have been immensely lucky that, since then, my job as a journalist has allowed me to meet a lot of different people and that those people have generously shared stories about their lives and their struggles. But for me, like a lot of us, June 2020 was a reminder to stop waiting to be told, to stop letting other people do the labour, and instead to go and seek out that information for myself.

In the weeks that followed the conversation with my friend in the garden, I noticed how many other white – usually middle-class and sometimes queer – friends were behaving differently: talking more about inclusivity, sharing fundraisers on social media, and picking up books and educating themselves. This clearly seemed to mark a positive change, but alongside this shift a severe form of cancel culture was erupting. A new group of liberal white people emerged online, policing others whom they viewed as ill-informed or whom they saw to be participating in systems of inequality, and, quickly, those deemed in the wrong or considered not to be doing enough were torn down. Seeing this play out, I felt that, while a person's education, naivety or class does not mitigate racist attitudes or – very importantly – equate to them, a conversation around these kinds of nuances did seem to be lacking. I saw a lot of 'pick up a book' sentiments thrown around by highly educated liberal friends without consideration of who has access to higher education, for example, or acknowledgement of the fact that school curriculums in the UK continue to under-teach about the racist history of Britain. There was also a distinct lack of understanding that people from all walks of life inherit views that they will need to work actively to deconstruct, and that this journey can take some time. And a lot of the people I saw called out online were people whom I knew to be participating in certain systems – like being employed by certain companies who have poor track records on inclusion – because they simply can't afford not to. Yet it seemed that the default response had become cancelling people rather than correcting or questioning them, expecting people to be better than 'the system' overnight.

At moments, it felt like call-out culture online had become a way for some metropolitan liberals to attempt to mitigate or distract themselves from their own white guilt, rather than inspecting it. But as well as a pervasive 'I know better' attitude, there also seemed to be a lot of hypocrisy at play: many of the people doing the cancelling online were still existing in their all-white microcosms, like a lot of the companies paying lip service to diversity while not actually doing anything to improve it. The individuals preaching inclusion were still surrounded exclusively by those who look and act like them, still trapped in their socio-economic bubbles, or their specific cultural class milieu of others who share the same very narrow ideas around good taste, beauty or success. People in power at the companies posting messages of solidarity were doing little to correct biased hiring processes or diversifying teams. Watching all of this unfold left me with several questions: Can we really talk about equality when our own social choices exclude those who look or act differently from us? To what extent can we improve our ability to empathise with other people if we never leave our echo chambers? Are we well prepared enough to confront our own shortcomings and do better?

Sociologists explain that like attracts like. 'Homophily' is the technical term. It refers to the tendency for people to have ties with other people who are similar to themselves in socially significant ways. 'Birds of a feather flock together' is another simple way of putting it. There are reasons that humans do this. For instance, sometimes finding groups of like-minded people is legitimately integral to our survival – like if we are from marginalised communities, for example. As a queer person, being around other queer people has helped me to understand that I am not 'abnormal', and among other queer people I feel accepted and empowered. More dominant groups may congregate in order to retain their power, or to protect their views from being challenged, or just to stick together out of apathy or bias, remaining in cloistered friendship groups from universities and other institutions that promote a homogenised white middle-class image of success. There are many material reasons why people might exist in a microcosm that lacks much difference too. Some of us live in rural spaces where there is not much diversity; others work in institutions or industries that still hire relatively few BAME people or people with disabilities, for instance, and do not tend to have social lives outside of these spaces. Even online – as J. K. Rowling seemed to experience – we exist in echo chambers, whereby algorithms show us more of what we want to see based on what we are already engaging with or searching for, suggest like-minded people for us to follow and essentially reflect our ideas back at us.

These are explanations, not excuses.

However, now feels like the time to question them, and ultimately to break out of the echo chambers we so often find ourselves in. You don't have to *be* something to understand it, but I believe that *being around it* could help. Opening up ourselves to greater difference, in the time we are living in, does not have to result in tokenising behaviour. This is an era of global travel, of the internet, of mass social movements and protests taking place online or on the streets. Even if not in person, or indeed permanently, there is no excuse not to leave our comfort bubbles, ones constructed of 'people just like us', unless our mental health or physical abilities dictate otherwise. Change starts from listening to one another, but in order to listen to other people, we need to expose ourselves to what they have to say.

The pandemic, I think, for all the death and destruction to people's lives that it caused, has at least provided us – in unique ways – with the opportunity to make changes that result in leaving our echo chambers and empathising more. Personally, as a Londoner, I found myself talking to and forging relationships with my neighbours for the first time in years. I was afforded more time to read stories written by people from worlds outside of my own. I noticed that my friends in fashion or the media (two industries I work in) stopped caring so much about where they could be seen or how they could spend their money – because there was nowhere to go and much less money to spend – and started caring about how to help other people. Many of us started volunteering and meeting people we might not usually meet through this work. In a broader sense, much of society (and the media that reflects it) adopted a more global perspective in the face of a global threat.

By the time you read this, things may have gone back to 'normal', they may have not. But these habits and mental shifts don't have to stop once we are out of a worldwide pandemic, free to roam around and spend our time as we like. They can be carried forward as the starting point for immersing ourselves in company, experiences and voices that differ from our own. We can, as Jamison says, exert ourselves, *choose*.

So, I am writing this here to remind myself of some of the lessons I have learned from 2020. I learned that I can't condemn J. K. Rowling's lack of empathy with trans people without asking whether I am being empathetic enough. That it's not constructive to cancel someone well-meaning for not being 'woke' enough until we all take a long hard look at how we might be reinforcing patterns of discrimination in our own lives. That we need to escape our tired and safe social confines in whatever ways we can, and be open to learning if we are to expand our thinking.

The incredible black queer writer, Buddhist priest and activist angel Kyodo williams says that true transformation will only come from 'a willingness to be flexible, open, soft-bellied enough to be moved by the truth of the other.' She says: 'For us to transform as a society, we have to allow ourselves to be transformed as individuals. And for us to be transformed as individuals, we have to allow for the incompleteness of any of our truths and a real forgiveness for the complexity of human beings.' This is, she says, 'the only way . . . to not just replicate systems of oppression for the sake of our own cause.'

With this in mind, I resolve, going forward, to take the initiative to ask people 'What was that like for you?' more often, to listen carefully and not to assume that I already know the answer.

Here's Looking at You
Lauren Bravo

Lauren Bravo is a freelance journalist and the author of two books, *What Would the Spice Girls Do?: How the Girl Power Generation Grew Up* and *How to Break Up with Fast Fashion: A Guilt-Free Guide to Changing the Way You Shop for Good*. She writes about clothes, pop culture, food, travel and feminism, among many other things, for titles including the *Guardian*, *Grazia*, *Stylist*, the *Independent* and *Refinery29*. You'll find her tweeting and Instagramming @laurenbravo, because the perk of having a weird name is no competition for a handle.

I t's hot as I write this. At last. We've had weeks of mediocre weather – the endless woolly grey an insult after the glorious spring that bloomed outside the window throughout those early weeks of lockdown. The weather felt border-line obnoxious in the circumstances, but nonetheless became the back-drop to the crisis. Golden sunshine as a foil for grim reality. 'That's weird,' I found myself thinking when it rained sometime in late April. 'I swear it's always sunny in a global pandemic.'

But now it's hot again. In London it's unnervingly hot; the kind of swamp conditions that see us retreating from parks and balconies to gasp quietly in darkened rooms with bags of frozen peas on our bellies. Heat is harder to ignore this year without the sweet relief of our air-conditioned offices. I'm braving the swamp, however; sweating beneath my face mask, which I have put on long before I reach the supermarket. Because first I have to walk along a strip of railway arches which house various garages, workshops and joineries. The men who work there stand outside between jobs or sit in chairs on the pavement, watching the world go by. Which is a nice way to say 'staring at women.'

Hot weather brings it out, famously; the gawping is an inevitable seasonal side effect, like sun-baked dog turds. I've put my mask on because I hate this part of the walk, this self-conscious procession past an uninvited jury. It's worse if I'm late to catch the train and have to do my signature hobble-run, which is inevitably slower than walking.

But with a mask, even a pretty one made of vintage bedsheets, I feel purposeful. *None of your shit, please. Don't you know there's a pandemic on?*

Back when I was a baby feminist in my early twenties, street harassment was my personal crusade and lively retorts were my sport. I shouted back, I scowled, I swore. I was a coiled spring, always ready to leap into action. I'm sure I chanced my safety more than once in a bid to make my fury felt. Sometimes I would flip an angry finger so fast that I had to style it out into a nose rub when I realised that my potential harasser had actually been talking to a colleague, flagging down a bus or pointing at a funny bird on a bin.

These days I don't get catcalled as often. I'm not sure if this is because men have changed or I have. Maybe it's just that my muscle has softened and my expression has hardened. In the two years I've lived here, I have never once heard the men in the railway arches say anything directed at me – and yet I still hate that walk, feeling their heads swivel like tennis spectators at each woman who walks past. I keep my eyes fixed on the pavement.

When I was asked to contribute to this book, I immediately thought of an essay I started writing a year ago, during another heat-wave. Perhaps 'essay' is a grandiose term for a few scrappy paragraphs hammered into my phone on the bus, but I remember feeling at the time like I'd tapped into something urgent and profound. Although I felt the same about a note that just read: 'the particular smell of WHSmith.'

She was angry, Past Me – that sweet summer child who had never knowingly used the word 'droplets' or considered instant yeast an aspirational luxury item. Who thought the biggest threat on the horizon was Brexit. Aw, babe.

But that day she was taking on something more ever-green, and much harder to condemn: literally just being looked at. This is what I wrote:

I ALWAYS THOUGHT that if we could get them to stop yelling, it would be enough. But it isn't. Not to have them muttering under their breath or whistling at our departing backs is nice, but it isn't enough either.

I want to escape the up–down glances, the following eyes, the craned necks from men who haven't decided if I'm worthy of harassment yet. It's a kind of micro-harassment so micro that I'm almost embarrassed to try to explain it. But here goes. I hate the tiny attentions of men designed only to remind me they are watching.

I'm thinking of the ones who stand back showily to insist you get on the bus first, even though they were first and you're still rummaging for your Oyster card and this whole daft performance is holding everyone else up. The male drivers who slow down to let you cross the road in front of them, when there's a gap in the traffic behind. The men at the swimming pool who are determined to greet me with 'good morning' every day, whether I welcome it or not. They hover in my peripheral vision at the end of the lane, waiting for me to look up so they can catch my eye and say it – 'Good morning!' Job done, on they go while my forced smile fades into the water. To them I think it feels like politeness; a little old-fashioned gallantry in a world that has forgotten how to be friendly. To me it feels like further evidence that I am eternally being observed.

Do I sound paranoid? I'm sure I do. But then para-noia is part and parcel of womanhood, and so many more marginalised experiences. Because there's always the voice in the back of our minds telling us that the one time we let our guard down – chat to the friendly stranger, take the leap, trust people, enjoy the attention, neglect to put our key through our knuckles on the late walk home – is the time we'll end up regretting it.

While we might make tiny strides towards a society where being yelled at in the street is not the norm, to say to men 'Do not even look at me!' feels like the kind of 'feminism gone too far' that is never going to fly. Yet often, and especially this week, when the city is a soup and virtually no walk to the corner shop for a Magnum is unaccompanied by eyes on flesh, it is exactly what I want to say.

Just don't look at me.

I'll happily sit out this and all future rounds of the pageant.

Of course, I'm projecting. I know I wouldn't hate it so much if I could believe they were looking with neutral curiosity, the way they might look at a cloud or a signpost – because for god's sake, a person's eyes have to fall on *something* – instead of evaluating me against some vast social tick list and finding me lacking.

I know that this 'don't look at me' exists uncomfortably on a spectrum with the 'Don't look at me!' I have yelled on more than one occasion when my boyfriend sees me struggling into my swimsuit. It's a sturdy one that has to be tugged on firmly; bent over, yanked, wiggled, wobbled. He looks wounded when I yell, as though I have hurt his feelings. Which I suppose, in a way, I have. Because I am hurt and I am his feelings.

I say 'looked at,' you note. I don't say 'seen.' To be *seen* is different; it suggests a gaze that passes through the superficial trappings and tries to understand. 'Seen' is positive; 'I feel seen' is the bugle call of a generation perpetually looking for themselves online. It's why we crave memes and relatable #content. Our innermost selves, reflected back at us wholesale? We love to see it.

No, it's my outermost self I often want to hide behind a hoarding, like a building site in progress. *Sorry, having a spruce-up! Business as usual inside!*

It's not always about body image, though, so much as the sheer awkwardness of being a body in the world. There's the worry I might trip over and look stupid, and the nagging feeling that there is perpetually food in my teeth. The fear of mispronouncing a word, or pushing on a door marked 'pull'. The learned self-consciousness that inhabits and inhibits, in a million small ways, my life and the lives of almost every other woman I know.

'Don't look at me!' can morph into 'Don't ask me!' any time we feel out of our conversational depth. It's a bruise that throbs every time a female politician is torn apart and thrown to the tabloid wolves. Being looked at doesn't just mean a pressure to look pretty – it also feeds into a kind of primal self-preservation instinct. Whatever you do, don't put a foot wrong. They're watching.

And we know it isn't really benign, the looking.

Ask women in their fifties and sixties who find themselves suddenly rendered invisible; routinely barged into on pavements, curiously absent from board-rooms, screens and magazines. Ask them if the gaze is simply human nature in flow, or a torrent of unasked-for attention that one day, just as unfairly, dries up.

Ask the women of colour who are relentlessly othered by a white-supremacist society, routinely silenced and

erased from public view while at the same time being fetish-
ised, sexualised and scrutinised more harshly than every
white counterpart.

Ask plus-size fashion lovers, begging to spend
their money in an industry that's determined to ignore
them.

Ask disabled people, fighting the dual battle to be
remembered and represented where it matters – in design,
in legislation, in the arts – while also being allowed to live
their lives without stares.

Ask virtually anyone who has ever found themselves
outside of society's blinkered beauty standards and they
will tell you: looking is loaded. In a culture that tells us we
are decorative before we are anything else, it can be both
a currency and a weapon.

But what do you want, *Lauren?* you might well ask. *A
world where nobody glances at each other without prior
written permission? An embargo on all unsanctioned eye
contact?*

Well, no. Obviously not! Don't be ridiculous.

Although if you ask me in the worst moments – burning with self-conscious heat, staring determinedly at my
lap as the guy on the train opposite continues his leisurely
appraisal of my body, my face, my lunch – then, yes. That
is exactly what I want. A visa for looking, signed off in six
to eight weeks.

LITTLE DID I know, when I wrote that a year ago, that I
would get an embargo. Of sorts. Four months behind closed
doors, away from the eyes of the world. No buses, no coffee
shops, no swimming. Amid all the fear and pain and uncertainty, it felt like a small gift, this opportunity for a personal
experiment. The chance to fully unclench and unbutton, to

sit back and let myself grow over like an abandoned garden. I was excited to see what would happen.

What happened was, I put mascara on for the first NHS doorstep clap.

'Are you wearing *make-up*?' asked a friend, incredulous, on an early Zoom call. I felt like I'd broken the first law of the lockdown sisterhood. And the second: dress like nobody's watching. And as the weeks went by and everyone evangelised about their new braless existences, as the headlines declared death to the underwire, I sheepishly carried on strapping myself in most mornings. I could pretend the reason was backache, but really my clothes just looked 'better' with a bra on. Was it internalised misogyny to prefer my tits supported? Probably. But then, my boyfriend didn't stop wearing pants.

I've always been conflicted about the 'I do it for myself!' line on beauty and style. In its purest form, painting your face and adorning your body can be an incredible tool of creative self-expression. But if that was really the reason we put make-up on, wouldn't we all be walking around with bright purple eyelids, green chins and turquoise butterflies daubed across our foreheads? Rather than spending wads on products that promise to perfect and disguise? If I really did it for myself and myself only, I wouldn't wince in horror when I walked past a mirror, barefaced with my fringe doing a flock-of-seagulls impression. I'd just think, 'What a lovely canvas!'

We could chew over the nuance all day long, but the truth is that we'll never really be able to separate out the social pressure from the personal choice while we still live in a world that treats female beauty as a Minimum Viable Product, not a 'nice to have.' For most of us, the personal pleasure we take in our appearance is bound up with the way we want society to see us, whether it's the tribal conformity of this season's must-have dress or the anarchic thrill of a neck tattoo.

John Berger had it right in *Ways of Seeing* when he said that a woman is 'almost continually accompanied by her own image of herself' – and forty years later, we can scroll through that image daily, on a device that lives in our pockets. With social media, no room is truly empty. On Zoom, every work meeting becomes a mirror. A global pandemic was the closest thing to test conditions I've ever had, and there I was, diligently filling in my eyebrows every morning. 'For me.'

A mask, on the other hand, definitely wasn't for me. It felt curiously liberating to wear something for the sake of protecting other people rather than impressing them. I'm not sure I've ever done that before.

In fact, it was liberating full stop, to get dressed without outside validation. Certainly it was a luxury, when key workers were still wearing a uniform every day. There was something joyful about putting together outfits the way a six-year-old does. Clashing fabrics and prints, finding beauty in the comfortable and comfort in the fun. I relished the chance to wear socks and Birkenstocks without apologising.

For a while, it felt like we might smash the mould entirely. When lockdown lifted, we would stride out together – a Boots-advert army of confident women in protective visors and Velcro sandals, who would never care about contouring or what we're told is 'flattering' again. But the trouble is we also craved normality. My normal was mascara and bras. Our normal is a world where we chip at the mould slowly, over decades. Two steps forward, one step back.

When I did leave the house during those first few eerie

weeks, wearing outfits best described as 'reclusive potter caught out by a hotel fire alarm', seeing another person felt like an event. On daily walks round the block, I found myself saying 'Good morning!' brightly to strangers. I didn't linger at the corner of the street waiting to bark it at them the way a man might, but still. I understood that urge for fleeting human connection a little more. I don't owe anyone a smile, but it turns out that choosing to give one can sometimes be good for the soul. My younger self would be furious.

I missed being seen, too, just a little. I craved the far-away faces of friends and family; even approximations of faces, distorted into cubist portraits by a bad Wi-Fi signal. The best bit of every Zoom call was the 'Ahh!' noise we made when one another's faces popped up. As though we were all beautiful fireworks, just by dint of being alive.

I don't disagree with what I wrote a year ago, but I have notes. Living through everything we have in the past few months has made me realise that the whole business is far more complicated than some binary Andy Williams–soundtracked vision of 'boys watching girls watching boys watching girls go by.' Sometimes it is an act of dominance, whether that's objectifying women or anyone else robbed of their power. The gaze can be political, and its withholding even more so. But sometimes looking at each other is an attempt at forging connection from a place of isolation, however clumsy. I've realised that my ideal world isn't one in which I exist as a disembodied invisible gas, or as a green-chinned, free-titted peacock. It's a world where we all get to own our images, and nobody else can detract from that value.

I have all too often been blind to my privilege and the power of my own gaze. It could be braver. It could look for the people who are missing, and help them feel seen. It could notice injustice, stare it down and call it by name, instead of waiting until 'speaking up' becomes an act of public performance. It could probably do a lot of good if I wasn't so busy picking over my own flaws through the eyes of imaginary strangers. If I didn't waste time holding other women up to myself for comparison, under society's fluorescent glare.

Life is exhausting enough without doing the patriarchy's work for it.

You have to wonder what we lose of ourselves and our potential because we're too busy trying to make ourselves invisible. If we eternally keep our heads down, what do we miss?

This morning, I walked back past the railway arches and this time I kept my eyes up. Grateful to feel the sun on my skin while we still have it, before the grey wool descends again – and after it, who knows? That first cool breeze that hits your face after you've taken your mask off is a treat specific to These Times; the new cold side of the pillow. Perhaps I'll describe it to my future children one day, and they won't relate to it any more than they'll relate to the way WHSmith used to smell. I kept my eyes up, and when the men looked at me, I looked straight back at them. As though I had every right to. As though they were just a funny bird on a bin.

Am I saying I've missed the micro-harassments? Well, no. Obviously not! Don't be ridiculous.

But I refuse to let them ruin another summer. In a few days I'll go for my first post-lockdown swim, and part of me hopes the 'good morning' men are still there. This time, maybe I'll say it first.

2020: The Failurey, Non-Chrononormative Year That I Can Finally Relate To

Virgie Tovar

Virgie Tovar is the author of *You Have the Right to Remain Fat* and *The Self-Love Revolution: Radical Body Positivity for Girls of Color*. She holds a master's degree in sexuality studies, with a focus on the intersections of body size, race and gender. She is a contributor for *Forbes*, hosts the podcast *Rebel Eaters Club* and is the founder of Babecamp, an online course designed to help people break up with diet culture. Virgie has been featured by the *New York Times*, *Tech Insider*, BBC, MTV, Al Jazeera and NPR, and you can connect with her on Instagram @VirgieTovar. She lives in San Francisco.

T he first indication that something had changed was when I would idle at stop signs in my car and watch others at the intersection cede their right-of-way and flag two, sometimes three cars to go ahead of them. It was early spring 2020, and where there had once been the relative ubiquity of impatient honks, there was now silence. Rushing had become not only rude, but actually absurd. Where was anyone going in a hurry during a pandemic – when schools, salons, office buildings and nearly every shop was closed?

2020 has been a slow year, with people waiting around – for a pandemic to end, to see if they will get fired, if the market will crash, if Trump will be impeached, if they'll meet their soulmate during a socially distanced, masked open-air speed-dating hike, if their restaurant will make it, to see if maybe we are *finally* experiencing the revolution we've dreamed of. Time slows down when you're afraid, when you're bored, when you're unsure of what might happen next, when you want something badly, and when you're waiting to get into a grocery store and you're twenty-seventh in the line (because you had time to count).

When it comes to the standards to which the United States of America holds itself, 2020 has been an epic fail of a year as well. Our country's laser focus on economic growth at any cost? Halted. The belief that each of us can pull ourselves up by the bootstraps, reality be damned? Gone. Covid-19 doesn't give a fuck about your religious commitment to neoliberalism, bro. The cultural entitlement of the police to murder Black people with no consequences? No more. Straight cisgender men are expected to wear masks that would indicate they are capable of being *defeated* by illness? The government is giving out stimulus checks, à la, what, *socialism*? People are expected to skip meals at restaurants because they have a duty to the rest of the world? This is *not* the country I know.

As a fat woman of color, I know a lot about being slow and about being rendered a failure by your culture's standards. And this essay is about that – how Covid-19, fear, the unknown, a racial-justice revolution and a halted market all slowed down time and rendered a culture a failure in its own eyes – and how I experienced it. I use Mark Rifkin's theory of 'settler time' (according to *Beyond Settler Time*: 'an account of time defined by the coordinates of settler governance and sociality') and its opposite – what my friends and I call 'POC time'. Additionally I enlist the concept of 'fat time', the subject of a 2017 special issue of the *Fat Studies* journal; Jack Halberstam's notion of 'queer time'; and Elizabeth Freeman's notion of 'chrononormativity' (defined as 'the use of time to organize individual human bodies toward maximum productivity') to discuss my experience. This is an essay about how 2020 temporarily suspended settler temporalities and how for a few months I lived – I think we all lived – on fat time, on POC time.

'Slow' is a relative term that relates to – and goes against – the widely accepted idea of time that exists where you are. When describing a clock as slow, it refers to showing a time that is earlier than the 'correct time', according to the *Oxford English Dictionary*. In order for there to be a concept of time, there has to be a 'correct' way to mark time and an incorrect way. I've learned that my fat body messes with both 'correct' time *frames* (the expected duration of time it takes to do a discrete task) and with 'correct' time-*lines* (the way life events are supposed to unfold in the United States).

I am the proud owner of a body that is understood in the USA as 'incorrect', and I guess I've settled into that fact. I'm proud of that fact, maybe even, because, hey, who wants to be the 'correct' version of something derived from colonialism, sexism, racism and fatphobia? Not anyone I'm itching to have coffee with.

In short, time functions differently when you're fat. Things take longer. I'd like to introduce you to the concept of 'fat time', derivative of queer time and defined by the editors of *Fat Studies: An Interdisciplinary Journal of Body Weight and Society* on fatness and temporality as 'abundant and spacious . . . it moves bigger, resists containment, "lets itself go," and stretches boundaries.' To me, fat time is both about the interesting ways that the fat body stretches and destabilizes settler time, and also the ways that fatphobia renders fat people as non-chrononormative because it impedes participation in rituals of cultural importance that signal 'real' adulthood (childbearing, marriage, career and home ownership).

When it comes to fat time, there's the small stuff. Like the way I take whatever Google Maps tells me is my estimated walking time to a destination, multiply it by .3333 and add that number to the original figure to get my actual ETA. And then there's the bigger stuff, the timeline stuff. It took longer to get into my first serious relationship, get my first job, my first well-made outfit, my first pleasurable sexual experience, not to mention a sense of dignity or belonging.

I learned that my body moves at a pace that is slower than what is considered normal or appropriate through a series of very clear social cues and just plain old overt shaming. It started out when I was a little Mexican nerd in enormous round glasses, running laps in PE. Even when I walked as quickly as my chubby little legs could take me – gasping and wheezing all the way as my thin counterparts breezed by chatting easily with one another – I was a permanent member of the The Rear.

After PE class, it would take me longer to get dressed because I tried to put on my street clothes while still wearing my sweaty uniform. Have you ever tried to do this? It's like trying to get dressed inside of a cocoon. It's uncomfortable and potentially more awkward and attention-garnering than whatever you fear may happen if you just took your clothes off. I didn't care about that line of reasoning. I was terrified that my classmates would see my body and make fun of me because that was what happened all the time.

When you're fat, it typically takes a very long time to find an outfit for a special occasion. I know that shopping will take longer because there will be very few options in my size. I will have to go to multiple stores or websites. I will have to check if those stores or sites carry anything in my size. I will have to talk myself through cycles of disappointment, rationalization, rage and confusion before finally settling on the least ugly (but still undoubtedly covered in ruche) garment. It will take time to talk myself into wearing it. It will take time to make it look cute.

Like the year 2020, my romantic life has been slow because it took me quite a long time to figure out that though there are seemingly innumerable men (the kind of human I date) who love sleeping with fat women, there are almost no men who will be seen publicly dating one. Once

I located my prospect pool (comprised of the men who would), it took a long time to find ones I liked, and then liked and respected, and then liked, respected and could imagine sharing a life with.

Many fat people experience this and that's why many of us don't marry or have children, and this fact renders us permanent non-adults in a culture that sees marriage and childbearing as markers of adulthood and full citizenship.

Fat time reminds me of the inside joke I shared with friends who are also people of color. During college, at any time, we could call 'POC time' the way someone might yell 'shotgun' to claim the front seat. It was an inalienable, no-backsies carte blanche for sometimes absurd levels of lateness, a courtesy we lovingly granted each other in a culture otherwise inhospitable toward our cadence.

And I saw that cadence when I went to Mexico by myself for the first time, there to write a novella based on my family and hoping to understand my grandparents better by visiting the place they came from. I saw the easy gait, the kind of walk that would get an elbow and a shove in any major city in the USA. I understood it immediately because in that time and place, it seemed not only perfect but inevitable. It was hot as hell. No point rushing, because rushing caused sweat, and sweat caused chafe, and chafe was unnecessary if you just worked with the natural world instead of against it.

I saw that cadence in the working-class neighborhood where I lived on and off for a few years in New Zealand. There was so little to do in the South Island town of Christchurch that I began to talk at length with the white-haired mother of my partner, and she began to explain to me that to avoid boredom one must extend tasks and errands. Walk slowly. Speak slowly. Relish the jaunt outside, the walk into the village; take your time and look through every aisle in the grocery store. Check the bargain-bin meats. Chat leisurely with a neighbor on the walk back. Take on massive knitting projects. Serve elaborate tea rituals from morning until 3 p.m. and then promptly begin cocktail hour until time to retire to bed. Start over tomorrow.

My California town of San Francisco, where I've lived for thirteen years now, is not normally a place permeated by fat time or POC time. And yet, in the early spring of 2020, time had undoubtedly changed. I began to wonder if maybe the people deemed successful in this culture had been forced to face their mortality, their weakness – which, as far as I can tell, already structures and texturizes the lives of marginalized people. Their lives had been bent to forces bigger than their personal wills to succeed at conforming. The same people who had been so out of touch with their fellow Americans that they actually cried when Trump won the presidency – *those* Americans had been faced with the kinds of facts that can change a person forever. Maybe?

They had been forced to face the terrifying truth that so many people of color live with every day: they might not survive to the end of the month.

They had been faced with the humility that something out of their control was now running their lives, a bitter pill I had to swallow when I was maybe five or six.

They had been faced with the fact that their hopes for relationship- and family-building timelines – for finding a partner and having children – would have to wait and might never come to fruition if they were dealing with sensitive reproductive windows, a devastating feeling I know well as a fat woman.

I felt my own internal clock adjust as my work halted. My terror and anxiety rose, pushing me to spend more time crying, meditating, talking with friends, offering support to others. My appetite withered, and it took hours to eat a meal because I wanted to throw up after every third bite, but knew that if I didn't have a full meal my brain would spiral into worst-case scenarios. By May, things seemed less terrifying (or more normal? this is the perpetual philosophical question), but I still wasn't leaving my home. I tried to create purpose through making increasingly elaborate schedules and events of my own creation, including a failed attempt at a solo film festival featuring very obscure documentaries.

Then something clicked.

I could just surrender.

I could just be fat, be brown, be slow, be a failure, be alive.

I WRITE THIS in late July, unsure of the lasting impact of the culture's tenure in fat time, in POC time. But for me, 2020 is and will always remain a year when a country that is essentially the metaphorical equivalent of a perpetually adolescent frat boy was reminded that even it could fail.

Thankfully, when done correctly, failure can be generative.

There are two types of failure, I think. The first type is systemic and therefore contrived. The failure of marginalized people exists by design. This type of failure is dehumanizing, stifles change or growth, and is therefore necrotic. This is the type of failure the US relies on for its so-called success. The second type is both deeply inevitable and deeply human: to want one outcome and end up with another. This type can be an opportunity to do work that is important to the individual and collective spirit: grieve, grow, face reality, abdicate egocentric and immature thinking, name our limitations, rely on others, collectivize resources, be creative and dream of something else, something new. This type of failure is humanizing, and therefore it is useful and reparative.

The year 2020 has offered us an incredible opportunity: to decide which flavor of failure we want to be. In my humble opinion, I'd say let's not pick the necrotic one.

'I'm here, I'm queer and I'm alive'

Shaz

in conversation with Feminist Book Society

Shaz, twenty-two, was born and raised in India up until the age of twelve. She moved to the UK with her family in 2011 and discovered social media at a very young age. Shaz is now a growing Social Media Influencer on platforms such as TikTok and Instagram, where she shares her experiences of growing up surrounded by hate from social media and overcoming the hardships of being a Queer Muslim. She now holds a 'safe space' on her platforms being a role model for young kids struggling with accepting their sexuality.

The media is full of stories about how dangerous and negative it can be to have a profile
online, especially if you don't conform to social
'norms'. But you've described TikTok as a safe space
for you.

I'd like to say that posting about being proudly queer
Muslim is not for everyone. Not everyone can hack it but
I have a strong mentality when it comes to people on the
internet saying the worst things that come to their mind. I
know a lot of people would not be able to handle that. We've
got people in our group chat who get very overwhelmed.
They're fourteen, some of them sixteen. So they're very
young and, being exposed to so much hate, they think that
this world is such a hateful place. But it's so much more
than that. Just because your videos are getting forwarded to
the wrong people, to people who think negatively, doesn't
mean that the world is full of it.

The reason I joined TikTok instead of posting things on
Instagram mainly, was because I was outed in 2018 by my
aunt to my mum. My mum had thought I'd stopped being
gay, basically. So my aunt outed me again saying, 'No, no,
she's still doing this thing. She's with a girl.' Everyone knew
my Instagram. Everyone from India, my extended family,
they knew my Instagram. TikTok was this new app and I

was like, okay, no one that I know is on TikTok. So I started posting videos on there. I started posting about the conversion therapy that I've been through and the counselling sessions that my mum made me go to because she wanted me to fix the gay side of me. I started posting about things like that with humorous videos, humorous concepts.

I got a few comments from young girls saying, 'Oh, I went through that as well. My mum did that to me when I was fourteen or when I was thirteen.' Things like that. And I was really taken aback by that because I didn't know someone else had gone through similar experiences. That was the time – the end of 2019 – where I started meeting more queer Muslims who were closeted or who had just come out and just started standing up for themselves. That was really amazing to see because I didn't know that we had this little community hidden away in the closet, scared to share their story but still connecting with people.

People now DM me to say, 'You're the first queer Muslim that I've seen on social media that's proud to be herself, that doesn't let hate get to her.' When I do get hate comments, I just make fun of it and I get clout from that. People ask, 'How do you deal with it so well?' And I say, 'No one can tell you who you are.'

And there are people that hate on me and then, a few months later they come back and they're like, 'I'm sorry for hating on you. I'm bi now. I'm bisexual now,' or 'I've realised I'm this now.' This is why I don't block my haters. I do not block people that troll me because they're the ones that need to see my videos more than anyone else. They're the ones that need to be educated.

As we now approach the end of this difficult year, we'd love to know what 2020 has been like for you.

I ended 2019 with a Harry Styles concert, and I caught a viral infection there. I was sick from the start of 2020, on and off, and getting secondary infections. So my quarantine really started before everyone else's. I came back to work [in retail] and because I see hundreds of people every day (this was around March, when everyone was panic buying, so there were a lot of customers we had to take care of) I eventually developed Covid-19 symptoms and I was isolated for two weeks. The Covid-19 symptoms had infected my lungs pretty badly so I had to use an inhaler all the time when I went back to work. Then I was put on furlough from May to July.

It was a great time. I don't regret taking that time off because during that time I met people on TikTok and Instagram going through the same thing as me: being LGBT, being queer, being closeted. During lockdown these people, who are closeted, had to spend a lot of time with family because unis were closed. A lot of people's mental health suffered because they were forced to stay with their toxic family members. So we bonded on Instagram. We used to do Zoom calls, Zoom group-chat calls, and things like that. We'd just talk about our days, reassure each other that this lockdown was going to be over soon.

Lockdown, really, was a lot about growth, personal growth. I got out of a four-year relationship, because I finally realised that it was not healthy. And I spent a lot of time trying to gain my health back. I started doing things I enjoy: doing my painting, writing, running, things like that, which I never got time for because I was so busy at work previously.

The past couple of months, I really focused on posting more content, putting my story out – about being queer, mostly, and the struggles of isolating yourself at home with family members you don't want to be around, and just making light of the situation, so people can laugh and they can have a good time with me and relate.

The online community is pretty informal. We all just wanted to have a nice time, have a laugh, because everything was so stressful at home, for everyone who was either recently outed or who'd come out to their family members. They were getting so much backlash from their family, and they had nowhere to go.

I live with my family. I've got a little sister and my parents. My dad found out that I'm gay because of the BBC video ['I didn't know other LGBT Muslims existed,' BBC.co.uk]. Before the BBC video ran in November 2020 it was only my mum and my close cousins and my sister that knew. My mum tolerated it. My cousins were very supportive, my sister was very supportive. She's young, so she's very much like, 'Oh, you know who you are.' But, yeah, my dad found out and things have been very rough since the BBC video.

And have you found support since that happened in your online community?

Yeah, of course. And from the editor from the BBC. He's been in touch with me. He's Asian as well, so he knows how bad it can get. And in terms of community, we have a little group chat on Instagram. We've got thirty-two queer, LGBT Muslims on there. Whenever anyone's struggling, really, or wants some advice, we just go on the group chat and instantly someone replies. It doesn't matter who it is. There are people on there with a million TikTok followers, there are people with two hundred followers or zero followers. It's become a really . . . a little family for us, one that we can turn to when our own families are not there for us.

So, coming to the end of this year, how do you feel?

Overwhelmed.

So many things have happened. So many good things but there have been quite a few bumps along the way.

Back in 2015, I came out on Instagram. I casually just made a post and I came out on Instagram, and from then on I got a lot of hate because I was young. I used to wear a hijab. I've worn a hijab for eleven years of my life. People would say, 'You can't be gay and you can't be Muslim at the same time. That doesn't work.' My DMs were full of people telling me to leave Islam or telling me to end my life because I'm a bad example. And me, being fifteen, I was like, 'Huh? What?' It was very overwhelming because I'd never questioned my sexuality.

I never questioned it until people of my culture, of my background, started making me question it. Even in school, I was the first person to come out. And I would tell people if you don't like gay people, don't be my friend. I don't want to talk to you. I was very straight up about it. I used to do a lot of debates back in secondary school. I have always been very excited to debate people about equal rights for women and men, equal pay, LGBT issues, things like that. Feminism is such an easy concept, but some people can't grasp it. A lot of people, especially men, get very scared of the word *feminism* because they think it's an extreme thing but we're fighting for you as well. You benefit from feminism. Feminism is about equality and that benefits everybody.

When I came out, they never really came for me because I was a woman but they came for me because of my religion. But you could argue that people didn't take me seriously because I'm a woman, because I was a girl, a 'little girl', coming out. I was told, 'No, that's not true.' And, women are so heavily sexualised in culture. . . . So being an LGBT woman, I've found people think, 'Oh, my God. All you think about is sex.' No. We're just trying to love. And that's one thing that my parents, my aunts, thought of me as: someone who was sort of sex crazed just because I came out at a young age. They thought I was possessed, first of all. They got Imams over to our house to do prayer on me, to pray the gay away because they thought something had possessed me. They couldn't grasp the concept that a teenager could fall in love with a girl. All they were thinking was, 'Oh, she's thinking about sex.' And they thought it was such an evil thing.

My partner was outed in August because someone saw my Instagram close friends story. They screen recorded it and sent it to her parents. It's been very rough and obviously she hasn't been able to go out of the house because of lockdown. It's been a struggle for her. But we've been there for each other and we've been that support system. So it's been okay. It could have been worse.

Hopeful is another word I'd use, actually, to describe this year.

There's so much shame around women's sexuality. I'm just not bothered. That's what I really like about myself. I don't let people get to me. And I think that's one of the benefits of being exposed to social media at a young age. Because you're given shit left, right and centre for whatever you do. Anything you do, you're doing it wrong. So I kind of just grew a thick skin, I guess.

I could have done without the bullying. But a life lived on social media toughens you up.

What have you been most proud of in 2020?

I already post pretty publicly on TikTok and Instagram but one of my first achievements was being featured in *Refinery29*. They did a little article on queer Muslims and it was really exciting. All this time I've been trying to share my story and trying to be for people what I didn't have growing up. So getting that *Refinery29* article out and then the BBC video that followed was a massive thing. Growing up I saw zero queer Muslim representation in the media and on the news. And that really made me struggle with accepting myself. I didn't see anyone like me. If I saw queer people, it was gay men on YouTube, for example, doing vlogs and things like that, being openly gay. But I never saw anyone from my culture, from my background. And never a hijabi girl saying 'I'm queer, I'm Muslim. This is who I am.'

I went on a little journey with religion. I did my own research and I learned that religion is not hateful, it's people that make it hateful. And it's the culture that influences people more than religion to say the things that they do and act the way that they do. So from then on I was just like, 'You know what? Fuck it.' Everyone's got their interpretation of religion and I decided to take the positive interpretation. It's really about how you choose to live your life.

I struggled with mental health so much. Being here was a struggle because I was seeing my family hurt every day because they wanted me to be someone that I wasn't. After a while you just have to say, 'You're the reason you're unhappy, because you can't tell someone to be something that they're not and make them feel guilty about it.' When the BBC video came out, I got quite a few DMs saying, 'You're so inspiring. Thank you for being the first queer role model for me.' That makes me really happy because this is what I've been fighting for. Getting my story heard. Yeah, it's going to put me in shit with my family but if it helps someone to feel like they're not alone – even if it's one person – if it can make them feel like they belong here, it makes it all worth it.

What do you know now that you didn't know at the beginning of March 2020?

Initially, the idea of lockdown was pretty scary, with everyone panic buying and just losing their minds. A lot of people assumed that with lockdown they'd feel very isolated. For me it was the complete opposite. I didn't know I would feel that. I found more people to connect with during lockdown. Because so many people were bored out of their minds, so many people downloaded TikTok, so many people downloaded whatever they could to keep themselves occupied. And there was this amazing, amazing community that I did not know about, and that me and a couple of friends put together.

We were isolated at our homes but we would just open our phones and talk to someone, reach out to someone, because everyone is always online. Lockdown gave us the time to connect with so many people all over the world. I mean, I found my partner during lockdown.

What makes you hopeful?

There are a lot of people trying to represent the LGBT community in the media. And that's a big thing that I did not see at the beginning of 2020 or 2019. Plus the fact that there are so many articles and so many people reaching out to different LGBT people and saying: 'Listen, I want to put your story out.' Or, 'I want to represent you in a good light.' I'd never seen anyone talk about being queer and being Muslim on the BBC, before a journalist reached out to me. So that was a big thing. Things like that make me very happy because, finally, these minorities are getting that positive attention.

Is there a form of allyship that you have found supportive during this time?

A lot of straight Muslim people have said, 'I'm not LGBT but I still support you. You're still a person. I still respect you.' That's good to see because a lot of the hate that I get is from Muslim people, saying, 'You're a shame to this religion.' But then you see the good side of the religion, where there are good people. So yes, the Muslim community has been pretty helpful.

On social media in general, a lot of closeted people act as allies when they're actually members of the community. But I understand they do that for their own safety or if they're not ready to come out. I understand that. There are so many people that have reached out to me from so many different backgrounds. So it's been pretty amazing.

Is there a book that's meant a lot to you this year?

One book that I did read this year was *Heal Your Mind* by Mona Lisa Schulz and Louise Hay. It's about being aware of your mental well-being, and how you deal with mental health in this day and age. For me it brought things into perspective when I'd got one hundred tabs open in my mind and I was juggling thoughts left, right.

When my mind is running I just write it all down. And then that turns into spoken word.

In my secondary school I wrote a lot about self-growth and self-acceptance. When my poems started becoming really dark in terms of struggling with mental health, I stopped performing them. I thought that people would not be able to handle it. You never want to trigger someone or upset someone. So I just write for myself now. During lockdown I've been writing without thinking and there are so many intense things in there. I want to share it on TikTok in the future, or on Instagram. I'll just sit down and read one of my poems. Poetry makes people think in different ways.

What's the one thing you want readers of this book to take away?

Putting yourself first isn't a selfish thing. I've always been called selfish by my family for choosing my happiness and for choosing to live my life the way I want to. But what they don't see is that I spent four, five years of my life, just praying every night to God to turn me straight. And I've taken my family's feelings into account so much that it deteriorated my mental health completely. I just gave up. And then I thought, 'Do you know what? It's not worth it.' We live once. I don't want to look back at my life and think that I was just sad all of the time because I wanted to make everyone else happy. You can't make everyone else happy. What you can control is your happiness. Caring about yourself doesn't make you selfish. You can't give *everyone* the time of day. You can't. Don't feel guilty about putting yourself first.

Look at You
Lisa Taddeo

Lisa Taddeo is the #1 *New York Times* bestselling author of *Three Women* and a two-time recipient of the Pushcart Prize. She is currently developing the adaptation of *Three Women* as a limited series for Showtime, and her debut novel, *Animal*, will be out in summer 2021.

think about my dead mother on an hourly basis because I have a daughter she has never met. I think about her because I am constantly assessing what it means to be a woman, and then I think about how the phrase itself – what it means to be a woman – sounds trampled. Heavy with self-importance, light with the freckles of its Hallmark history.

I think about it for myself, I think about it for my daughter. Every minute I am trying to be strong, not too strong, loud, quiet, conciliatory, unremitting. I am trying to be the best woman, so she can see what that looks like. But every minute I fail, I scream, I am neurotic, I am too frightened to act suave, I am too self-absorbed so I overcorrect with plaintive affection, and she feels it, and looks at me side-long, and refuses to eat her eggs, which I have cooked perfectly, lovingly, at the expense of not engaging with her little ponies. So I cheer myself with the idea that I am the worst woman, and so my child will have an easy path, simply striving to be the opposite of me.

I know this is too facile a point. I am searching for a deeper meaning. My daughter is at once simple and impossible. In her mischievous eyes I see the clockworks of her future. Saul Bellow wrote of the 'hauteur of the female child who knows it won't be long before she is nubile and has the power to hurt.' Said by a man, that line. It will be true, if we continue to live under their gaze. If we continue to fear *not* doing so.

But how do we get out from under it? Even feminists, lesbians – they are defined not by themselves but by the larger society, as women who are choosing to live outside of the male gaze. Like a straggling population of outliers, drinking their own kombucha, twirling their undyed hair.

Before the pandemic I went to a playground with my daughter. Early fall – bright leaves on the trees, but hot outside, little boys sweating as they played. By the basketball courts there was a bouncy castle, powered off. It looked wilted, depressed by the heat. By the monkey bars there was a nerdy-looking boy wearing glasses, orchestrating his younger brother through a hastily assembled obstacle course. They were showing off to each other, to us. Walking on the bars. Climbing them backward. Can the lady do this? Bet the lady can't do *this*.

I wanted to show my daughter that women can do the same, and more, than boys. I easily swung through the monkey bars. I did them backwards and forwards. Pretty good, said the boys.

Then one of the boys ran to the bouncy castle. He turned the power on. My daughter, almost three then, was zealous about bouncy castles. She ran over and I followed. The older boy told me the castle was left over from a church picnic. His father had been left in charge. She can come in, he said, pointing to my daughter, who already had her shoes off. Come on, lady, you too.

I left my shoes and glasses on the ground and followed my daughter inside the bouncy castle. The boys jumped high. I jumped high. My daughter squealed in delight.

Then the older boy said, Knock the lady down! Get her!

The older boy came at me with his hands. Swiped at my chest, nearly brought me down. Then the younger one threw himself at me and hung from my oxford like a small monkey, swinging. My daughter was nervous, but still jumping. I became afraid before realizing I was afraid. Had my daughter not been there, I could have knocked the boy down. That's what I was thinking. I can take this child down. Instead, I said, Stop! – but with a laugh in my throat. They didn't back off. I said, Stop, enough.

At this point, my husband, who'd been doing some work, walked over from the car.

He didn't seem to realize I was nervous. Even as he approached, I felt vulnerable, with my child there. I felt vulnerable also because I didn't want the boys to know I was scared of them. For me that has always been the main objective. Don't show fear. I treat the world like it is a bear in the forest.

But there's been some enlightenment that has come from these terrible times. I've decided that it's okay to say, I am scared, not because you are strong and I am weak, but because you are being an asshole.

In the early days of March, I bought a big, ugly freezer from WalMart. I am still thinking about how, in the parking lot, a man offered to help me load my items and I said no and he kept approaching and I said no again and he still kept coming. And I said no again, loudly, and he looked at me like he was going to kill me. I am pissed that I felt the need to tell him why. I am pissed that I was scared. I wanted to tell him I was scared he had the virus. Instead I told him, I have the virus.

I chastised myself afterwards. I felt I'd been a coward. But I no longer feel that way. The things I had to do that day, stockpiling the house with dried broccoli and gasoline, were more important than setting that man straight. We don't have to school men the way they have schooled us. We only need to stop entering their classrooms.

I find it funny that men will become uncomfortable when women speak of a good-looking man in their midst. They are too used to being the gazers. Nearly every story or essay I have written that involved a good-looking man who was perhaps also charming and wealthy, a male reader, editor or professor has taken issue. This man does not exist, they have told me. I overdid this, or withheld that. And yet why are there so many nubile women floating around? I have never been told a gorgeous, young, bemused female character of mine did not exist. That she was *too* beautiful, too sensual. That's because men want to believe those women are all around us, while there is a dearth of beautiful, good men, perhaps, like themselves.

It's up to women to change the script. It's up to women to hail one another on. To gaze at one other with a sort of platonic desire.

I believe we start like that. By gazing. Not by looking at men with excellent muscles and degrading them the way that women have been herded into hot and not-hot pens for centuries. Not like that at all. But the idea is right, I think, to gaze, instead of merely being on the receiving end of the gaze. To look *first*. This can be anywhere – in the classroom, the boardroom, on the tennis courts. Hit the ball. When you are on the right, say it is yours, even if it is a little left of center. Look at a kid on a monkey bar with an intense look, to let him know your daughter will be taking her turn next. A warning shot.

Why were you scared? my husband asked me, that day at the playground. They are children. You could have easily shoved them off if they got any rougher.

I know, I said, but, in the moment it just felt wrong. It felt violent.

That's how boys play, my husband said, ruffling our daughter's hair.

I wanted to kill him. I told him so.

Whoa, he said. Relax.

But, I said, looking at my daughter, this is how girls are going to play.

Create

Hold Your Pen Torches High

Molly Case

Molly Case is a spoken word artist, writer and nurse born and brought up in South London. She currently works at St George's Hospital, London, as a cardiac nurse specialist. In April 2013 she achieved national recognition after performing her poem 'Nursing the Nation' at the Royal College of Nursing's Annual Congress. Molly has appeared in the *Guardian*, the *Independent*, *The Times*, *Elle* magazine and the *Huffington Post*, as well as being included in the *Health Service Journal*'s list of 'Inspirational Women' and the BBC's '100 Women'. Her book *How to Treat People: A Nurse at Work* was published in 2019.

I wrote 'Hold Your Pen Torches High' during the first national lockdown in the UK, with a brand-new baby. I was torn between feeling immeasurable love and happiness with my daughter but also overwhelming guilt that I wasn't standing beside my National Health Service colleagues during this unprecedented time.

That feeling was hard to manage.

I spoke to friends who are nurses. They were exhausted; many of them traumatised from seeing people die without loved ones around.

I wrote this poem as a gift to them, and to everybody affected by the virus: nurses, midwives, patients. I couldn't be with them in person, but I wanted them to feel seen and heard; words have the power to do that.

I

The earth is nursed on her front.
First light brings end to a dreamless night,
the earth lies face-down,
infusion pump sounds,
busy gloves and gowns
surround her bed.
Outside the sun rises like a crown,
a halo that gleams around her head.

Night-shift rounds are coming to an end,
hot coffee and tea,
the earth's leaves return to green
now that there is oxygen supplying her trees.
The nurse finishes, takes off her PPE,
looks in the mirror,
her name badge reads:
Hello my name is Florence.
She thinks,
I am glitter and dust and light in the dark,
I am PEEP and peak and burnt out stars,
I am thousands of pen torches lighting a well-trodden
    path.
And today is new,
it is the twelfth of May
and Florence Nightingale was born two hundred years
    ago today.

II

The earth wakes at dawn,
she sits up stretches and yawns.
Today is the twelfth of May,
her first baby's due date.
The earth waits,
holds her egg-warm roundness,
in the curtain-y dark.
She has found this last bit hard;
midwife smiles that are hidden behind masks.
But now she calls her midwife who lives across the street,
she comes running with cambium hands and heartwood
    feet:
the earth has tending to her the very tallest tree
cut with knowledge and skill and kindness beneath.

Her baby is coming,
streaks of red and gold
flashes of hot and cold,
lavender, chamomile and marigolds –
the earth's breath is controlled
and her baby is born,
three souls forever notched on bark
where a new growth ring forms.

III

The earth has grown older,
she feels this in her bones
when the weather grows colder.
Her chest is a bird's nest of brittle sticks
no longer so easily fixed.
The earth worries about her lungs
since she is to *stay at home* –
frightened now she'll spend each day alone.
Her phone rings, a specialist nurse
who teaches her
with one simple click,
a flipped
screen and suddenly less lonely in all of this.
It is,
a video call
across her deserts and forests,
an oceanic ridge,
a tectonic shift,
children's hope-filled drawings
on the smooth banks of her snow-drifts,
a voice she had missed
and from her living room she is no longer adrift
nor alone,
moored to a nurse that picked up the phone.

IV

We look to what came before,
at Florence's lamplight quivering against half-open doors,
and to Cronk and Cavell,
Saunders, Seacole and more.
We look now to these nurses and midwives
who cared for the earth
who look after others
and didn't put themselves first.
Hold your pen torches high
to carpark cries and angry tweets asking why,
to those that rejoined
and those on stand-by.
To the earth's clearer waters and cloudless skies,
to the people that stayed at home
with the days drifting by.
To the nurses and midwives and all those who lost their
    lives,
to all of them we know that didn't have to die,
hold your pen torches high.
Here's to healthy days and hopeful nights
Thank you, NHS, the one and only, the very best.

This Is Who We Are, This Is How We Rise

Kuchenga

in conversation with
Feminist Book Society

Kuchenga is a writer, a journalist and an avid reader of Black women's literature as a matter of survival. She is a Black transsexual feminist whose work seeks to cleave souls open with truth and sincerity. She is currently writing a novel telling the tale of a young Black trans girl from North London whose triumphant journey takes her down a path of sexual scandal, substance abuse and a mission to prove the Jamaican family legend that she is a descendant of Admiral Horatio Nelson. Connect with Kuchenga on Instagram @kuchenga and via kuchenga.com.

What thoughts from lockdown do you want to share? Is there anything you didn't know at the beginning of March 2020 that you do now?

The thoughts are not necessarily pandemic related, but they arose because of the circumstances that the pandemic has created. During the summer of 2020, the political touchstones which affected me the most were, obviously, the Black Lives Matter upsurgence and #PublishingPaidMe – both of which smacked right into my life with intense ferocity, not least because with this upsurgence there was a more potent conversation around the fact that *all* Black lives matter. So, as a Black trans woman who faces discrimination and has social media feeds filled with the murder of my sisters, that has been difficult to navigate, but has also compelled me to consider *what* I prioritise, *who* I fight for – even if they're not fighting for me – and, more broadly, how I am excluded from institutions and the job market. As a writer and a journalist, seeing such a stark disparity in what Black writers receive, financially, was really painful, and I felt compelled to share my way through it on social media, because it's such a fraught, intense conversation. Sharing my anxieties and struggles led to a flood of support and I'll be forever grateful to those who really showed up for me in ways I couldn't even imagine happening at the time.

There's one quote that really stuck with me recently, from an interview between Trixie Mattel and Alyssa Edwards from *RuPaul's Drag Race*. Trixie said, 'Winning isn't everything – but wanting to *is*.' Because of everything that's happened politically and where I'm positioned professionally, I've felt more comfortable about the fact that I am relatively ambitious. I do want to be read by a wide number of people, be published and have my writing enter the public sphere. And I'm not sure if I would have felt so encouraged in my ambition outside of the current political climate.

I think if I were American, I would have been a bit more declarative about how difficult a position I was in and not had as much shame around it. Sometimes I wonder if my reluctance was due to an evolution of the British stiff upper lip. I'm an older millennial who graduated into the recession and have heard constant accusations about my life being centred around avocado toast at brunch, so I absorbed that a bit too.

I read Nathalie Olah's *Steal as Much as You Can*, which threw my perspective on my own professional life wide open because I hadn't understood why I felt stuck. I felt like I was part of this cottage industry of journalism, that I wasn't being considered for longer-form writing, like I'd been somewhat ghettoised because of my identity. That book clarified the political machinations which have led to my generation in particular being shepherded into these professional positions, which have proved very limiting. That was then expanded upon by Dr Tressie McMillan Cottom in *Thick*, a collection of essays published last year that spoke from a Black feminist perspective about how there's a stratification within the media industries, where Black women specifically are not given those healthiest salaried paid roles that come with the benefits and which mean that you don't need to be constantly on the hustle.

Sometimes I feel like I am being asked to be a trauma merchant, to speak from the seat of my pain and give readers a 1000-word trip into how difficult my life is so that they can clutch their chests, say 'how *awful*' and then move on. As a writer who is also an avid reader, my desire has always been to achieve a whole lot more than that. I want to elicit a whole load of other emotions for those whose lives are nothing like mine.

What are some feminist books that made you?

Rock My Soul: Black People and Self-Esteem by bell hooks did what it said on the tin and transformed my perspective on my own life but, moreover, my academic approach when entering into my university education: that as much as I was learning what I needed to become more employable once I graduated, I needed to understand the structures that I was living in for my own survival. And it also alerted me to cultural practices of the political movements of the '60s and '70s, namely the Black Panthers and the Black feminist movement – with their reading groups and education programmes – helping me realise that I would grow to depend on myself for education and to transform my living space, for my home to become a sanctuary.

I always have a library with me. In a world where the beauty standard is so Eurocentric and fatphobia exists, I know that my bedroom walls deserve to be covered with people that look like me.

As a result, since reading bell hooks, my bedroom went through a complete transformation, from being exclusively covered with images of white femininity to a wider range of bodies with much darker skin, and it has absolutely revolutionised the way that I feel about myself. And that's an ongoing thing. So, funnily enough, because of that Black feminist's text, I now live with a village of images of people who make me like myself a whole lot more.

In 2015, I read *Woman on the Edge of Time* by Marge Piercy. It is now rightly deemed a feminist sci-fi classic, and addresses the dichotomy of dystopia and utopia. The way that book specifically wrestled with the impacts of gender, race and cosmic oppression was so clarifying for me. The world that Piercy describes is a promised land of decolonisation and left-wing politics that sees gender and sexuality as a spectrum, and returns to indigenous living practices.

Throughout my life, people have told me that what I desire and who I am is impossible. But now, if I see someone being dismissive of non-binary gender identities or being markedly transphobic or misogynistic, I'm able to return to that mental place in my head, to that novel where transitioning one's gender is mundane and raising a family outside of a nuclear family unit is normal. And that's what has kept me going until now. It's been five years since I read it and there has been many a time when I've had to question, 'Is this worth it? What am I fighting for? Why do I bother doing this? Why do I bother writing?' and the visions Piercy's book gave me sustain me in the fight for freedom and equality.

What makes you hopeful about our immediate feminist future? And what makes you hopeful about the long term?

This summer's upsurgence of the Black Lives Matter movement, being fuelled by Black feminist discourse, has introduced abolitionist politics into the mainstream in a way that we hadn't anticipated. Black feminists like Barbara Smith and Angela Davis have always highlighted that this is a fight for the long haul, that we're fighting for things that we may not see, and that we need to dig our heels in. When I read *Are Prisons Obsolete?* by Angela Davis, I had to wrestle with huge ideas – what justice looks like for survivors of sexual assault and childhood abuse, what we're going to do with our murderers, how to end the war on drugs – and I wouldn't have been as prepared to have those conversations if it weren't for the works of Black feminist theorists. Of course I worry about things being co-opted by capitalism, but I'm glad that they are now in the mainstream.

The backlash to Cardi B and Megan Thee Stallion's single 'WAP' has shown how anxiety-inducing that idea of women celebrating their own sexual desire is. More so than just wanting to enjoy sex and sexuality, what made their commentators really scared is the idea that respectability politics can be shed to an extent where women question their need for men beyond sexual encounters, and stop centring their lives around men at any given moment.

So I'm looking forward to the next twenty years of women feeling like they have less pressure to have children, and their ability to have kids without a partner. What would a society look like where single mothers weren't so beleaguered, where we are able to provide the childcare, the freedom and the fresh opportunities that have historically been ripped away from someone? I want more liberal relationship models. That's where my long-term hope is.

I know that queer and trans liberation has led the way for us to rethink those things. Sure, we are obviously going through a very intense backlash. But we've got an expanding section of society that is declaring who they are, the way they want to live, irrespective of how they were assigned at birth, or what they were told they needed to be; who ensure their gender makes sense for them. In spite of the violence and resistors, it has a knock-on effect for cisgender heterosexual people, and I look forward to when they can taste the joys and the freedoms of manifesting themselves the way that we do.

So if you have one call to action for readers of this book, what would it be?

I struggle to have a blanket statement because of how we're structured as people in a society. With us all being in different subjective positions, I feel it's difficult for me to have something that's applicable to everyone (that isn't just shallow and schmaltzy!).

What I'm hoping for from the allies who have become a lot more vocal about their desire to undo a system of white supremacy – if I was to speak to white feminists specifically – it would be to encourage them to continue to become scholars of whiteness. Because Black people have many different things we have to learn about race and for our own survival. White supremacy has depended upon the ignorance and the fear of white people who refuse to look into themselves about the way that whiteness has impacted their own lives. It's more than just white privilege. The system of white supremacy is pernicious in a number of ways.

I'm not fully convinced that white feminists in particular are ready to look at the ending of the system as part of a white-saviour mission. It's just about making our lives better. My relationships with white people have shown me that white supremacy doesn't make white people happy. It may provide a certain amount of safety, it may even feel familiar and the thought of it ending without some sort of vengeful bloodbath is difficult for certain people to comprehend. There are revolutionary relationships to be had once we're able to learn how to respect each other and find an end to these oppressive systems. I look forward to us being able to do so.

Relief and Revelation

Jude Kelly

in conversation with Feminist Book Society

Jude Kelly is the Founder and Director of The WOW Foundation, which runs WOW – Women of the World Festivals across the globe to celebrate the achievements of women and girls and confront global gender injustice. Starting at London's Southbank Centre in 2010, where Jude was Artistic Director for twelve years, the festival now takes place in thirty locations across six continents. In 2018 Jude established The WOW Foundation as an independent charity dedicated to building the WOW movement as a force for change.

Jude Kelly has directed over 200 theatre and opera productions, including at the Royal Shakespeare Company, English National Opera, National Theatre, and the Châtalet in Paris including Ian McKellen in *The Seagull*, Patrick Stewart in *Johnson over Jordon* and Dawn French in *When We Are Married*. She is the recipient of two Olivier Awards, a BASCA Gold Badge Award for contribution to music and a Southbank Award for opera. She was headhunted to join the bidding team for the 2012 London Olympics and create the programme for culture and ceremonies, and subsequently advised both Rio and Tokyo on their successful bids.

Jude Kelly has founded a range of arts institutions and has commissioned and supported the work of thousands of artists across all genres.

First, let's get personal: how you are feeling right now and what is the feminist issue that has been most in your mind as the pandemic crisis unfolded?

I would say I'm pretty energetic as I tend to be when I can see that there are lots of jobs to be done. And I think that maybe I benefit from being older so I know that progress isn't linear, that it takes a number of zigzags. I'm a windsurfer, so I have to tack and gybe to get somewhere. You can never sail in a straight line. You have to navigate by the wind. And with the wind against us, we have to take different directions. It doesn't mean to say we can't get somewhere.

It is okay to be fed up, it is okay to be blue. I'm not trying to be holier than thou about being an optimist, because you just can't always be like that. But I think that for those of us who are saying to people: *there is another world, a different world. It doesn't look like this one. We haven't seen it yet, but we will get there – as in equality –* we have got a duty, really, to keep on demonstrating that we still believe that, even when the circumstances look very hard.

I feel both personally energetic because there are things to do, but I also feel philosophically determined to build resilience at this moment because it's bleak so you have to dig deep. You have to look at progress over hundreds of years, not just at the knock-backs of the last twenty-five.

I'm conscious that, like all crises, this one disproportionately affects people who have less power. And women have less power in so many different ways that interconnect. They have less power economically, they have less power in terms of their time control. They have less time in terms of their access to emotional choices because they have got so many responsibilities and people have so many expectations of them – and then we have so many expectations of ourselves. I mean, it's very obvious who jumps in and starts doing stuff all over the place – it tends to be women straightaway.

Over these last months I've done lots and lots of connecting with people and still am, and you hear an awful lot about what is so wrong. It's much harder to get around a kind of model for change that is working. Much harder. I am a great believer in celebrating good stories because I don't think you can find stamina and hope unless you do.

We've done an awful lot of introspective thinking, and we'll have to carry on doing it, but a question I am thinking about a lot at the moment, in terms of how we move forward from here: What is action-based learning?

You talk about digging deep, and finding stamina and hope. What does building resilience mean for you? And how has that manifested over these recent months?

Part of my thing is reaching out. Reaching out to friends and people who might not even be close friends, but retaining connections and saying, 'I need to stay in touch for my sake.' Being able to express one's own needs is something a lot of people – women – aren't encouraged to do. We don't encourage ourselves. There's a sort of imagery as well around leadership and stoicism.

I've been working with a group of people I formed myself. People who aren't necessarily my friends, as such, but they're people who I admire. And we've been practising what vulnerable leadership looks like – being able to really share fears and also past mistakes so that we are using this time for reflection, in order to build new methods of being more courageous and more open. For example, there are so many people who have no choice but to suffer in public. They've got no choice but to have their pain in evidence – their poverty, or their anxiety. So it isn't appropriate for people who have less insecurity to model the idea that you can hold it all together all the time.

Tell us more about vulnerable leadership.

I'm looking back through years of leadership in the arts and in women's areas. We still have this idea that leadership looks strong in a particular way. Even though people say: *take your whole self to work* and *be your authentic self*, and so on, we're still quite chary about revealing ourselves to each other.

And that's not a very tender thing to do – to be closed like that leadership model demands. It's not respectful because it doesn't acknowledge the fact that other people's issues have to also get closed down if you only present the 'strong' part of yourself. So I'm interested in, and a lot of us have talked over many years about, women's leadership being more compassionate, more collaborative. And it is because we know what it is like to be shut out of spaces and excluded.

But I think we're still very affected by male leadership and demonstrations of strength, and we still imitate it and audition to be legitimised by men, even though we vow to not behave that way. So, as a leader, what does it look and feel like to have the courage to really be emotionally available, both to yourself and to other people, including vulnerability? That's the thing I have done the most thinking about during this lockdown period.

That feels like a pretty revolutionary approach. Where are you and fellow leaders at in your conversations around that?

I think that there's a sense of relief and revelation once you reveal to yourself how much you carry that idea of always being fine and always presenting positiveness. Because, as I said at the beginning, it's a kind of a duty to be optimistic, and that's a philosophical position, but I think you can go too far with always looking as if things haven't got to you, or you haven't gone through lots of doubts, or you don't hold doubts.

And I also think, in terms of conversations I'm having with my Black friends, and women of colour friends and disabled friends, that it's important for a white woman to openly demonstrate the things that are difficult, scary and unknowable. I'm not talking about white fragility here. I'm talking about your own journey, because, like I say, some people are made especially vulnerable by the structures of society. Whether they like it or not, their jeopardy is exposed. And for those around them to model leaderships that close their own vulnerability down is unacceptable.

I think women leaders have done an enormous amount

to shore themselves up, not look like victims, which is good, but I think it can make for quite a difficult cross-fertilisation of empathy because you look like you're the sort of person who is secure and the person who would give advice and the person who can give your wisdom. And that's useful too, but for models to change, those of us who hold leadership positions, well – you've sort of got to demonstrate the holes in your own cheese!

In terms of our discussions so far, it's been very rich; it's very rewarding and it's very important.

Let's talk more about the power of vulnerability. It's such an important word, but so horribly charged.

It is. And of course, in some ways, it's very fashionable as well. So that's part of its problem at the moment, isn't it? Because yes, we give TED talks on vulnerability, but leadership, for me, involves embracing your own and others' vulnerability.

I don't see how you can think in real compassionate ways unless you also factor in compassion for yourself, and to do that you have to acknowledge why you need compassion. And that might mean breaking down some of the things that you have built up around yourself in terms of coping.

That's as far as I've got with this thinking, so far. I don't believe that leadership needs to look invulnerable at all. And I think that if, as leaders, we're really saying that we want other people to be empowered and included, that means that they have to come into our force fields. They have to be allowed inside and witness our turmoil and give advice and wisdom to us . . . it's got to be equal transfer.

Yes. And if we're truly serious about breaking down white-centric, male-centric binary concepts of how we lead and how we structure society, there's got to be that collectivity you mentioned earlier, hasn't there, and that reaching out and communicating? The singular leadership role – that one 'strong', privileged person in control – that narrative no longer works if truly empowering other people is what you're trying to do, does it?

No. And that model precludes you from having lots of fun. Deep, deep, deep fun, which you can get, I think, in collective leadership.

There's no doubt collective leadership is hard, because it requires a huge amount of trust, and you've also got to give trust in advance.

This is an area that I feel we can do more thinking about together as women. We get a bit confused because on the one hand we see women's leadership as fantastically important, but on the other I'm not sure how far we've got in trying to actually model it.

So often we're just glad that we've got women leaders, but then there's so much more to it than that . . .

You talked about 'deep fun', which has particular resonance when it comes to leading an arts organisation. Is that something that excites you, looking forward?

Yes. When people ask me about WOW – the Women of the World Festival and Foundation – I explain it is actually a piece of art that I have tried to make, rooted in the idea of a mosaic of stories. That, to me, is the most important thing:

it's the mosaic. The Islamic tradition of mosaics has an idea that you place each tile and that they're all worth . . . you can't have the floor in the way that it looks unless every tile is in place and every tile has a value, a virtue.

When I was creating WOW, to begin with, it was partly out of reaction to directing hundreds of plays where no matter how I tried, they just reinforced the status quo in terms of where men were and where women were. And even though you might try to reframe that, reinterpret it, and you might be directing some plays by women that challenged all of that, they were still single narratives that didn't include the wider story.

And most people's stories were never there because they were unheard, unseen or ignored. So WOW was my kind of rewriting of the story to make it possible for multiple stories to happen. And to try to build into it – and that's why it's a festival – the joy that you get from the arts, or can get when you travel through story. Either through a music piece, or a dance piece, or a theatre piece, or a film . . .

And you know that when you reach the other end, you feel happier and richer, emotionally richer, and more fulfilled, and often more giving towards the human race. You rejoin the human race at the end and you think, well, I still love humans or I love them more, or I love them differently. I have always felt that what I was trying to do in WOW was build in that journey that is essentially a kind of a storytelling that ends with some level of transformation, and that's a great happiness.

And with WOW I was trying to say that there has to be room for silliness, there has to be room for jokes, there has to be room for light-heartedness. Hence, again, the idea of a festival, not a symposium, not an academic conference.

There's a place for all of those things, of course, but I also wanted to let women feel that having happiness and light-heartedness was incredibly important, and that you can explore human rights alongside that. The human right to be silly, for example, which lots of people are never allowed to be.

So, for me, the whole idea of the range of choices that women can have, has to include the question of what range of emotional choices women can have, and how can those be valued both by ourselves and by others. The making of WOW is to acknowledge that massive gamut of emotions, not just subject matters.

One of the things about movements, like feminism or any human rights movements, is they still have to allow for very individual experiences to be awakened in you. This is what art does. Art is both a very collective experience, but it's also a very individual experience. And consciousness-raising, too, which I suppose is what WOW is doing: you're not trying to take a group of people and have the same thing wash through their brain so they all think the same thing. That's not what feminism should be.

Feminism has got to be something which is very nuanced in terms of me being able to be more of the Jude Kelly I'd like to be, but also less of the Jude Kelly that I've been taught to be, when it's been about my power as opposed to somebody else's power, or white power as opposed to Black power. So as a leader, a leader in the arts and a leader experimenting with new models of leadership in a pandemic, and as a feminist, I'm both learning and unlearning, and it's about our own lives as well as a societal belief system.

Where do you see WOW going next? What is your team's vision for the near future, and the long-term future of the WOW Festival and Foundation?

Well, I think it's fair to say we're still finding out. We're excited and we can clearly see that WOW is global, which it has been for years in terms of different WOWs happening all over the world, but we can really operate and connect now at a global level, digitally. And fast. So we will build on all of those connections.

I'm more convinced than ever that the global movement that WOW has been building can significantly increase. But we have to also think very carefully about how to ensure that the digital advantage that a lot of people have – not just the access to digital, but the time to access digital – doesn't then create another sort of superstructure of privileged people who are able to operate in that space, thereby neglecting the local community, which is where the action should happen. So we must build those local community connections.

WOW will build a much bigger global connectivity, but we also are very interested, as I think everybody is at the moment, in what 'hyper-local' looks like. Where does the connection of living your life in your own community come in; how does WOW impact those conversations at a local level?

Which takes me back to the point about reaching out to your friends and your neighbours and saying, 'Here's what I need. And this is what I've been thinking about. And can we work together on this?'

I don't want WOW to become a global movement of global movers and shakers, and then *not* be informed and co-curated by the girls and women at a very local level who are making their alliances and their friendship circles. Those are the places that we need to connect to for our mutual learning.

And what has that local connection looked like for you in 2020?

I have been running the Creative Women's Forum on Thursdays. When lockdown happened I put a call out to women working as creatives, and any contacts and said, 'Look. Let's just meet every Thursday, find out what you're all doing. Find out what's going on.' Because I knew how lonely a lot of women would be and how hard it is to feel creative when actually what you're doing is homeschooling or you haven't got a job. So quickly thoughts like 'Are you still a writer? Are you still an actor? Are you still a designer?' can take over. That sense of identity can disintegrate so quickly and we've fought so hard to get women to be perceived as legitimate cultural creators. And in many countries women are still not perceived as that. And I can see that Covid-19 could drive all that back again.

I often talk about the tremendous problem of every theology in the world, basically maintaining the idea that divinity and creativity are seen as almost twin properties and that divinity is male. And therefore, that challenge runs very deep inside women; 'Am I actually as creative as a male artist, and am I as entitled to the time and the space?' And then once children arrive, society basically says, 'No, you're not as entitled.' So I'm very interested – on a global level and a local one – in the progress of women owning their creativity because I think that is at the core of owning the right to exist as an equal.

Oh, Freedom Suite: Journal Poems

Akasha Hull

Akasha Hull, Ph.D., is a poet, literary activist and professor emeritus, University of California, Santa Cruz (akashahull.com). Her publications explore the interlocking personal-political-spiritual dimensions of Black women's lives. These include short stories, articles, reviews, a novel (*Neicy*, 2012), *All the Women Are White, All the Blacks Are Men, But Some of Us Are Brave* (co-edited), *Healing Heart: Poems* and *Soul Talk: The New Spirituality of African American Women*.

Currently based in Little Rock, Arkansas, Akasha spends rewarding time writing, communicating with her son, friends and family, plus organizing her papers and photographs – while sorely missing travel, theater and nice restaurant dinners.

My contribution to this anthology is excerpted *from a manuscript of journal poems (August 2019–July 2020) for which I am seeking a publisher. Initially triggered by my continuing fifteen-year struggle with a degenerative autoimmune disease, it interrogates physicality-sexuality, death and dying, and potential rejuvenation, all backlit by global culture and the Covid-19 pandemic.*

1/31/20

Spirit says:
Don't judge
Just write

2/2/20

'EmPeaches Recall: Washington, DC

The fruit and flora
      every bit as corrupt
      as the stink fauna tweet bird at the top

Out of season, sour
      rotten at the core

If unchecked
      invasive blight
      on a lethal course of control

2/6/20

California Dreaming

A haze of eucalyptus breezes
in a transformed Compton
Open spaces, populous trees
     and a vacant lot for me

I can't explain
the churchy building at the center
Or why that woman
     had her hands on me
Or who was the girl
     in the second bedroom

I still had a lovely walk –
     unafraid –
through the kids crisscrossing on bikes
and the clean green air

Then woke up rested in Little Rock

2/9/20

Tired of
putting on clothes
eating food
getting up
returning phone calls ......

Until I do

Then, everything changes

One foot
     follows the other

2/28/20

Last Spring Here

At this fetching house
as winter loosens its climate-warmed grasp
and new life ambushes from every corner
rushing into my disgracefully unkempt yard

Ten years I've seen brave quince
        stand up to killing blasts
        and shake their pink behinds
        at stone-cold sunshine
Watched the daffodils and wild onions
        begin their predictable march
        along the backyard fence
By then bold, big-breasted robins
        have staked out their territory
        and decided to chirp at dawn

It's a riot of budding pear trees
        fresh salads on the maple branches
        that the squirrels can't wait to eat
        (no grace proffered)
Rabbits morning and evening
        grass greener on every side

Soon, the snakes will come out of hiding
Long-disappeared turtles renew faith
        in everlasting life
Azaleas and roses peeping – hyacinths, hydrangeas,
        figs and day lilies still sleeping

A game little *Salvia greggii* biding its time
      maybe dreaming of kisses
      from hungry Arkansas hummingbirds

Crepe myrtles – awaiting pruning – are
      as true as Billie Holiday's snowy gardenias
And the two great pin oaks – stanchion –
      perpetually standing guard

Yes. It's time to turn another page
of the calendar

3/4/20

And What If
(with thanks to my friend Geraldine)

What if Bernie said:

You know, of course, that
I'm working for the disfranchised
for the masses catching crumbs
the exploited and discounted
all the forgotten ones

But what I haven't said yet is
I'm working for the 1 per cent too
for the obscenely rich billionaires
who really don't give a poot about you
don't see you, don't want to see you,
don't know who you are
as they grind out commerce and corporations
from the marrow in your bones

I want to sit all of us down
at one huge welcome table
for the feast of plenty we already possess
and have that bounty feed us
Hunger here, homelessness here, hopelessness
here really doesn't make any sense
I want the top and the bottom both
to dream big, inclusive, God-blessed fair
and honest from the pure unified heart
that beats inside us as humans on this earth

I want us to multi-create the vision
and hammer it into a glorious reality
from the bottom up to the skies
We can do that, I know we can do that
In our best moments, our best selves –
when we kiss the bloodied stranger,
rescue our flooded neighbor's beloved pet –
that's who we are
We can make those moments lasting
we can draw on them to manufacture
a just and equitable world
Let's sit at that welcome table
and work it out, together

And what if Bernie smiled – a lot!
Happy at the sight of the new day coming –
and that smile ignited more smiles,
put a grin on other faces

And we became the sun

3/4/20

Liberation?

Trapped in a dream
I found out who the elephant was –
A beautiful and handsome, richly dressed mulatto
man
who didn't know what to do with himself
I'm grateful for him telling me, 'Listen to your body'

We women were sexual slaves
a pack of them arrayed against lone me
subtle and frightening as a den of mating snakes

He housed us in our individualized cabins
with wooden-plank doors and special makeshift
symbols –

Until the night I finally escaped
through moonlit mountains
in a purple fog

Now, I would like not to need or want him anymore

[I, Akasha, faithful to the call, write this narrative and hereby
set my sign and seal]

8A8A

3/14/20

No, Not Finished

I was wrong
(about the wrong things)

I was right
(about the right things)

And I may well be mistaken
about it all

Still
It's better to bleed
than to be bloodless

3/15/20

Geraldine Said UnhUnh

Re the What if Bernie poem:

Too soft

And he needs to find somewhere
     inside him
that can connect to all these people
     who are not like him

(But it's a nice poem ☺)

That's her smile
I'm still frowning
     (like Bernie)

3/21/20

Free at Last

Tell pretty massa'
No handprints
Left on me

I'm in Nova Scotia
Looking 'cross another part
Of the ocean

My my . . . . . .
What a long journey
That was

3/25/20

Tragically Belated / Future Possible
(A Collective Work in Progress)

Why does it take a virus pandemic
for mass society to act like:

We're all one
We're in this together
The government should care
        for its citizens
Our food supply depends upon
        undocumented workers

Doctors with degrees from abroad
        are qualified to practice medicine
Supermarket shelf stockers
        deserve a living wage
Every worker needs at least
        a two-week vacation
Our economy is pleasure-bloated
The 'health care' system
        is a broken mess
Congressional laws must
        hold corporations accountable

Nurses should be treated
        like royalty
The homeless can be housed
        in nice, empty hotels

The creative genius of people
     far exceeds passive consumerism,
     sports events and video games
The most vulnerable among us
     should be remembered and protected
Price gouging is a crime
People deserve better than eviction
     from their homes and apartments
It is perilous to ignore science
We belong to the earth
     and Spirit moves among us

The list goes on . . . .
The question is
Can we make the realizations stick
     and institutionalize the lessons
Truth and justice are not
     convenient umbrellas
To be summoned
     when the sky is falling
We cannot emergency manage our way
     out of systemic social failure

4/4/20

Conviction

'At the end of the day
we all want to belong
to somebody.'
   – Funeral home director, Chicago
         NPR *Weekend Edition*

Trying to figure out
who on earth
I belong to

And what
that possible belonging
actually means

Being more determined than ever
to let what's for me
come to me

4/10/20

Like Jesus
> (recalling Lucille Clifton)

i.

Being crucified
is extremely exhausting

No wonder it needs
entombed nights of sleep

ii.

It looked like I was dead
Even I myself thought so

Unbeknownst to me
I was just waiting on Easter

Resurrection
Is a powerful thing

Four Months
Michelle Tea

Michelle Tea's work includes the cult classic *Valencia*, the dystopic *Black Wave*, the PEN Literary Award–winning *Against Memoir* and the children's book *Tabitha and Magoo Dress Up Too*, inspired by Drag Queen Story Hour, the international sensation that she helped create. Find her on Twitter @TeaMichelle.

March 2, Moon in Gemini

It's my seventeen-years-sober birthday. Seventeen years ago today, one of my favorite people in the world brought me to my first AA meeting, and I listened to a missionary, of all people – an old white cisgender straight, have I forgotten anything, missionary – talk about his alcoholism. If I could create a pastiche of an individual I am more at odds with in our world, I don't know what it would be. And yet everything that he expressed wrong with him was wrong with me also. The cheeks of the people in folding chairs around me were flushed and smooth. Mine were splotchy, both dry and oily like my hair, which no longer held on to the colors I applied to it and looked vaguely green, not in a cute way. I say that vanity got me sober. I wanted what these people had, even the horrible missionary – health, a flush of life in their faces, glossy hair. When the secretary asked for newcomers to raise their hands, my favorite person assured me I didn't have to. I could just listen, take it in. But I've always been a joiner. My hand shot up. I was the most important person in the room. All my life I'd thought my defining story was my girl-ness, my poverty, but I was wrong. All my life it had been *this*.

Tonight, on the stairs, my spouse halted. They'd forgotten. They were on their way to their girlfriend. The look on their face, they'd failed me again. Yesterday, when I was meant to take a cake, my spouse had tensed – they had a date. Fine. Never mind. Who cares. Of course, it was manipulative, but I was doing us a favor. I was providing them an opportunity to walk back to me and take my hands, look into my face and say, *No, this is so important. You are so amazing. You've done the hardest thing. Go and get your cake and then come home and we'll celebrate.* I was always arranging the setting for something cinematic to occur. I could see a scramble of stress like a child's scrawl in the air around their face. *No, go get your cake, I'll go on my date a bit later.* But after the cake, I would want to celebrate. Go get a taco at the place in Los Feliz, the one with the picnic benches arranged under a tarp. I imagined rushing into a Lyft to relieve my partner from childcare duties, so they could go see their girlfriend. It made me feel sad and heavy, self-sabotaging. Fuck it, I don't want a cake. So I didn't get one.

I did get a donut. Because I had a boyfriend, one who didn't identify as a boy, exactly. A theyfriend. They came over with a little cardboard clamshell from Donut Friend and some bags of sugar-free gummies from Sprouts. We sat on the couch and ate. I planned to leave the Donut Friend trash on the table for my spouse to see when they returned, hoped that it transmitted 'sober birthday celebration' vibes. My theyfriend was not eating sugar because their body was very somatic; they had become shut down after we had expressed our love. After a spell of sex that had suddenly, powerfully, fallen into a sphere that felt luscious and Plutonian, I mean dark, as if we had been leaning our full weight on a tank of perverse fantasy and suddenly tipped in and drowned, emerged dazed, in my case, delighted. In my theyfriend's case, walled. I was trying to work with it, but between my spouse barely touching me

– coming back from each date with their girlfriend wearing a new piece of matching jewelry, falling asleep early on our nights together versus pounding Red Bulls and dashing out the door in their new wardrobe of animal prints to complement their animal-printed lover – between that and my theyfriend's haunted libido, I was distraught. My theyfriend had recently stroked my arm while lying beside me in bed and claimed that it felt just as intimate to them as sex. Despair plumed inside me.

That was right before everything fell apart, the season of pre-destruct, but I felt it all in my chest. When my theyfriend showed up at my house unable to do more than give me a thin-lipped kiss, I asked them to leave and then broke up with them via a lengthy, hysterical text message, as is my way. The medium ruins the message. We got back together and went to a play party, having sex for what felt like hours on a chair tucked halfway behind a sofa and a hobby horse–like contraption. They had taken a Xanax, and had felt loose and easy and somewhat mischievous, until the madam who was having a birthday got into the sling and began receiving a round of birthday fists in her vagina. The noise of it got to them, and we left. After that, everything between us went away again, if it had even ever come back. And my spouse. Despite all proclamations to the contrary, and the knowledge that made my veins itch, they were also already gone.

Friday, 13, Moon in Scorpio Sextile Pluto in Capricorn

All day I walked around Silverlake and Echo Park with Ben, hanging posters for our show – a live talk show with mystical themes. There would be feminist writers and queer artists, a tarot creator, an herbalist who taught plant medicine to people of color. A podcast influencer. I would host alongside an Aries co-host, a comedian who had recently scored a role on a broadcast show. It was Aries season, we'd broken out of Pisces, that doldrum, Charybdis, rumble fish. Ben was adamant that the world was going to shut down, even as we invited the world to come to our show in the little black box theater on Hyperion. I scoffed. I had mistaken Ben to be an Aries, but really he is a Taurus, grounded, attuned to the earth's movements. I am mostly Sagittarian, and never believe the worst will happen. Perhaps it renders me a little bit simple, but I wouldn't change it. Our show would be fine, I thought. So would the one we'd just booked in Portland, and San Francisco and certainly we should be curating one in New York City, don't you think? 'You watch,' Ben said.

That night I met my ex-theyfriend for a Coca-Cola at the Hermosillo because they wanted the dignity of an in-person breakup, even though once I was there they couldn't say the thing they'd wanted to say because it didn't feel *safe*. But when were breakups safe? I bristled at the suggestions I was a monster. I was simply cold, as was appropriate. Inside the Hermosillo, at the dark, wooden bar top, my eyes watered. I was annoyed that they had brought me out in the rain to withhold their processing from me. It seemed they most wanted to communicate that when they told me I had bad breath the other night, they were only trying to help. Their shaman had suggested I avail myself of our poly-amory during this period of shutdown, and so I had swiftly booked two dates on Lex with an ad that referenced *Dirty Dancing*, a movie I had never actually seen but that my dating demographic seems to hold dear. Upon learning this, my ex shared with me the bad news. The bad-breath news. When I got home, I told my spouse what I had learned. Their face fell a bit in empathy. 'Well, it's your teeth,' they said knowingly. 'You have tooth problems.'

After I finished not-talking to my ex, I called a car to take me to Akbar, where a new 'they', one who had responded to my ad, was having a birthday party. This 'they' drank coffee and smoked cigarettes and drank alcohol in spite of having recently been in AA; they'd realized they were in the wrong twelve-step program, and their problem was people, not booze. I shrugged, open to becoming a problem. We had met earlier that afternoon, when I had arrived in the rain at a home, where they were cooking Frito pie for the first phase of the night's celebration. Akbar was phase two, and phase three would be, they said with some bravado, maybe an orgy. I wondered if being informed of an orgy equaled being invited to one. The new they made me a French press and read my tarot cards, and eventually I climbed on their lap and kissed them. I had hoped to bring a friend to Akbar, as I feared it would be awkward, but my friends were spooked by whispers of the world shutting down, and had opted to stay in, and so I sat on the sofa at the rear of the bar, where people were definitely not six feet apart, and fielded such questions from the new they's friends as, 'Where did you guys meet?' (an app) and 'How long have you known each other?' (a few hours). When the scant revelers willing to brave the strange moment and blustery weather went home, I and the new they walked across the street to the twenty-four-hour Del Taco. The streets were empty and the graffitied stretch off Sunset felt like an abandoned section of Brooklyn, not LA. The Del Taco was closed. Because of the thing, the cold. 'Weird,' we said, and they lifted me off the ground with their kiss and got into their Lyft, while I waited under the narrow fast-food awning for my own.

April 11, Moon in Sagittarius Opposition Venus in Gemini

This was after I had started therapy to learn why I was so unhappy all the time; why I cried; how I could be better, not provoke my spouse with my emotions, not be so triggered by their polyamorous choices; how could I hear them when they told me everything was OK; what was this alarm system that had been tripped, 'bitches' intuition', it had never failed me, but now it seemed to have gone haywire, hadn't it, hadn't it, hadn't it. My therapist affirmed that my spouse should probably come to couples counseling but if they didn't want to – and they didn't, because of the money, they would say, though they injected botulism into their face regularly to ease the effects of their aging, no judgment – there was no use nagging them, since such visits rarely paid off. This was after I had tried to talk calmly to my spouse and they had mocked me, which had made me cry, and I had gone into the living room where our child sat on the sofa in a YouTube haze, and I tried not to cry, and I couldn't believe they would leave to go to their girlfriend's with me in such a state, but it would not be the first time and they just had to *get out*, and when I told them it was *very hurtful*, what they had said, using a phrase my therapist had suggested, they turned to me and mocked me again, in front of our child, 'Oh, I'm very hurtful, am I very hurtful?' in that voice, like I was a fucking idiot, like I was the stupidest worst person to ever be married to and I watched it like watching a movie, *wow*, but one I was maybe psychotically invested in, because look how I cried, and they left and somehow I got the baby to bed, he's not a baby, he's five, and I thought that for someone who is able to *leave the house*, for someone who actually has *someplace they can go*, a different *environment*, a *new face* they can look at, *make out with* and *fuck*, for someone with such *privilege*, they should be a whole lot nicer to someone like me, who has not left the house in nearly a month except to risk my life buying organic chicken at Whole Foods and smoking cigarettes and crying in the alley around the corner.

This was after that night, when I moved into the guest room with the little bathroom, when I moved my toiletries onto the shower floor, when I moved all the books I was reading, and my perfume bottles, my department-store boxes filled with eyeliner and lipstick. When I moved that little barrel I bought on the street in San Francisco and used as an end table. When I moved a deck of tarot cards and a journal, a little ceramic dish filled with lavender and amethyst and that piece of heart-shaped glass found half-buried in the muck of the LA river, the tiny piece of pink rhodochrosite my spouse had given to me. And I texted my spouse that we were separating and that I had moved into the guest room, and they called me and wanted to come back to the house and I said, 'No, no, don't, I don't want you to,' and then sat on the front porch smoking, waiting, as I had set the stage for another cinematic moment to happen, for my spouse to come bounding around the corner, their bleached hair lit white by the streetlights, rounding the box hedges and coming up the path to tell me they'd ended it, they'd ended it with their girlfriend because it wasn't working, something about it was not working, it was tearing us apart, they couldn't bear to see me like this and they were so sorry for the way they had treated me and we would start anew, in couples counseling, we would get back to what we were the day after our son was born, a bulb packed tightly into the earth, tight green petals clutching at one another, we were so beautiful and strong and fragile and my heart broke for us, what would become of us, what an undertaking, a family, what ridiculous hope, so many forces could tear us asunder, not the least ourselves, we were more precious than I could articulate then, hormonal and morphined, but truly I saw it, I saw us glow in the dim hospital room, like light beings, benevolent and blind. And my spouse did not come home. I sat on the white wicker chair and smoked until I shook, talking to Ben. 'They have got to come home,' he said. 'They have got to get their shit together.' But I knew, even as my heart leaped each time a suburban white SUV rounded the corner, that it was beyond them.

July 13, Moon in Taurus Sextile Mercury in Cancer
My ex-spouse sat on the sofa while my child detailed the mechanics of the Lawbringer, a Nerf gun I had not only now allowed into the house but also had purchased for him on the internet, because my ex's new house, where they live with their girlfriend, has a swimming pool and a dilapidated but useful trampoline, not to mention the sunny vibes of two people in love, whereas my house, my ex's ex-home, has a scrubby backyard littered with crusty mounds of poop and bloody tufts of feathers from the resident dog and cat, respectively. My house is minus the vibes of two people who stop to hug each other and play in tandem with a child, an only child, a Libra who basks in the rays of beloved dyad attention. My house, I fear, feels cold, as if blown through with November weather; imagine some awful neighborhood, say a financial district on a Friday evening, the heartless buildings creating tunnels for the wind to race through, paper trash rustling in the gutter. Into this house must come, well, anything the child desires,

for now anyway, so guns, and Minion gummies and Minion sunglasses and camo clothing and the expensive grapes that taste like cotton candy, and more gummies, these in weird shapes and combinations, like witch's fingers and strawberries. A Slip 'N Slide. A Would You Rather? book, a horror coloring book, slime, sticky hands, squishy sea creatures, a pouf to sit upon, anything you like, kid. I didn't know this woman seven months ago and now she's raising my child. The school won't reopen next month. I'm moving my mother in to the guest room, she can't work anymore, not with her lungs, a nurse. I think I am going to get a Black Lives Matter flag for the house, I mean we have a flagpole, we should use it. I applied for Medi-Cal. I applied for rent relief. I applied myself. I mean, I know I did, because it's just how I am, and the way you do anything is the way you do everything. I did what I could, because my Venus is in Capricorn, my Saturn in Taurus, I'm loyal that way. John Waters says not to fuck people with no books on their shelves and this is the advice I shall take into the future. Don't think that someone locks down their emotions because their feelings are so raw and deep. They might simply be an accumulation of cat dander and dust, the way those cysts grow from hair and teeth and excess fat inside the body. Don't marry someone for whom emotions are a cyst. Eileen told me they'd never been left for someone who was their equal. Which soothes my Leo rising and bristles my Aquarian sun, but also, they wrote, 'I / write because / I would like / to be used for / years after / my death. Not / only my body / will be compost / but the thoughts / I left during / my life.' And Stevie sang, 'So I'm back to the velvet underground / Back to the floor that I love.' And Yoko sang, 'Bless you for your anger / It's a sign of rising energy . . . Bless you for your sorrow / It's a sign of vulnerability / Bless you for your greed / It's a sign of great capacity . . . Bless you for your jealousy / It's a sign of empathy.' Locked in my house for the duration, all I have are words. Good thing they're everything. And what do I say? Bless me. I kiss my floor like a beloved country I've been returned to. *At the end of the pandemic, I am my prose.*

Inheritance
Kerry Hudson

Kerry Hudson was born in Aberdeen. Her first novel, *Tony Hogan Bought Me an Ice-Cream Float Before He Stole My Ma*, was the winner of the Scottish First Book Award and shortlisted for the Southbank Sky Arts Literature Award, *Guardian* First Book Award, Green Carnation Prize, Author's Club First Novel Prize and the Polari First Book Award. Kerry's second novel, *Thirst*, won France's prestigious award for foreign fiction the Prix Femina Étranger and was shortlisted for the European Premio Strega in Italy.

Her latest book and memoir, *Lowborn*, takes her back to the towns of her childhood as she investigates her own past. It was a Radio 4 Book of the Week, and a *Guardian* and *Independent* Book of the Year. It was longlisted for the Gordon Burn Prize and Portico Prize and shortlisted in the National Book Tokens, Books Are My Bag Readers Awards and the Saltire Scottish Non-Fiction Book of the Year.

You can find her on Twitter @ThatKerryHudson and on Instagram @KerryEatsALot.

'm on the Victoria line. The same blue line I rode every day to work in my mid-twenties and wept on more than once because I felt ugly in the way that particularly grips you when you're a young woman alone in a large city. Now, in my mid-thirties, I grip a burning paper coffee cup between my knees. A make-up bags spills out across my lap.

A mum gets on and sits opposite me, a smaller girl on her lap, a baby boy in a buggy and two girls of perhaps four and five in school uniforms who sit snugly together in a single seat beside me. They bring the smell of cold outside air and a sense of just-finished laughter into the carriage.

'Bethan, pull your skirt down, cover yourself.'

One of the girls beside me squirms in her seat, pulling at her grey school skirt. I smile at the mum, who rolls her eyes, and carry on with my make-up. Powders and pastes, mascara, lipstick, several brushes. The two girls tilt their faces towards me, watching me clamp the coffee between my knees, balance the make-up, hold the mirror at different angles to paint over my dissatisfied expression. I wonder how, if they asked, I could explain what I am doing. Why I would sit there on a swaying train staring at myself, trying to change my face to one I find acceptable. I wonder what I would tell those girls if they asked why it mattered that the people on the tube could see their thighs. Why they have to learn to cover themselves.

FOUR YEARS LATER we got the results of the test that, along with any genetic markers for 'abnormalities', would identify our own child's gender.

The email came one night while our baby, still ungendered, danced away in my womb like a fractious, exotic insect. Since we were in Prague, the email was in Czech, and it took some internet wrangling, but the symbol at the top of the email, a light blue circle with an arrow emerging at a jaunty angle, needed no translation at all. We were having a wee boy. Or that's what he was now, said my partner, for who knew what our child would end up being in the future? Who could imagine what the binaries of sex and gender would look like once he was grown?

I was surprised and slightly betrayed by own my relief at the result. I realised that from the moment I'd found out I was pregnant, there had been some part of me cataloguing the litany of indiscretions and indignities meted out to me as a woman: assault, rape, the male gaze, unattainable body image, the exhausting double standards in every single arena. Without knowing it, I'd already been panicking about social media and body image and raising a strong woman in a society where I knew how strong women – and fragile women, for that matter – are treated. Later I would tell a respected older female colleague that I was having a boy and she would reply pragmatically, 'Probably for the best.'

And, yes, we'd need to worry about toxic masculinity and the propensity for schizophrenia in the young men in my family on both sides, but my instinctive motherly response was still to be glad my child would have an easier life. My feminist response was deep disappointment in the mother I was becoming.

I reminded myself we could also raise a gentle, good man who might move through the world aware of his privilege. That we'd teach him to be mindful of all he inherited through the sheer luck of genetics. I told myself we'd raise a feminist and an ally. It seemed a lot to put on the shoulders of a child who had not yet drawn a breath of air, but the fight is intersectional and it never stops. And it's so much less than what would be asked of him if he were a woman.

'BETHAN, PULL YOUR skirt down, cover yourself.' Bethan giggles and wriggles her grey school skirt down.

I finish my make-up, watching the girls watching me.

So: What would I answer if they asked why I would sit there on a swaying train staring at myself, trying to change my face to one I find acceptable? What would I say if one of those girls asked why it mattered if the people on the tube could see their thighs? Why did they have to learn to cover themselves?

I would have told them I didn't know. That I was still trying to make answers from fragments of clues myself. If they asked me why I was putting on make-up, I would never tell them it was because somewhere it had been dictated that my face as it was wasn't quite right. I'd tell them instead about the man we hope to raise. The different future so many of us are trying to shape for them. That we'll do our best to give them the tools and words and space to do that too.

They got off at Oxford Circus. I stayed on until Vauxhall. They didn't ask me anything and I didn't get to say. So instead I wrote it here.

On Joy

Juli Delgado Lopera

in conversation with
Feminist Book Society

Juli Delgado Lopera is an award-winning Colombian writer, historian, speaker and storyteller based in San Francisco. They're the author of the *New York Times* acclaimed novel *Fiebre Tropical*, a finalist for the 2020 Kirkus Prize for Fiction, *Quiéreme* and *¡Cuéntamelo!*, an illustrated bilingual collection of oral histories by LGBT Latinx immigrants, which won a 2018 Lambda Literary Award and a 2018 Independent Publisher Book Award. They are the former executive director of RADAR Productions, a queer literary non-profit in San Francisco.

What has your experience of lockdown been like in San Francisco?

It's been depressing, inspiring, terrifying – all at the same time. The joy of being in a city is being in relation to other people, right? The possibilities that appear when you're surrounded by others. You see different things outside, you see that other people are different, there are gatherings – in all of that, there is joy. In lockdown, all of this changed. The stark inequality of the city really came through in various ways – for instance, there are a lot of homeless people on the streets who are not being provided with safety. Also, I live in the Mission, which is where a lot of Latinx people live, and that's the neighborhood with the highest number of cases of Covid-19 in San Francisco, because most people are essential workers. Low-income people are being hit the most with the virus.

However, it's been incredible to see the creativity of people. In the first month there were people who had already set up their mask-selling businesses on the street. The way public space has been reimagined is also really interesting and hopeful for me – public art started popping up because people were doing a lot of graffiti when everything was boarded up.

But overall, the sense of dread is really intense. I'm going next week to the river with my girlfriend, and I'm excited to take a week just being in nature. Nature is the one thing that has saved me.

Your book *¡Cuéntamelo!* features the oral histories of LGBTQIA+ Latino immigrants in San Francisco. Given that our book is capturing narratives of the pandemic, what would you say is the importance of personal history?

The power of personal story is huge. It has such a deep impact in our understanding of that person when we listen to their story, which is the reason why the feminist movement, the gay movement, the civil rights movement, the immigration movement here in the USA, the dreamers, used personal stories to be able to open a door for compassion from other people, and empathy. Personal story unlocks a sense of connection between people. Maybe somebody else didn't experience exactly the same as you, but they understand pain and grief and loss, and in that way there's connection, empathy.

The amnesia around the legacy of colonialism plays an important political role. As a society we are taught that because slavery happened many years ago, it doesn't have an impact on the way our lives are structured right now. History, the way that we remember it, how we remember it and the stories that we tell about it, impacts the way that we currently exist, in our personal lives, collectively and in what we feel is possible. The other power of personal stories is in creating an archive of our humanity at a specific time. And the more people we include in it, the more complex the narrative is going to be. It's so crucial for us in the future.

Has this period of crisis made you reassess your priorities, or has it made you reaffirm them?

In a very personal way, in a very intimate way, I've had to reevaluate a lot of things because I've been disconnected from a lot of my network of people. I've been reflecting on how I took for granted a lot of little things before, about the people that I have around me, and really, really valuing the relationships that are sustaining me through this, especially the relationship I have with myself.

My own trauma is bubbling up, so I've had to prioritize my well-being and mental health, and I'm caring about my intimate relationships in a different way. I show people way more kindness than I did before, having asked myself: 'How do I access my own kindness?' and 'How do I access my own compassion and generosity for other people?' because it's crucial for me to be able to show that to others.

How have your writing habits or intentions changed (or not) in the past five months?

When it first started in March, my book had just come out and I had to cancel my book launch and tour. I thought, *This is temporary. I will go back to my library soon.* So I was waiting for my life to come back in three weeks – it never did. Then I felt I had to start reconnecting to my writing. And I started small.

Beth Pickens has a book called *Your Art Will Save Your Life*, in which she argues that, as artists, we need our art to process the world, not only because it's healing, but just because that's the way that we connect with the world and ourselves, and to gain a sense of self. So I kept reminding myself of that, and I started pushing myself.

Writing is the one thing that I need to do for myself right now. It's becoming something around survival – not in that I'm going to die, but a survival of my soul and my spirit, so I don't fall into a horrible depression or completely disconnect from myself and others. I said to myself, *This is something that is important to your heart and to your soul*, so writing became a priority. I've been reaching out to people to get more support, tapping into the resources that I have in order to be able to help myself. I feel humbled and amazed at people tapping into the networks that we had previously and figuring out how to make those networks work for us right now, because we need each other so much. I also reached out to my agent and told her: 'You have to give me deadlines. I need deadlines!' Being given deadlines is a very, very good technique to start writing again.

Which feminist issue is most on your mind right now?

I keep thinking about how the inequalities that have always been in the fabric of capitalism and white supremacy, and in the way that this country functions, are being highlighted in such a stark way. For people who have no safety because of the way that the economic system has been structured – like Black, undocumented and Latinx people – those communities are getting worse off. (For example, in the beginning of lockdown, some Indigenous people didn't have access to water.) I keep thinking about how all these capitalist systems really rob us of our joy.

To me, joy is a feminist issue. As human beings we need that; we need the place of connection. Joy is so important, but it's stolen from us by these systems. Who knows when the new world order is going to be established, as this continues? I keep thinking about how to center joy and celebration. Capitalism and white supremacy are robbing us of the ability to tap into our intuition, our sense of kindness and generosity for other people. I'm trying to intentionally make space for myself to find moments of joy.

I think a lot about how we can center joy in our social movements as we move forward and rethink economic systems so joy is at the center instead of capital, so humans are not being commodified. Sometimes, for people who have a long history of activism, it feels as though the fight has to be driven by anger. I do believe that anger is a great vessel and channel, but we tend to forget that it's important that we also have joy. We need to ask: 'What are we really fighting for, and what is the dissolution of all the systems for?'

Anger has been really important to feminism, and crucial for communities of color, and I'm in no way rejecting anger as a response to social inequalities. But how does that anger get channeled in a way so that we create the optimal conditions for people to be able to access and experience joy?

What do you want us to let go of?

This is definitely a moment for reflection, and for a lot of us to ask questions. Some of the oldest narratives that we hold dearly and pass down – and I include myself in this – about ourselves and our role in society, they harm a lot of people. The most important thing right now is self-reflection, to question why a lot of the population does not have the same access to resources, or sources of joy, as everybody else; so we can work to dismantle these structures and so that everybody has access to a sense of themselves and to humane conditions. What is fueling white supremacy is that people in this country are so attached to the 'bootstrap narrative', that it is all about yourself. Capitalism blooms out of this notion that you should pull yourself up – alone – and if you're not successful, that is your own doing. The entire economic history of this country is wiped out with this narrative, so that there's no collective responsibility.

And so, what I'm talking about is that we should question why this pandemic is hitting everybody so differently. Where does this come from? How are some of these narratives giving me privilege and blinding me from really seeing what's going on? And because we are all going through a lot of pain, although we're all presented with challenges right now, we can maybe have more compassion for other people.

If we're holding on to our privilege then we're holding on to narratives about ourselves, which keeps us from being more compassionate and from being able to see how the systems are made to keep wealth among very few people. Sadly, in a capitalist society, the people that hold the wealth also hold power and, because of a less burdened life filled with resources, have easier access to joy.

And so, off the back of that, what makes you hopeful?

Well, I have a lot of hope right now, because of the protests. I've been in San Francisco for twelve years, and the Pride protest of this year was one of the best – if not the best – that I've ever been to, mostly because there were no corporations. There were no banks. There was no police. Black people were leading the protests with flags and music. It was a party on the streets, and everybody was wearing a mask, and it felt like it was *the people* leading this. People showed up for it, and demonstrated the most beautiful parts of what it is to be a queer person and to carry our history.

We weren't being commodified and sold to, so that Bank of America can make more money. It's a reminder that we're here to disrupt; to fuck shit up; that we need to take action for the people who are the most underprivileged, uplift everyone, and that's how we all get liberation.

It was a great reminder of the power of queer people. It was pretty incredible to see a lot of Black women taking over, with a message of queer liberation: a message that we're dancing for the death of the prison-industrial complex. Dancing is a protest, and drag is a protest!

Everybody's going to remember this, and remember the way that the Black Lives Matter protests and uprisings here, in this country, created a sense of hope for a lot of people who really needed it. We've been under lockdown, a lot of people are being hit extremely hard. Then, all of a sudden, there are all these protests happening, all over the country (and they're still happening), but also, what's happening now is that the question of race, and its relationship to access, to power, its relationship to the police and incarceration, is very much at the forefront right now of conversations that we're having about anything that we as a country want to do.

This kind of conversation makes me feel hopeful, as does the way in which people did not wait for the government to come and organize things – rather, everybody has been organizing themselves and sharing resources.

At the beginning of lockdown, I lost a lot of my income, but I was able to access artists' grants and resources by connecting with other people. Sharing of resources has been happening widely, such as sharing food. And all from networks that have always been there, especially those of queer people and of people of color; they're not waiting for the government. Thanks to banking apps, we are using our own local economies to share wealth quickly; people are using crowdfunding pages to get protesters out of jail, to support gender-affirming surgeries; these people are often working class, sharing with each other, no questions asked. The power of collective well-being is felt in the protests and in this sharing of resources.

Things will pass, because they always do. Big changes have to come. And people are creating solid networks of connection. That's hopeful to me, because, however much time it takes us to move on to whatever is next, those networks will be there.

Finally, if you have one call to action for readers of this book, what would it be?

A feminist act that I really want to point out – which is tied to hope – is the act of imagining. To imagine a possible future, to be able to imagine ourselves outside of this, to be able to empathize. Imagination is a place that cannot be policed.

While on the outside we police each other and we have to wear masks, the role of imagination is crucial right now – as is the creation of art, the creation of a future and the creation of ways we can come together. I want to emphasize how important it is to nourish our imagination, and how as feminists we can imagine collectively.

Inspire

The Feminist Book
That Made Me

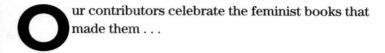

Our contributors celebrate the feminist books that made them . . .

Amelia Abraham

Cookie Mueller, *Walking Through Clear Water in a Pool Painted Black*. Her friend said about her: 'Cookie was a great character, and anytime she walked out the door, her life was a story. I mean, she would say, "I'm going to get the milk," and something lunatic would happen to her. Her life was like that all the time.' I think she showed me that women can be wild and make trouble and have near escapes, in the way that so many male writers do.

Yomi Adegoke

Black Feminist Thought by Patricia Hill Collins.

Rosanna Amaka

I was unknowingly brought up on feminist books, mainly because of the women in my life and their influences, so I naturally gravitated towards books such as *Anne of Green Gables* that had strong female characters. They prepared me for more adult books like *Beloved*, which had a profound effect on me, not only from a feminist viewpoint, but also from a cultural perspective.

Laura Bates

Gloria Steinem's *My Life on the Road* made me a better activist, a better ally and a better listener. It is impossible to read the story of her life and work without feeling awed and humbled by her humour, wit, tenacity and generosity of spirit.

Fatima Bhutto

The poems of Forough Farrokhzad.

Lauren Bravo

I could lie and say something more highbrow, but honestly? The book that made me a feminist was *Bridget Jones's Diary* by Helen Fielding. It's problematic, but then so is the world. I fell in love with it aged fourteen, and I think the messy, funny, thoroughly flawed snapshot of '90s womanhood she represented did more to make me a feminist than many 'strong' female characters have done since. I never want to count another calorie as long as I live, but I will remain primed against emotional fuckwittage forever.

Molly Case

The feminist books that made me are Sylvia Plath's collected journals. They are honest, erudite, stunning in their lyricism and offer an unmediated look at the woman who so desperately wanted to encompass all the things a woman can be: wife, mother, home-keeper and brilliant writer. I am sad that society didn't allow her to marry all of those things when she was living.

Catherine Cho

A Tree Grows in Brooklyn by Betty Smith. I loved this novel when I first read it as a child; I thought Francie Nolan's descriptions of life in a tenement building were fanciful and romantic. It wasn't until I was older that I considered the hardship in the novel, and I felt that it helped me better understand my mother's upbringing as a girl growing up in post-war Korea. The women in the novel are survivors; they are strong and determined, even as life is stacked against them.

Sara Collins
Angela Davis: An Autobiography.

Melissa Cummings-Quarry and Natalie A. Carter
Melissa: The book I always go back to is *Their Eyes Were Watching God* by Zora Neale Hurston. It cemented what 'feminism' meant and gave it a language. The book taught me about financial freedom and also about being able to be in charge of my sexuality and autonomy. It was an awakening. That's the book I always go back to when I'm unsure of myself, or if I have a friend who's trying to figure out what's going on in their lives, I would always give them that book.

Natalie: Two stories gave me comfort as a Black woman. *The Color Purple* by Alice Walker – Celie is one of my favourite kinds of characters; it's the watching her grow and what she goes through trying to be an independent woman, trying to raise her family and seeing how she's battered and bruised but still triumphs. And reading Maya Angelou's *I Know Why the Caged Bird Sings* gave me an idea of the progression of Black women and the story of coming from nothing and claiming a space for yourself.

The book that I was inspired by most recently has been *Hood Feminism* by Mikki Kendall . . . [it] perfectly sets out a manifesto for feminism that needs to be adopted.

Juli Delgado Lopera
The Second Sex by Simone de Beauvoir.

Lindsey Dryden
There are so many writers who opened up the universe of feminist thought, adventure and possibility, my favourite of which include Jeanette Winterson, Barbara Kingsolver, Anna Gavalda, Sara Maitland, Jackie Kay and Stella Duffy; scholars Judith Butler and Jack Halberstam; songwriter Skin; and goddess-screenwriters Lucia Puenzo, Jane Campion, Céline Sciamma and Ava DuVernay. Also the authors 'Fynn' and Garth Nix, who showed me the way towards valuing myself as an odd, curious and self-determining little girl. But if I have to choose one, it's Angela Carter's glorious *The Bloody Chamber*. It threw everything upside down in the most delicious way when I was a teenager, and made me want to go out into the world and bite it, hard.

Stella Duffy
Alice Walker's *The Color Purple*. I read it when it came out; I was nineteen. I already considered myself a feminist; I didn't know about being womanist. I was hungry for books with all women in them, not just white women, not just middle-class women. I was hungry for novels that told stories that were of me, even if they were not about me. I remember reading it and sobbing and raging and roaring. All very good things.

Sarah Eagle Heart
Waterlily by Ella Cara Deloria. *Waterlily* is a historical fiction novel about a young Yankton woman in the late 1800s that provided the framework to understand my responsibility as a Lakota woman to my people and the world.

Fox Fisher

Germaine Greer's book *The Whole Woman* had a huge effect on me until I read the chapter about trans women. Other books include *Gender Outlaw* by Kate Bornstein and many of Judith Butler's books, particularly *Gender Trouble*.

Shirley Geok-lin Lim

The feminist book that made me is Tillie Olsen's *Silences*. Her speaking out loud that women's silences come from 'the unnatural thwarting of what struggles to come into being' gave me courage to send my books out into the world.

Mireille Cassandra Harper

Although I identify as a womanist, I would recommend bell hooks' *Sisters of the Yam* as one of the most seminal feminist texts one can read. Reflecting on relationships, beauty, self-worth, passion, grief/loss and so much more, hooks shares how Black women can heal in a world built of institutions and structures which assault them. It has had a dramatic effect on how I view the world and is a tool of empowerment in fighting against racism, sexism and consumer capitalism (aka the hell-hole in which we live).

Kerry Hudson

I read the *The Color Purple* by Alice Walker in my teens and it entirely changed the way I thought about womanhood. As did so many of The Women's Press books I found in my local libraries by searching out that ironic/iconic iron logo on the spine, knowing that whatever they published would nourish and challenge me.

Akasha Hull

I don't think I would voluntarily say that any book 'made me'. However, because that phrase so perfectly evokes the response it is looking for, I will name two books: Betty Friedan's *The Feminine Mystique* and Toni Cade Bambara's *The Black Woman: An Anthology*, both of which I read around 1970.

In the prior four years, I had earned my B.A. and – like the girls around me – married my college sweetheart; given up a three-year graduate fellowship so that I could accept a teaching assistantship to study at the same school as my husband as he pursued his doctorate; and expertly timed the birth of our son between passing my M.A. exams and beginning the Ph.D. program. Friedan's manifesto resonated. Shortly thereafter, I was blown away by Toni Cade's *The Black Woman* – for example, the raw, searing honesty of Nikki Giovanni and Kay Lindsey in their opening poems; the revolutionary socialist perspective; the fine craft of a story like Paule Marshall's 'Reena'. Without completely knowing it, I had models for what I instinctively moved toward as my life work.

Juliet Jacques

The feminist book that made me: *The Empire Strikes Back: A Posttranssexual Manifesto* by Sandy Stone.

Jude Kelly

I'd definitely say *Little Women* by Louisa May Alcott had a big effect on me as a girl. I'm one of four daughters too and Jo's determination to be a writer and earn her own money, and marry for intellectual and emotional stimulus not security gave me permission to be independent.

Dorothy Koomson

I can't really think of a book that made me a feminist – no one thing did – but one I read that left a lasting impression was *Fat Is a Feminist Issue* by Susie Orbach. It put into context a lot of the way society sees and constantly tries to claim tacit ownership of women's bodies. It also explained a lot about why women put on weight and how we can use it as armour and protection. Like I say, this wasn't the book that made me a feminist, but it did expand my knowledge of the world.

Kuchenga

The feminist book that made me was *Woman on the Edge of Time* by Marge Piercy. The spectral perspective on gender identity and expression clarified what I have fought for throughout my life. Furthermore, it has a vision of the future where abolitionism, decolonisation and a harmonious relationship with nature are fundamental to an enduring and healthy human existence. The politics that underpin the novel clarified my own relationship with feminism and how expansive and liberatory the pursuit of equality should and will be.

Helen Lederer

Fear of Flying by Erica Jong.

Francesca Martinez

Eleanor Marx: A Life by Rachel Holmes. Such an inspiring woman and life!

Gina Miller

I studied English at A-levels and had to choose a book to critique. I chose *A Room of One's Own* by Virginia Woolf – she wrote about female independence and creativity with such passion, energy and humour. I wouldn't say it made me, I was born a Feminist, but I found it quite intoxicating.

Jessica Moor

Their Eyes Were Watching God by Zora Neale Hurston.

Kate Mosse

The Women's Room by Marilyn French, first published in 1977, opened my eyes to the realisation that sexism and female inequality are everyday issues, often tiny issues that, when put all together, have a huge impact on women's lives. The power of the novel is that change can begin at home, the very definition of 'the personal is political'!

Jess Phillips

How to Be a Woman by Caitlin Moran, because she spoke like I spoke about the things I had experienced and made me want to stand on a chair and shout that I was a feminist.

Layla F. Saad

Ain't I a Woman by bell hooks and *Sister Outsider* by Audre Lorde.

Radhika Sanghani

A Room of One's Own by Virginia Woolf. Reading this book as a teenager gave me the drive to get myself a room of my own so I could live life on my own terms. I've never looked back.

Jenny Sealey

When I was growing up, the first feminist book I read was Betty Friedan's *The Feminine Mystique*, but in all the books I read back then, I could not find me as a Deaf young woman in any of them, and I sort of stopped reading and sorted what I meant for myself as a feminist. Still doing that now!

Shaz

Heal Your Mind: Your Prescription for Wholeness through Medicine, Affirmations, and Intuition by Mona Lisa Schulz and Louise Hay.

Lisa Taddeo

Later the Same Day by Grace Paley.

Michelle Tea

The Re/Search book *Angry Women*! I had never seen such a bunch of countercultural women talking about sex and feminism and art and revolution before, and I became aware of so many of my heroes, and about the potential for art and activism to merge, and to become not just a project but really the fabric of a life.

Virgie Tovar

There are so many books that could make this list! Inga Muscio's *Cunt* was my first-ever introduction to feminism. Right after that, I read Audre Lorde's *Sister Outsider*, which showed me that feminism could be gorgeous and poetic.

Phyllis Chesler's *Women and Madness* really helped me understand how mediocrity is demanded of women so that men can retain a societal advantage and how that lifelong process makes us lose our minds.

Sophie Williams

Everything Roxane Gay. *Bad Feminist, Hunger, Difficult Women* – Roxane Gay's writing means the world to me!

Thanks

First, a HUGE thank you to every contributor to this collection and to every person who helped us make the connections we needed to make, and smooth the process of bringing together many creative voices, from many backgrounds and all around the world.

In the publishing journey of this book, we collaborated in new ways, and the creative and supportive network we created is, hopefully, just one of the new beginnings this book will bring about. So, heartfelt thanks go to the entire creative, pioneering team at And Other Stories – Stefan Tobler, Tara Tobler, Nichola Smalley, Javerya Iqbal, and Emma Warhurst; the ever-calm, dedicated and transformational Feminist Press team – Lauren Rosemary Hook, Jamia Wilson, Nick Whitney, Jisu Kim, Lucia Brown, Rachel Page and Drew Stevens. Thank you to Sarah Whittaker for our striking and beautiful cover design.

It was essential to us to support writing womxn in their work, not simply add to their workload in an intensely difficult year. Though we have not been able to pay much, we have remunerated our contributors for their creative work, with some choosing to donate their time as part of the fundraising mission of this project. No womxn or non-binary person should be expected to work for free. Thanks to all who made that possible. A project like this depends on many hands on deck. I am so very grateful to our collective of super-talented and passionate editorial/creative volunteers, honourary Feminist Book Society members all, who made managing and delivering this project a reality: Ebyan Egal, Frankie Edwards, Katherine Cowdrey, Rosanna Hildyard, Salma Begum and Vera Sugar. Gratitude and much love go to Rosie Beaumont-Thomas, Hannah Boursnell, Katy Loftus and Parastou Khiaban of Feminist Book Society. You always make me, for one, feel stronger.

Thank you to Women's Aid and Imkaan, and to the Third Wave Fund in the US. We hope this is only the beginning of our work together.

Thank you for every single person who has supported us in this endeavour – partners, loved ones, family, friends, professional contacts.

And thank you to *you*, for buying this book, for reading it, and for (hopefully) telling everyone you know about it!

Eleanor Dryden
Co-founder of Feminist Book Society
January 2021

Twenty per cent of the cover price of every copy of this book sold will be donated to and shared equally between Women's Aid and Imkaan, two organisations working on the frontline in the fight against gender inequality.

women's aid
until women & children are safe

Women's Aid is a grassroots federation working together to provide life-saving services in England and build a future where domestic abuse is not tolerated.

www.womensaid.org.uk

imkaan

Imkaan is a UK-based, Black feminist organisation. We are the only national second-tier women's organisation dedicated to addressing violence against Black and minoritised women and girls i.e. women and girls which are defined in policy terms as Black and 'Minority Ethnic' (BME).

www.imkaan.org.uk

Feminist Book Society
is a UK-based literary organization that celebrates
feminist authors of brand new fiction and non-fiction,
from escapist beach reads to literary novels and Big Ideas,
via monthly sell-out author panel events and an ever-growing
international network. It brings people together in
lively discussion to share ideas and actively
champion the fight for equality.

And Other Stories
publishes the best in contemporary writing,
including many translations, with authors including
Yuri Herrera, Rita Indiana, Deborah Levy and Gerald Murnane.
Launched with a select list in 2011, And Other Stories has built
a reputation for combining boundary-pushing literature
with bold social action, including a commitment to
environmentally-minded publishing practices,
and the 2018 Year of Publishing Women.